JOURNALS

OF

RALPH WALDO EMERSON

1820–1872

—

VOL. V

Ralph Waldo Emerson, about 1846

JOURNALS

OF

RALPH WALDO EMERSON

WITH ANNOTATIONS

EDITED BY

EDWARD WALDO EMERSON

AND

WALDO EMERSON FORBES

1838–1841

BOSTON AND NEW YORK
HOUGHTON MIFFLIN COMPANY
The Riverside Press Cambridge

CONTENTS

CONTENTS

JOURNAL XXX

1839

(From Journals D and E)

CONTENTS

CONTENTS

JOURNAL XXXI

1840

(From Journals E and F)

Guy learns friendship. Man before measure; Character brings Theocracy. Plato's "Politician." Estimating nations. One miracle. Scholar. Church's poverty. Balzac. Character *plus* sensibility. Course on *The Present Age;* disappointment in it. The maiden; gems. The elect. Wealth in thought and senses. Bible priceless, yet not final. Shakespeare. Things the divine language. Instinct speaks for Immortality. Nature flows. Writing and speech. Confessions help. Power of manners, yet humanity greater. Death in

CONTENTS

ILLUSTRATIONS

ILLUSTRATIONS

JOURNAL

JOURNAL XXIX

(Continued)

1838

(From Journal D)

[All page references to passages from the Journals used by Mr. Emerson in his published works are to the Centenary Edition, 1903–05.]

Sunday, *July* 1, 1838.

IN Boston, Friday, and rode to Charlestown, and afterward to the Cambridge bushes with George B. Emerson. A beautiful thicket like a mat of South American vegetation. Arcadian ladders did the dead vines of the smilax make; a delicate fruit the *Pyrus villosus* offered; the azalea was in profuse flower; the tupelo tree and the *Ilex canadensis* I had never seen before. It seemed not June, but August or September. The pines have a growth and twisted appearance that I do not remember elsewhere. *Hamamelis. Asper indentatus. Aralia nudicaulis.*

[During July and the exciting events connected with the delivery of the Divinity School

Address and its reception, Mr. Emerson did not forget to care for the interests of his friend Carlyle in this country. (See the *Correspondence*, vol. i, letters xxv to xxxii.)]

Most of the commonplaces spoken in churches every Sunday respecting the Bible and the life of Christ, are grossly superstitious. Would not, for example, would not any person unacquainted with the Bible, always draw from the pulpit the impression that the New Testament unfolded a system? and, in the second place, that the history of the life and teachings of Jesus were greatly more copious than they are? Do let the new generation speak the truth, and let our grandfathers die. Let go, if you please, the old notions about responsibility for the souls of your parishioners, but do feel that Sunday is their only time for thought and do not defraud them of that, as miserably as two men have me today. Our time is worth too much than that we can go to church twice until you have something to announce there.

If you rail at bodies of men, at institutions, and use vulgar watchwards, as bank; aristocracy; agrarianism; etc., I do not believe you.

I can expect no fruit. The true reformer sees that a soul is an infinite, and addresses himself to one mind.

Look for a thing in its place and you will find it, or tidings of it. The red leaf of the straw-berry-vines is mistaken for a berry; but go to it and you will find a real berry close by.

Read Herbert. What eggs, ellipses, acrostics, forward, backward and across, could not his liquid genius run into, and be genius still and angelic love? And without soul, the freedom of our Unitarianism here becomes cold, barren and odious.

Never compare. God is our name for the last generalization to which we can arrive, and, of course, its sense differs today and tomorrow. But never compare your generalization with your neighbor's. Speak now, and let him hear you and go his way. Tomorrow, or next year, let him speak, and answer thou not. So shall you both speak truth and be of one mind; but insist on comparing your two thoughts; or in-sist on hearing in order of battle, and instantly you are struck with blindness, and will grope and stagger like a drunken man.

We think too lowly altogether of the scholar's vocation. To be a good scholar as Englishmen are, to have as much learning as our contemporaries, to have written a successful book, satisfies us, and we say, "Now, Lord, we depart in peace!" A true man will think rather, All literature is yet to be written. . . .

I think Tennyson got his inspiration in gardens, and that in this country, where there are no gardens, his musky verses could not be written. The Villa d'Este is a memorable poem in my life.

There is a limit to the effect of written eloquence. It may do much, but the miracles of eloquence can only be expected from the man who thinks on his legs. He who thinks may thunder; on him the Holy Ghost may fall, and from him pass.

July 2.

The price of the picture indicates the common sense of men in regard to the chance there is for the appearance of equal genius. The chances are millions to one that no new Raphael is born today, and therefore pictures as great as the actual Raphael painted express that chance in their nominal value. But it is beautiful to see that when genius does arrive, it writes itself out in every word and deed and manner, as truly and self-same as in its masterpiece. A leaf in the forest, or a flower, as a violet, would be as highly prized as the Transfiguration, if they were the solitary productions of human genius, and would administer the same gratification and the same culture.

July 8.

We shun to say that which shocks the religious ear of the people and to take away titles even of false honor from Jesus. But this fear is an impotency to commend the moral sentiment. For if I can so imbibe that wisdom as to utter it well, instantly love and awe take place. The reverence for Jesus is only reverence for this, and if you can carry this home to any man's heart, instantly he feels that all is made good and that God sits once more on the throne. But when I have as clear a sense as now that I am speaking simple truth without any bias, any foreign interest in the matter, — all railing, all unwillingness to hear, all danger of injury to the conscience, dwindles and disappears. I refer now to the discourse now growing under my eye to the Divinity School.

July 10.

A true man can never feel rivalry. All men are ministers to him, servants to bring him materials, but none, nor all, can possibly do what he must do, he alone is privy, — nor even is he yet privy to his own secret. They can never know until he has shown them what that is. Let them mind their own.

[On July 15, Mr. Emerson delivered before the graduating class at the Divinity School in Cambridge the address which raised such a storm of dissent. Now a memorial tablet to him may be seen on the walls of the Divinity School Chapel.]

July 16.

The object catches your eye today, and begets in you lively thought and emotion which, perchance, arrives at expression. Tomorrow, you pass the same object, — it is quite indifferent: you do not see it, although once you have been religious upon it, and seen God through it, as we worship the moon with all the muses at midnight, and, when the day breaks, we do not even see that scanty patch of light that is fading in the west. They who have heard your poetry upon the thing are surprised at your negligence of a thing they have learned from you to respect. Tonight I saw fine trees. Trees look to me like imperfect men. It is the same soul that makes me, which, by a feebler effort, arrives at these graceful portraits of life. I think we all feel so. I think we all feel a certain pity in beholding a tree : rooted there, the would-be-Man is beautiful, but patient and helpless. His boughs and long leaves droop and weep his strait imprisonment.

Little Waldo cheers the whole house by his moving calls to the cat, to the birds, to the flies, — " Pussy-cat, come see Waddow ! Liddle Birdy, come see Waddow ! Fies ! Fies ! come see Waddow ! " His mother shows us the two apples that his grandfather gave him,[1] and which he brought home in each hand and did not begin to eat till he got nearly home. " See where the dear little angel has gnawed them. They are worth a barrel of apples that he has not touched."

July 17.

In preparing to go to Cambridge with my speech to the young men, day before yesterday, it occurred with force that I had no right to

1 Dr. Ripley.

go unless I were equally willing to be prevented from going.

[Mr. Emerson drove in a chaise from Concord to Hanover, New Hampshire, to deliver the "Literary Ethics" address, with John Keyes, Esq., a leading citizen and lawyer of Concord, and a Dartmouth graduate, and the young son of the latter, John Shepard Keyes, later United States Marshal under Lincoln, and Justice of the Middlesex Central District Court, who died in 1910. The northward journey must have taken three days. It is interesting to consider that, although the Divinity School Address had startled the clergy and the Harvard professors into denunciation of the views therein expressed, no ripple of the storm at Cambridge seems to have reached the orthodox New Hampshire college six days later, and Mr. Emerson was kindly received.]

August 6.

At Dartmouth College, Tuesday, 24 July.

Lidian wonders what the phrenologists would pronounce on little Waldo's head. I reply that his head pronounces on phrenology.

It is bad of poverty that it hangs on, after its lesson is taught, and it has a bad side; poverty makes pirates. The senses would make things of all persons; of women, for example, or of the poor. The selfishness in the woman, which hunts her betrayer, demands money of him, exposes him, swears a child on him, etc., is only the superficial appearance of Soul in her, resisting forevermore conversion into a thing.

As they said that men heard the music of the spheres always and never, so are we drunk with beauty of the whole and notice no particular.[1]

August 9.

[The entry of this date is the criticism on Wordsworth with which the *Dial* paper, "Europe and European Books," opens.[2]]

The poet demands all gifts, and not one or two only. Yet see the frugality of nature. The men of strength and crowded sense run into

---

1 The two twilights of the day
   Fold us, Music-drunken, in.
          Poems, "Merlin," II.
2 *Natural History of Intellect,* pp. 365, 366.

affectation. The men of simplicity have no density of meaning.

August 10.

If that worthy ancient king, in the school-books, who offered a reward to the inventor of a new pleasure could make his proclamation anew, I should put in for the first prize. I would tell him to write an oration, and then print it, and, setting himself diligently to the correction, let him strike out a blunder and insert the right word just ere the press falls, and he shall know a new pleasure.

Hateful is animal life resembling vegetable, as when a pear-worm is mistaken for a twig of the tree, or a snake for a stick.

Limitation. — I told Mr. Withington at the Medical Rooms in Hanover that this melancholy show of bones of distortions and diseases was one of the limitations which the man must recognize to draw his plan true.

August 14.

Sanity is very rare : every man almost, and every woman, has a dash of madness, and the combinations of society continually detect it. See how many experiments at the perfect man. One thousand million, they say, is the population of the globe. So many experiments then. Well, a few times in history a well-mixed character transpires. Look in the hundreds of persons that each of us knows. Only a few whom we regard with great complacency ; a few sanities.

Herbert's piece called "Constancy" is noble, and seems to have suggested Wordsworth's "Happy Warrior."

August 15.

The sun and the moon are the great formalists. I woke this morning with saying or thinking in my dream that every truth appealed to a heroic character. This does not seem to hold of mathematical as of ethical science.

The Understanding possesses the world. It fortifies itself in History, in Laws, in Institutions, in Property, in the prejudice of Birth, of Majorities, in Libraries, in Creeds, in Names ; Reason, on the other hand, contents himself with animating a clod of clay somewhere for a moment, and through a word withering all these to old dry cobwebs.

The little girl comes by with the brimming pail of whortleberries, but the wealth of her pail has passed out of her little body, and she is spent and languid. So is it with the toiling poet who publishes his splendid composition, but the poet is pale and thin.

August 17.

Saw beautiful pictures yesterday. Miss Fuller brought with her a portfolio of Sam Ward's, containing a chalk sketch of one of Raphael's Sibyls, of Cardinal Bembo, and the angel in Heliodorus's profanation; and Thorwaldsen's Entry of Alexander, etc., etc. I have said sometimes that it depends little on the object, much on the mood, in art. I have enjoyed more from mediocre pictures, casually seen when the mind was in equilibrium, and have reaped a true benefit of the art of painting, — the stimulus of color, the idealizing of common life into this gentle, elegant, unoffending fairy-land of a picture, than from many masterpieces seen with much expectation and tutoring, and so not with equipoise of mind. The mastery of a great picture comes slowly over the mind. If I see a fine picture with other people, I am driven almost into inevitable affectations. The scanty vocabulary of praise is quickly exhausted, and we lose our common sense, and, much worse, our reason, in our *superlative degrees*. But these

pictures I looked at with leisure and with profit.
In the antiques I love that grand style — the
first noble remove from the Egyptian block-
like images, and before yet freedom had become
too free. The Phocion, the Aristeides, and the
like. The Dying Gladiator, too, is of an archi-
tectural strength. What support of limbs in
these works, and what rest therefore for the
eye! A head of Julius Cæsar suggested instantly "the terror of his beak, the lightning of
his eye," a face of command, and which pre-
supposed legions and hostile nations.

Thorwaldsen is noble and inventive, and his
figures are grand, and his marchers march, but I
see in him all the time the Greeks again. I could
wish him a modern subject, and then an ignorance of Greek sculpture. Besides, it seemed to
me that Alexander wanted a divine head.

Raphael's heads seem to show more excellent
models in his time than any we have now. His
angel driving out Heliodorus is an ideal. The
purity, the unity of the face is such that it is instantly suggested, *here is a vessel of God*. Here
is one emptied of individuality, nothing can be
more impersonal. This is no Gabriel nor Uriel,
with passages of private experience, and a long
biography, — but is a dazzling creation of the

moment, a divine wrath, as the resisted wave bursts into dazzling foam. Again the expression of the face intimates authority impossible to dispute.

The crest of the angel's helmet is so remarkable, that, but for the extraordinary energy of the face, it would draw the eye too much; but the countenance of this god subordinates it, and we see it not.

The Sibyl to whom the Messiah is announced is a noble, daring picture with a radiant eye and a lovely youthful outline of head, and admonishes us that there is a higher style of beauty than we live in sight of.

The Persian Sibyl of Guercino is an intellectual beauty. A single expression lights the whole picture.

How much a fine picture seems to say ! It knows the whole world. How good an office it performs ! What authentic messengers are these of a wise soul, which thus stamped its thought, and sends it out distinct, undecayed, unadulterated to me, at the end of centuries, and at the ends of the earth.

Life is a pretty tragedy, especially for women. On comes a gay dame, of manners and tone so fine and haughty that all defer to her as to a countess, and she seems the dictator of society. Sit down by her, and talk of her own life in earnest, and she is some stricken soul with care and sorrow at her vitals, and wisdom or charity cannot see any way of escape for her from remediless evils. She envies her companion in return, until she also disburdens into her ear the story of *her* misery, as deep and hopeless as her own.

August 18.

It would give me new scope to write on topics proper to this age and read discourses on Goethe, Carlyle, Wordsworth, Canova, Thorwaldsen, Tennyson, O'Connell, Baring, Channing, and Webster. To these I must write up. If I arrived at causes and new generalizations, they would be truly valuable, and would be telescopes into the Future. Elizabeth Hoar says, Add the topic of the rights of woman; and Margaret Fuller testifies that women are slaves.

[Here follow quotations from Heeren's *Ideas on the Politics, Mutual Relations and Commerce of the Leading Peoples of the Ancient World*, which are used in "History" in the First Series of Essays.]

Dr. Ripley prays for rain with great explicitness on Sunday, and on Monday the showers fell. When I spoke of the speed with which his prayers were answered, the good man looked modest.

I think it must be conceded to books that they are grown so numerous and so valuable that they deserve to have imperfect characters, half-witted persons, and the like persons who are confessedly incapable of working out their own salvation, appointed to study these, and render account of them. For want of a learned class, here, I am in ignorance where valuable facts and theories are found until years after their promulgation.

August 19.

Always that work is the more pleasant to the imagination which is not now required. Ah! how wistfully, when I have been going somewhere to preach, I looked upon the distant hills!

A scholar is a selecting principle.[1] . . . So in every community where aught new or good is going on, God sets down one of these Perceivers

1 Here follows the passage in "Spiritual Laws" thus beginning, with the simile of the lumber-boom. *Essays*, First Series, p. 144.

and Recorders. What he hears is homogeneous ever with what he announces.

I think myself more a man than some men I know, inasmuch as I see myself to be open to the enjoyment of talents and deeds of other men, as they are not. When a talent comes by, which I cannot appreciate and other men can, I instantly am inferior. With all my ears I cannot detect unity or plan in a strain of Beethoven. Here is a man who draws from it a frank delight. So much is he more a man than I.

I noticed in fine pictures that the head subordinated the limbs and gave them all the expression of the face. In poor pictures, the limbs and trunk degrade the face. So in women, you shall see one whose bonnet and dress are one thing, and the lady herself quite another and wearing withal an expression of meek submission to her bonnet and dress; another whose dress obeys and heightens the expression of her form.

Sympathy. — He whose sympathy goes lowest, — dread him, O kings! I say to you, dread him. See you a man who can find pleasures everywhere, in a camp, in a barn, in a schoolhouse, in a stage-coach, in a bar-room, so that he needs no philosophy, but drops into heaven wherever he goes, because of the great range of his affinities; who is an observer of boys and admires so much the strokes of nature they deal, that he feels himself their inferior whilst he watches them; who is an observer of girls and lacks countenance to speak to them, so warm is his interest in their well-being; who is so alive to every presence that the approbation of no porter, groom or child is quite indifferent to him, and a man of merit is an object of so much love as to be a *fear* to him — see you such a man, and is he a worshipper also of truth and of Virtue? then mark him well, for the whole world converts itself into that man and through him as through a lens, the rays of the universe shall converge, whithersoever he turns, on a point.

Dr. Ripley preached from the noble text, "Trust in the Lord with all thy heart and lean not to thine own understanding. In all thy ways acknowledge him, and he shall direct thy paths." When he was to speak of its reasonableness he said, "Reasonableness! It is all Reason."

In perfect eloquence, the hearer would lose
the sense of dualism, of hearing from another;
would cease to distinguish between the orator
and himself; would have the sense only of high
activity and progress.[1]

. . . What makers are our eyes! In yonder
boat on the pond the two boys, no doubt, find
prose enough. Yet to us, as we sit here on the
shore, it is quite another sort of canoe, a piece
of fairy timber which the light loves and the
wind, and the wave,—a piece of sunshine and
beauty.

August 21.

The address to the Divinity School is published, and they are printing the Dartmouth
Oration. The correction of these two pieces for
the press has cost me no small labor, now nearly
ended. There goes a great deal of work into a
correct literary paper, though of few pages. Of
course, it cannot be overseen and exhausted except by analysis as faithful as this synthesis.
But negligence in the author is inexcusable. I
know and will know no such thing as haste in
composition. All the foregoing hours of a man's

1 This entry is followed by the passage on Eyes, printed in
" Behavior " (*Conduct of Life*, pp. 178, 179).

life do stretch forth a finger and a pen and in-
scribe their several line or word into the page
he writes to-day. I remember the impatience
Charles expressed of the frolicking youth who
had finished his college oration a fortnight before the day and went about at his ease; re-
membering the pale boys who worked all the
days and weeks of the interval between the appointment and the exhibition, and dreamed by
nights of the verses and images of the day.

Providence Library. — It seems to me that
every library should respect the culture of a
scholar and a poet. Let it not then want those
books in which the English language has its
teeth and bones and muscles largest and strongest,
namely, all the eminent books from the accession of Elizabeth to the death of Charles II, —
Shakspear, Bacon, Jonson, Marlowe, Herrick,
Beaumont and Fletcher, North, Sidney, Milton,
Taylor, Dryden, Cotton, the translator of Montaigne, Donne, Marvell. Not only in the masters,
but in the general style of the pulpit and the
history of that time, there is greater freedom,
less affectation, greater emphasis, bolder figure
and homelier idiom than in books of the same
classes at the present day.

Bell's *Bridgewater Treatise on the Hand*.
Davy's *Elements of Chemistry*.
Herschel.
Cudworth.
Landor.
Taylor's *Plato*.

August 22.

I decline invitations to evening parties chiefly because, besides the time spent, commonly ill, in the party, the hours preceding and succeeding the visit are lost for any solid use, as I am put out of tune for writing or reading. That makes my objection to many employments that seem trifles to a bystander, as packing a trunk, or any small handiwork, or correcting proof-sheets, that they put me out of tune.

Landor has the merit of knowing the meaning of character. I know no modern writer who gives traits of character with more distinct knowledge than he. He has also the merit of not explaining. He writes for the immortals only.

In a hot-house, should be a lotus, a mandrake, a century plant, a banian, a papyrus.

The great difference between educated men is that one class acknowledge an ideal standard and the other class do not. We demand of an intellectual man, be his defects what they may, and his practice what it may, faith in the possible improvement of man.

August 25.

What is more alive among works of art than our plain old wooden church, built a century and a quarter ago, with the ancient New England spire? I pass it at night, and stand and listen to the beats of the clock — like heart-beats; not sounding, as Elizabeth Hoar well observed, so much like tickings, as like a step. It is the step of Time. You catch the sound first by looking up at the clock-face, and then you see this wooden tower rising thus alone, but stable and aged, towards the midnight stars. It has affiance and privilege with them. Not less than the marble cathedral it had its origin in sublime aspirations, in the august religion of man. Not less than those stars to which it points, it began to be *in the soul*.

Samuel Hoar. — I know a man who tries time. The expression of his face is that of a patient judge who has nowise made up his opinion, who fears nothing, and even hopes nothing, but puts nature on its merits. He will hear the case out, and then decide.

The manners of society indicate every hour the consciousness of one soul. Put three or four educated people together who have not seen each other for years, and perhaps they shall be unable to converse aloud without force. Each predicts the opinion of the other, so that talking becomes tedious. All know what each would say. Why should I officiously and emphatically offer a pail of water to my neighbor Minot? He has a well of his own that sucks the same springs at the same level that mine does. Why should I drum on his tympanum with my words to convey thoughts to which he has access equally with me?

How expressive is form! I see by night the shadow of a poor woman against a window-curtain that instantly tells a story of so much meekness, affection, and labor, as almost to draw tears.

Almost every woman described to you by a woman presents a tragic idea, and not an idea of well-being. One most deserving person whom I commiserated last night with my friends, has such peculiar and unfortunate habits of conversation that she can say nothing agreeable to me. Say what she will, — rare and accomplished person that she is, — I hear her never, but only *wait* until she is done. I think with a profound pity of her family. Were she my sister, I should sail for Australasia and put the earth's diameter between us.

[Here follow long quotations from Heeren on the architecture of Egypt, its might, its dignity and repose, of which one is given below. Many are on the Ethiopians.]

" Since our acquaintance with these wonders wrought in the highest style of perfection, we feel convinced that so just and noble a taste could never have been formed under the rod of tyrants, but that there must have been a period, and indeed a long one, however different the form of government from ours, during which the mind could unfold its faculties freely and undisturbed, and could soar to a height in certain points never attained by any other."

The whole History of the negro is tragedy. By what accursed violation did they first exist that they should suffer always.[1] . . . I think they are

1 Here follow other quotations from Heeren, which were

more pitiable when rich than when poor. Of what use are riches to them? They never go out without being insulted. Yesterday I saw a family of negroes riding in a coach. How pathetic!

The Negro has been from the earliest times an article of luxury.

It is very fit that man should build good houses. Such an irritable, susceptible, invalid, beauty-loving creature as he is, should not dwell in a pen. His understanding, his eye, his hand are fitly employed on Persian Terraces, Egyptian Temples, and European Palaces. The wise man will prize and obtain the luxuries of baths, of ventilated houses, of gardens, of clean linen, of digestible meats and drinks, and thereon will spend time and money, and not on fine clothes, equipage, and rich living. Is not thought freer and fairer in a house with apartments that admit of easy solitude than in a foul room where all miscellaneous persons are thrown together, cheek by jowl, heads and points? I look upon the stately architecture of

used by Mr. Emerson in his address on Emancipation in the British West Indies.

In his poem " Voluntaries " the tragedy of the negro is portrayed.

Persia and of Egypt as a real part of the human heaven as much as a poem or a charity. Justice can be administered on a heath, and God can be worshipped in a barn. It is, nevertheless, fit that Justice should be administered in a stately hall open to the sun and air and to nations; and that God should be honored in temples whose proportion and decoration harmonize rather with the works of nature than with the sheds we build for the domestic animals.

It is a comfort to me, who neither build nor see built, that Egypt builded. It was done by the family: and I had as lief my brother did it as I. Is it great? Then the task that falls to me in the division of labor may be greatly done, as well.

How charming is the ignorance of children!

August 27.

A good subject for a sermon would be the Doctrine of Benefits. Benefit is the end of nature. Benefit is done to all by all, by good and bad, voluntarily and involuntarily. Air, water, sun and moon, stone, plant, animal, man, devil, disease, poison, war, vice, — all serve. But man is a voluntary benefactor. The meaning of good

and bad, of better and worse, is simply helping
or hurting. He is great who confers the most
benefits. He is base — and that is the one base
thing in the universe — to receive favors and
render none.[1] . . . In the order of nature we
cannot render benefits to those from whom we
receive them, or only seldom. But the benefits
we receive must be rendered again line for line,
deed for deed to somebody.

There is history somewhere worth knowing,
as, for example, Whence came the negro? Who
were those primeval artists that in each nation
converted mountains of earth or stone into
forms of architecture or sculpture? What is the
genealogy of languages? and when and what is
the genesis of man?

"A man and his wife," says Menu, "constitute but one person; a perfect man consists of
himself, his wife, and his son."

August 28.

It is very grateful to my feelings to go into
a Roman cathedral, yet I look as my countrymen do at the Roman priesthood. It is very

1 The rest of the passage thus beginning is in "Compensation" (*Essays*, First Series, p. 113).

grateful to me to go into an English church and hear the liturgy read. Yet nothing would induce me to be the English priest. I find an unpleasant dilemma in this nearer home. I dislike to be a clergyman and refuse to be one. Yet how rich a music would be to me a holy clergyman in my town. It seems to me he cannot be a man, quite and whole; yet how plain is the need of one, and how high, yes, highest, is the function. Here is division of labor that I like not. A man must sacrifice his manhood for the social good. Something is wrong, I see not what.[1]

August 31.

Yesterday at Φ B K anniversary. Steady, steady. I am convinced that if a man will be a true scholar, he shall have perfect freedom. The young people and the mature hint at odium, and aversion of faces to be presently encountered in society. I say, No: I fear it not. No scholar need fear it. For if it be true that he is merely an observer, a dispassionate reporter, no partisan, a singer merely for the love of music, his is a position of perfect immunity: to him no disgusts can attach: he is invulnerable. The

1 This passage is the theme of " The Problem," in the *Poems*.

vulgar think he would found a sect, and would
be installed and made much of. He knows better, and much prefers his melons and his woods.
Society has no bribe for me, neither in politics,
nor church, nor college, nor city. My resources
are far from exhausted. If they will not hear
me lecture, I shall have leisure for my book
which wants me. Besides it is an universal
maxim worthy of all acceptation that a man
may have that allowance which he takes. Take
the place and attitude to which you see your
unquestionable right, and all men acquiesce.

Who are these murmurers, these haters, these
revilers? Men of no knowledge, and therefore
no stability. The scholar, on the contrary, is
sure of his point, is fast-rooted, and can se-
curely predict the hour when all this roaring
multitude shall roar for him. Analyze the
chiding opposition, and it is made up of such
timidities, uncertainties and no opinions, that it
is not worth dispersing.[1]

1 A scrap of verse, of uncertain date, in which Mr. Emerson expressed the same idea, but with regard rather to mobs
than inquisitors, may be here given : —

> Look danger in the eye — it vanishes :
> Anatomize the roaring populace,
> Big, dire and overwhelming as they seem,
> Piecemeal 't is nothing.   Some of them [but] scream,

We came home, Elizabeth Hoar and I, at night from Waltham. The moon and stars and night wind made coolness and tranquillity grateful after the crowd and the festival. Elizabeth, in Lincoln woods, said that the woods always looked as if they waited whilst you passed by — waited for you to be gone. But as you draw near home you descend from the great self-abandonment to Nature, and begin to ask, What's o'clock? And will Abel be awake and our own doors unlocked?

A topic touched at Waltham was the metaphysics of the antagonisms, or, shall I say, elective affinities observed in conversation. Sometimes we have nothing to say to persons with whom we can talk well enough at other hours. What a lottery, for instance, are my own visits at Waltham. But it is one of the blessings of old friends that you can afford to be stupid with

> Fearing the others; some are lookers-on;
> One of them hectic day by day consumes,
> And one will die tomorrow of the flux.
> One of them has already changed his mind
> And falls out with the ringleaders, and one
> Has seen his creditor amidst the crowd
> And flies.   And there are heavy eyes
> That miss their sleep and meditate retreat.
> A few malignant heads keep up the din,
> The rest are idle boys.

them; whilst these visits are lotteries, the intercourse with others, as George Bradford, never is. He makes my Commencement Holiday usually : so that this year I feel poor in his absence at Bangor.

September 1.

Looked over S. G. Ward's portfolio of drawings and prints. In landscapes it ought to be that the painter should give us not surely the enjoyment of a real landscape, — for air, light, motion, life, dampness, heat, and actual infinite space he cannot give us, — but the suggestion of a better, fairer creation than we know; he should crowd a greater number of beautiful effects into his picture than co-exist in any real landscape. All the details, all the prose of nature, he should omit, and give us only the spirit and splendor. So that we should find his landscape more exalting to the inner man than is Walden Pond or the Pays de Vaud. All spiritual activity is abridgement, selection.[1]

September 3.

I have usually read that a man suffered more from one hard word than he enjoyed from ten

1 A portion of this paragraph is found in the opening passage of "Art" (*Essays*, First Series).

good ones. My own experience does not confirm the saying. The censure (I either know or fancy) does not hit me; and the praise is very good.

Is it not better to live in Revolution than to live in dead times? Are we not little and low out of good nature now, when, if our companions were noble, or the crisis fit for heroes, we should be great also?

September 5.

How rare is the skill of writing? I detected a certain unusual unity of purpose in the paragraph levelled at me in the Daily Advertiser, and I now learn it is the old tyrant of the Cambridge Parnassus himself, Mr. Norton,[1] who wrote it. One cannot compliment the power and culture of his community so much as to think it holds a hundred writers; but no, if

1 Andrews Norton, Professor of Sacred Literature in the Harvard Divinity School, a strong writer and good man. He was the father of Professor Charles Eliot Norton, Mr. Emerson's valued friend. A year after the latter's Address at the Divinity School, Professor Norton gave an address before its Alumni Association on "The Latest Form of Infidelity," an attack upon the "Transcendental Movement." For an account of this, see George Willis Cooke's *Ralph Waldo Emerson: His Life, Writings, and Philosophy*.

there is information and tenacity of purpose, what Bacon calls longanimity, it must be instantly traced home to some one known hand.[1]

George Bradford has been here, to my great contentment, and to him I have owed the peace and pleasure of two strolls, one to Walden water, and one to the river and north meadows. I like the *abandon* of a saunter with my friend. It is a balsam unparalleled. George says his intellect approves the doctrine of the Cambridge Address, but his affections do not. I tell him I would write for his epitaph, " Pity 't is 't is true."

I saw a maiden so pure that she exchanged glances only with the stars.

Of proverbs, although the greater part have so the smell of current bank-bills that one seems to get the savor of all the marketmen's pockets, and no lady's mouth may they soil, yet are some so beautiful that they may be spoken by fairest lips unblamed; and this is certain, — that they

1 This is followed by another passage, printed in " The Tragic," as to actions, opinions, prayers, loves, etc., being few in life, and therefore composure and readiness being all that it demands (*Natural History of Intellect*, pp. 412, 413).

give comfort and encouragement, aid and abetting to daily action. For example : " There are as good fish in the sea as ever came out of it," is a piece of trust in the riches of nature and God, which helps all men always. Is it so ? Is there another Shakspeare ? Is there another Ellen ?

September 8.

That which is individual and remains individual in my experience is of no value. What is fit to engage me, and so engage others permanently, is what has put off its weeds of time and place and personal relation. Therefore all that befals me in the way of criticism and extreme blame and praise, drawing me out of equilibrium, — putting me for a time in a false position to people, and disallowing the spontaneous sentiments, — wastes my time, bereaves me of thoughts, and shuts me up within poor personal considerations. Therefore, I hate to be conspicuous for blame or praise. It spoils thought.

Henry Thoreau told a good story of Deacon Parkman, who lived in the house he now occupies, and kept a store close by. He hung out a salt fish for a sign, and it hung so long and grew so hard, black and deformed, that the deacon forgot what thing it was, and nobody in town knew, but being examined chemically it proved to be salt fish. But duly every morning the deacon hung it on its peg.

September 9.

How attractive is the book in my friend's [1] house which I should not read in my own! At Waltham, I took up Jouffroy, and if they had left me alone an hour, should have read it well. But Goethe, Schleiermacher, lie at home unread. Many books are not so good as a few. Once, a youth at college, with what joy and profit I read the *Edinburgh Review*. Now, a man, the *Edinburgh Review*, and Heeren, and *Blackwood*, and Goethe get a languid attention.

September 10.

Fancy relates to color; imagination to form.

Stetson, talking of Webster this morning, says, " He commits great sins sometimes, but without any guilt."

How is a boy, a girl, the master, the mistress of society, independent, irresponsible, — Gore Ripley, for example, or A. P., or any other,

1 Mrs. Ripley was an eager reader of every new work on science.

looks out from his corner on such people and facts as pass by; tries, and sentences them on their merits, as good, bad, interesting, silly, eloquent, troublesome.[1] . . .

Teachers' Meetings everywhere are disturbed by the question whether . . . any sin can be repented of so as to place the sinner where he had been if he had not sinned at all. . . .

The question is answered by the consideration of the nature of Spirit. It is one and not manifold: when God returns and enters into a man, he does hallow him wholly, and in bringing him one good, brings him all good.[2]

September 12.

Yesterday, the Middlesex Association met here, with two or three old friends beside. Yet talking this morning in detail with two friends of the proposition often made of a journal to meet the wants of the time, it seemed melancholy as soon as it came to the details.[3] . . .

1 The above and a long passage which continues it are printed in "Self-Reliance" (*Essays*, First Series, p. 49).

2 Here follows the sentence about tacit reference to a third party in conversation ("The Over-Soul," *Essays*, First Series, p. 277).

3 This is followed by the passage on "The painful kingdom of time and place" ("Love," *Essays*, First Series, p. 171).

Alcott wants a historical record of conversations holden by you and me and him. I say, how joyful rather is some Montaigne's book which is full of fun, poetry, business, divinity, philosophy, anecdote, smut, which dealing of bone and marrow, of cornbarn and flour barrel, of wife, and friend, and valet, of things nearest and next, never names names, or gives you the glooms of a recent date or relation, but hangs there in the heaven of letters, unrelated, untimed, a joy and a sign, an autumnal star.

A sermon, my own, I read never with joy, though sincerely written; an oration, a poem, another's or my own, I read with joy. Is it that from the first species of writing, we cannot banish tradition, convention, and that the last is more easily genuine? Or is it that the last, being dedicated to Beauty, and the first to Goodness, to Duty, the Spirit flies with hilarity and delight to the last; with domestic obligation and observance only to the first? Or is it that the sentiment of Duty, and the Divinity, shun demonstration, and do retreat into silence; they would pervade all, but they will not be unfolded, exhibited apart, and as matter of science?

September 13.

Licence. — Consider that always a licence attends reformation. We say your actions are not registered in a book by a recording angel for an invisible king; Action No. 1, No. 2, up to No. 1,000,000, — but the retribution that shall be is the same retribution that now is: Base action makes you base: holy action hallows you. Instantly the man is relieved from a terror that girded him like a belt, has lost the energy that terror gave him, and when now the temptation is strong, he will taste the sin and know. Now I hate the loss of the tonic. The end is so valuable, — to have escaped the degradation of a crime is in itself so pure a benefit, that I should not be very scrupulous as to the means. I would thank any blunder, any sleep, any bigot, any fool, that misled me into such a good. And yet (as William Henry Channing said yesterday in reply to my remark), there is a certain intimation that joy is the home of the mind, in this new licence.

The analogous evil may be seen in literature. We say now, with Wordsworth, to the scholar, Leave your old books; come forth into the light of things; let Nature be your teacher; out upon your pedantic cartloads of grammars and dictionaries and archæologies; the Now is all. Instantly the indolence and self-indulgence of the scholar is armed with an apology:— Tush, I will have a good time.

Culture. — A cheerful face makes society; a cheerful, intelligent face shows the present end of nature and education answered; a sour face, a waiting face, dissatisfaction, unrest: impatience of the rain, of the company, suspense, care, betray imperfect culture or uncultivation. Cannot a man have so various parts of his nature unfolded that he shall have a resource when conversation flags, and dull men come, and there are no books or letters? Cannot he play? Can he not be domestical and affectionate, and crack nuts and jokes?

It is easy enough for a firm man who knows the world to brook the rage of the cultivated classes.[1] . . . Yet it is difficult not to be affected by sour faces. Sympathy is a supporting atmosphere, and in it we unfold easily and well. But climb into this thin, iced, difficult air of Andes of reform, and sympathy leaves you and hatred comes. The state is so new and strange and un-

1 Here follows most of the matter, though differently arranged, that is found on p. 56 of "Self-Reliance" (*Essays,* First Series).

pleasing that a man will, maugre all his resolutions, lose his sweetness and his flesh, he will pine and fret.

The person that has acted, fears; the person that looks on is formidable.

The Silken Persecution. — Martyrs with thumb-screws, martyrs sawn asunder, martyrs eaten by dogs, may claim with gory stumps a crown. But the martyrs in silk stockings and barouches, with venison and champagne, in ballrooms and picture galleries, make me sick — self-pitying.

After thirty, a man is too sensible of the strait limitations which his physical constitution sets to his activity. The stream feels its banks, which it had forgotten in the run and overflow of the first meadows.

True Science. — I do not wish to know that my shell is a *strombus* or my moth a *vanessa*, but I wish to unite the shell and the moth to my being.

September 15.

A disinclination to society will keep out more visitors than a good bolt.

I please myself with the thought that my accidental freedom by means of a permanent income is nowise essential to my habits, that my tastes, my direction of thought is so strong that I should do the same things,— should contrive to spend the best part of my time in the same way as now, rich or poor. If I did not think so, I should never dare to urge the doctrines of human culture on young men. The farmer, the laborer, has the extreme satisfaction of seeing that the same livelihood he earns is within reach of every man. The lawyer, the author, the singer, has not.[1]

Society seems to have lost all remembrance of the irresponsibility of a writer on human and divine nature. They forget that he is only a reporter, and not at all accountable for the fact he reports. If, in the best use of my eyes, I see not something which people say is there, and see somewhat which they do not say is there, instantly they call me to account as if I had un-

---

[1] It was only for a short time that Mr. Emerson's permanent income was equal to the needs of his modest housekeeping and large hospitality. It was absolutely necessary in later years that he spend most of the winter in lecturing far and near for modest fees to carry him through the year.

made or made the things spoken of. They seem to say, Society is in conspiracy to maintain such and such propositions: and wo betide you if you blab. This diffidence of society in authors seems to show that it has very little experience of any true observers, — of any who did not mix up their personality with their record. The Arabs of the desert would not forgive Belzoni with his spyglass for bringing their camp near to him.

Not the fact avails, but the use you make of it. People would stare to know on what slight single observations those laws were inferred which wise men promulgate and which society receives later and writes down as canons. A single flute heard out of a village window, a single prevailing strain of a village maid, will teach a susceptible man as much as others learn from the orchestra of the Academy. One book as good as the Bodleian Library.

I have learned in my own practice to take advantage of the aforesaid otherism [1] that makes other people's bread and butter taste better than

[1] The reference is to one reading books in a friend's house while ours at home are neglected.

our own, and books read better elsewhere than at home; and now, if I cannot read my German book, I take it into the wood, and there a few sentences have nothing lumpish, but the sense is transparent and broad, and when I come back I can proceed with better heart. So in travelling, how grateful at taverns is Goethe!

September 16.

Dr. Ripley prays, "that the lightning may not lick up our spirits."

Mr. Frost[1] said very happily in today's sermon, "We see God in nature as we see the soul of our friend in his countenance."

You must read a great book to know how poor are all books. Shakspear suggests a wealth that beggars his own.[2] . . .

It does seem as if history gave no intimation of any society in which despondency came so readily to heart as we see it and feel it in ours. Young men, young women, at thirty

1 Rev. Barzillai Frost, Dr. Ripley's colleague and successor as minister of the First Church in Concord.

2 The rest of the passage occurs in "The Over-Soul" (p. 289).

and even earlier seem to have lost all spring and vivacity, and if they fail in their first enterprise, the rest is rock and shallow.[1] Is the Stoic in the soul dead in these late stages? I cannot understand it. Our people are surrounded with greater external prosperity and general well-being than Indians or Saxons: more resources, outlets, asylums: yet we are sad, and these were not. Why should it be? Has not Reflection any remedy for her own diseases? Assume the Immortality. Say boldly, there is no trifle. I see before me the bended horizon. There hangs on high a lovely purple cloud. I accept these sublime pledges by which creative Love and Wisdom yet speak to you and say to you, I am. The memory assures me I have lived. Nature affirms that God is still with me. Then how can I doubt that as good and fair things remain for me as yet I have known? . . . Sadness is always the comparison of the Idea with the Act.

Sunday eve.

I went at sundown to the top of Dr. Ripley's hill and renewed my vows to the Genius of that place. Somewhat of awe, somewhat grand and

[1] The beginning of this paragraph is printed in "The Tragic" (*Natural History of Intellect*, p. 406).

solemn mingles with the beauty that shines afar around. In the West, where the sun was sinking behind clouds, one pit of splendour lay as in a desert of space,—a deposit of *still light*, not radiant. Then I beheld the river, like God's love, journeying out of the grey past on into the green future.

Yet sweet and native as all those fair impressions on that summit fall on the eye and ear, they are not yet mine. I cannot tell why I should feel myself such a stranger in nature. I am a tangent to their sphere, and do not lie level with this beauty. And yet the dictate of the hour is to forget all I have mislearned ; to cease from man, and to cast myself into the vast mould of nature.

A Stranger.—It is singular how slight and indescribable are the tokens by which we anticipate the qualities of sanity, of prudence, of probity, in the countenance of a stranger.

We see with a certain degree of terror the new physique of a foreign man; as a Japanese, a New Zealander, a Calabrian. In a new country how should we look at a large Indian moving in the landscape on his own errand. He would be to us as a lion or a wild elephant.

In such proximity stand the virtues and defects of character that a disgust at some foible will blind men oftener to a grandeur in the same soul. In describing the character of his wife a man may even omit to name a sensibility which is the costliest of attributes, which gives the person who hath it an universal life, and mirrors all nature in her face.

Is not the Vast an element in man? Yet what teaching or book of today appeals to the vast?

When the preacher begins to talk of miracles, I think immediately of the Capuchins.

The mural crown for an argument, the triumphal crown for one just and noble image.

Pericles was not yet ready. To keep order and to give him time, a man of business was in the rostrum mumbling long initial statements of the facts before the people, and the state of Greek affairs. After what seemed a very long time, the people grew nervous and noisy, and, at a movement behind him, he sat down. Pericles arose and occupied the rostrum. His voice was like the stroke of a silver shield. A cold, mathematical statement warmed by imperceptible degrees into earnest announcements of a heroic soul. He conversed with the people, he told stories, he enumerated names and dates and particulars; he played; he joked, though coldly and reservedly, as it seemed to me ; then having thus, as it seemed, drawn his breath, and made himself master of his place and work, he began to deal out his thoughts to the people: the conclusions of his periods were like far-rattling storms. Every word was a ball of fire.

September 18.

A Stranger. — What is the meaning of that? The fork falling sticks upright in the floor, and the children say, a stranger is coming. A stranger is expected or announced, and an uneasiness betwixt pleasure and pain invades all the hearts of a household.[1] . . .

Housekeeping. — If my garden had only made me acquainted with the muckworm, the bugs, the grasses and the swamp of plenty in August, I should willingly pay a free tuition. But every process is lucrative to me beyond its economy. For the like reason keep house. Whoso does,

---

1 Here follows the long passage thus beginning in " Friendship " (*Essays*, First Series, pp. 192, 193).

opens a shop in the heart of all trades, professions and arts, so that upon him these shall all play. By keeping house I go to an universal school where all knowledges are taught me, and the price of tuition *is my annual expense.* Thus, I want my stove set up. I only want a piece of sheet-iron 31 inches by 33. But that want entitles me to call on the professors of tin and iron in the village, Messrs. Wilson and Dean, and inquire of them the kinds of iron they have or can procure, the cost of production of a pound of cast or wrought metal, and any other related information they possess, and furthermore to lead the conversation to the practical experiment of the use of their apparatus for the benefit of my funnel and blower, — all which they courteously do for a small fee. In like manner, I play the chemist with ashes, soap, beer, vinegar, manure, medicines; the naturalist with trees, shrubs, hens, pigs, cows, horses, fishes, bees, cankerworms, wood and coal; the politician with the selectmen, the assessors, the probate court, the town meeting.

Is not the beauty that piques us in every object, in a straw, an old nail, a cobble-stone in the road, the announcement that always our road

lies *out* into nature, and not inward to the wearisome, odious anatomy of ourselves and comparison of me with thee, and accusation of me, and
ambition to take this from thee and add it to
me?

Alcott is a ray of the oldest light. As they
say the light of some stars that parted from the
orb at the deluge of Noah has only now reached
us.

Nomads. — We are all nomads and all chimney ornaments by turns, and pretty rapid turns.[1]
I fancy the chief difference that gives one man
the name of a rover, and one of a fixture, is the
faculty of rapid domestication, the power to find
his chair and bed everywhere, which one man
has, and another has not. In Paris, a man needs
not to go home ever. He can find in any part
of the city his coffee, his dinner, his newspaper,
his company, his theatre, and his bed, as good
as those he left.

A new degree is taken in scholarship as soon
as a man has learned to read in the wood as well
as he reads in the study.

1 Compare the pages on the Nomad tendency in "History"
(*Essays*, First Series).

This afternoon the eclipse. Peter Howe did not like it, for his rowan would not make hay: and he said, "The sun looked as if a nigger was putting his head into it."

The people say, when you shudder, that someone is walking over your grave: they describe and feel a murder and the insults done to a murdered body as a successful revenge; and to pluck out the quivering heart is thought to consummate the harm. They do not see that a man is as much a stranger in his own body as another man is.[1]

The Nomad and the Pivot are two poles, quite essential both to the intellectual culture. The intellectual nomadism is the faculty of objectiveness, or of Eyes which everywhere feed themselves. Who hath such eyes, everywhere falls into true relations to his fellow men. Every man, every object, is a prize, a study, a property to him, and this love smooths his brow, joins him to men and makes him beautiful and beloved in their sight. His house is a wagon, he

1 This is followed by the passage in "Self-Reliance," p. 57, about bringing the past into the thousand - eyed present.

roams through all latitudes as easily as a Calmuc.[1] He must meantime abide by his inward
Law as the Calmuc by his Khan.

We are by nature observers, and so learners.[2]

September 19.

I found in the wood this afternoon the drollest
mushroom, tall, stately, pretending, uprearing
its vast dome as if to say, "Well I am something! Burst, ye beholders! thou luck-beholder!
with wonder." Its dome was a deep yellow
ground with fantastic, starlike ornaments richly
overwrought; so shabby genteel, so negrofine,
the St. Peter's of the beetles and pismires. Such
ostentation *in petto* I never did see. I touched
the white column with my stick,—it nodded
like old Troy, and so eagerly recovered the perpendicular as seemed to plead piteously with
me not to burst the fabric of its pride. Shall I
confess it? I could almost hear my little Waldo
at home begging me, as when I have menaced
his little block-house, and the little puff-ball

1 Compare stanza in "The Poet" (*Poems*, Appendix,
p. 311).
2 Here occurs the passage so beginning in the last paragraph of "Love" (*Essays*, First Series).

seemed to say, "Don't, Papa, pull it down!"
So, after due admiration of this blister, this
cupola of midges, I left the little scaramouch
alone in its glory. Good-bye, Vanity, good-
bye, Nothing! Certainly there is comedy in the
Divine Mind when these little vegetable self-
conceits front the day as well as Newton or
Goethe, with such impressive emptiness.

The greater is the man, the less are books to
him. Day by day he lessens the distance between
him and his authors, and soon finds very few to
whom he can pay so high a compliment as to
read them.

September 20.[1]

. . . .

The fact detached is ugly. Replace it in its
series of cause and effect, and it is beautiful. Putrefaction is loathsome; but putrefaction seen as
a step in the circle of nature, pleases. A mean
or malicious act vexes me; but if I can raise myself to see how it stands related to past and future
in the biography of the doer, it becomes comic,

1 The first entries under this date are the passage in "Self-
Reliance," p. 48, about the boy who can speak strongly to
his mates, and that in "Friendship," p. 200, about the protection of delicate souls by the husk of bashfulness, etc.

pleasant, fair, and prophetic. The laws of disease are the laws of health masked.

All affections to persons are partial and superficial.

Aunts. —

> All Peggy heard she deemed exceeding good,
> But chiefly praised the parts she understood.
>
> JANE TAYLÔR.

They say Dr. Palfrey lost his countenance once at the baptismal font when the affectionate father whispered in his ear the name of his babe, Jacob Adonis. 'T is poor fun, but sometimes resistless—odd names. Zephaniah Tearsheet; Beelzebub Edwards, not the distinguished Beelzebub.

Every homely proverb covers a single and grand fact. Two of these are often in my head lately : " Every dog his day," which covers this fact of otherism, or rotation of merits ; and " There are as many good fish in the sea as ever came out of it " ; which was Nelson's adage of *merit*, and all men's of *marriage*. My third proverb is as deficient in superficial melody as either of the others: "The Devil is an ass." The sea-men use another which has much true divinity: "Every man for himself and God for us all."

September 21.

The equinox.

Subjectiveness. — "I wish I could forget there is any such person as William Channing," said my friend William Henry Channing the other day.

Originality. — How easy to repeat, how mys-teriously problematic to begin an action! To sit upon the merits of Plato, of Voltaire, of Shaks-pear, and simply judge them from our station seems very easy when it is done, and as fast as the author names his subjects it is half done. Yet we do it not. "Where 's kitty?" [1]

Teeth. — The greatest expression of limitation in the human frame is in the teeth. "Thus far," says the face; "No farther," say the teeth. I mean that, whilst the face of the child expresses an excellent possibility, as soon as he opens his

1 Mrs. Emerson was in the habit of diverting the child Waldo when he hurt himself, by saying, "Where 's kitty?"; so when the conversation took a tone of reproof disagreeable to him, he said to his mother, "Where 's kitty?"

mouth, you have an expression of defined qualities. I like him best with his mouth shut.

Scale. — Man, says Goethe, loves the unconditional. All or nothing, in blame, in praise. I like the scale, and hate the neglect of the scale, and, as I tell some of my friends who love the superlative, one day an angel will bring them a golden Gunter.

Inferior Nature. — The excursions of Poetry into lower nature, into the winds, waters, beast, bird, fish, insect, plant-tribes, are Man taking possession of the world on one side, as the classifications of Science are on another side, and the taming of animals and their economical use — on a third side.

Tennyson is a beautiful half of a poet.

September 22.

Nature a Deist. — The thermometer, the microscope, the prism are little deists. They stand like pagans, have a very pagan look when the creed and catechism begin; they are little better than profane: and so a doctor of medicine, a chemist, an astronomer do never remind one of St. Athanasius.

September 24.

Nature a Resource. — Nature is the beautiful asylum to which we look in all the years of striving and conflict as the assured resource when we shall be driven out of society by ennui or chagrin or persecution or defect of character. I say, as I go up the hill and through the wood and see the soliciting plants, I care not for you, mosses and lichens, and for you, fugitive birds, or secular rocks! Grow, fly, or sleep there in your order, which I know is beautiful, though I perceive it not; I am content not to perceive it. Now have I entertainment enough with things nearer, homelier. Things wherein passion enters, and hope and fear have not yet become too dangerous, too insipid, for me to handle. But by and by, if men shall drive me out, if books have become stale, I see gladly that the door of your palace of magic stands ajar,

> and my age
> Shall find the antique hermitage
> The hairy gown and mossy cell.

Nature-knowing. — Nature is no fool. She knows the world. She has calculated the chances of her success, and if her seeds do not vegetate, she will not be chagrined and bereft. She has another arrow left, another card to play, her harvest is insured. From her oak she scatters down a thousand seeds, and if nine hundred rot, the forest is still perpetuated for a century.

Every man projects his character before him, praises it, worships it.

The Indians say, the negro is older than they, and they older than the white man. The negro is the pre-Adamite. But the great-grand-father of all the races, the oldest inhabitant, seems to be the trilobite.

Le Blaie was a man who never printed a let-ter but straightway every country curate must read it, and, without saying a word, run to his barn, tackle up his old horse and chaise and take the road to Paris to know what he must think of this.

It is of great entertainment to read Goethe's notices of Kepler, Roger Bacon, Galileo, New-ton, Voltaire. Yet they consist of the simplest description, almost merely *naming* of the per-sons from his point of view. Nothing was easier than to strike them off. It implied no such labor as to write a Faust or an Egmont. Before it is done, one shrinks from such a dark problem as the estimate of a great genius, a Voltaire, a Newton. Yet he has only to address himself to it, to utter the name of the man in a self-contained, self-centred way, and the problem is solved.[1]

A religious culture to the intellect of men is needed. The intellect has been irreligious these many years, or ages.

The antique expresses the moral sentiment without cant.

Your Turn. — "Each Dog," etc. In childhood, in youth, each man has had many checks and censures, and thinks modestly enough of his own endowment. When, by and by, he comes to unfold it in propitious circumstance, it fills his eye and it fills the eye of all. It seems the only talent. He is surprised and delighted with his success, and carries that out also into the infinite, as man will, and accounts himself

1 The continuation of this passage, written four days later, on Goethe's mention of "the grandees of European Scientific history" from his own point of view, occurs in *Representative Men* ("Goethe," p. 287).

already the fellow of the great. But he goes into company, into a banking house, into a mob, into a mechanic's shop, into a society of scholars, a camp, a ship, a laboratory; and in each new place he is a fool; other talents take place and rule the hour, and his presumption, cowed and whipped, goes back to the timid condition of the boy. For every talent of man runs out to the horizon as well as his.

September 25.

The kiss of the Dryads is not soft; the kiss of the Oreads is still. A good woodland day or two with John Lewis Russell who came here, and showed me mushrooms, lichens and mosses, a man in whose mind things stand in the order of cause and effect, and not in the order of a shop, or even of a cabinet.

Casella[1] sang of love. A song of love that gave us to know and own the natural and the heavenly or divine — that were indeed uplifting music. It seems to me that in the procession of the soul from within outward it enlarges its

1 When Dante met his friend, the beautiful singer, in Purgatory, he begged him to sing, and the souls flocked to hear. — *Purgatorio,* Canto II.

circles ever, like the pebble thrown into the pond or the light proceeding from an orb.[1] . . .

Nature insures herself. Nobody cares for planting the poor fungus. So she shakes down from the gills of one agaric countless spores, any one of which, being preserved, transmits new billions of spores tomorrow or next day.[2] . . .

Let the scholar know that the veneration of man always attaches to him who perceives and utters things in the order of cause and effect.

The divine soul takes care for heroes. It inspires not only every animal body with sagacity and appetite that shall secure food to its belly ; and several individuals in every society, with skill to organize *social* labor, to build the dam, the road, and the boat ; to make the law and mend it ; but it transcends the zones of appetite and of prudence, and darts into some souls gleams out of the deeper heaven. So that here

1 Here follows the long passage thus beginning, printed in "Love" (*Essays*, First Series, pp. 183–186), although combined with sentences written in Journal C the previous year.

2 The long paragraph follows, which is printed in "The Poet" (*Essays*, Second Series, pp. 23–25).

came B. R. and said he never planted anything
which he expected to reap, except corn. He
plants forest trees and arranges improvements
of water and land which will be good for children
and towns to come.

September 28.

Like-minded. — Nothing seems so easy as to
speak and to be understood.[1] . . .

Sickness. — Our health is our sound relation
to external objects ; our sympathy with external
being. A man wakes in the morning sick with
fever; and he perceives at once he has lost his
just relation to the world. Every sound in the
lower parts of the house, or in the street, falls
faint and foreign on his ear. He begins to hear
the frigid doom of cold Obstruction, "Thou
shalt have no part in anything that is done under
the sun."

Famed Books. — It is always an economy of
time to read old and famed books.[2] . . .

Order of Wonder. — If you desire to arrest
attention, to surprise, do not give me facts in the

1 " Spiritual Laws " (*Essays*, First Series, p. 146).
2 See " Books " (*Society and Solitude*, pp. 195, 196).

order of cause and effect, but drop one or two links in the chain, and give me with a cause, an effect two or three times removed.[1]

Apples and Men. — The St. Michael's pear-tree of the present day is a vast forest scattered throughout the gardens of North America and England, yet subject in all the quarters of its dispersion to the diseases incident to the parent stock, and like a disease or an animal race, or any one natural state, it wears out, and will have an end. Each race of man resembles an apple or a pear, the Nubian, the Negro, the Tartar, the Greek; he vegetates, thrives, and multiplies, usurps all the soil and nutriment, and so kills the weaker races; he receives all the benefit of culture under many zones and experiments, but his doom was in nature as well as his thrift, and overtakes him at last with the certainty of gravitation.

"Faction." — A foolish formula is "the spirit of faction," as it is used in books old and new. Can you not get any nearer to the fact than that,

1 This was Mr. Emerson's own method in lectures, to keep attention on the stretch, and give the hearer the creative pleasure of supplying the link.

you old granny? It is like the answer of children, who, when you ask them the subject of the sermon, say, It was about Religion.

Why need you choose?[1] . . .

I wrote Margaret Fuller today, that, seeing how entirely the value of facts is in the classification of the eye that sees them, I desire to study, I desire *longanimity*, to use Bacon's word. I verily believe that a philosophy of history is possible out of the materials that litter and stuff the world that would raise the meaning of Book and Literature. "Cause and effect forever," say I. Those old Egyptians built vast temples and halls in some proportion to the globe on which they were erected, and to the numbers of the nation who were to hold their solemnities within the walls. They built them, not in a day, nor in a single century. So let us with inveterate purpose write our history. Let us not, as now we do, write a history for display and make it after our own image and likeness, — three or four crude notions of our own, and very many crude notions of old historians, hunted out and patched

[1] Here follows the passage thus beginning in "Spiritual Laws."

together without coherence or proportion, and no thought of the necessity of proportion and unity dreamed of by the writer, a great conglomerate; or, at best, an arabesque, a grotesque, containing no necessary reason for its being, nor inscribing itself in our memory like the name and life of a friend. But let us go to the facts of chronology, as Newton went to those of physics, knowing well that they are already bound together of old, and perfectly, and he surveys them that he may detect the bond. Let us learn with the patience and affection of a naturalist all the facts, and looking out all the time for the reason that *was*, for the law that prevailed, and made the facts such; not for one that we can supply and make the facts plausibly sustain. We should then find abundant *aperçus* or lights self-kindled amid the antiquities we explored. Why should not history be godly written, out of the highest Faith and with a study of what really was? We should then have Ideas which would command and marshal the facts, and show the history of a nation as accurately proportioned and necessary in every part as an animal. The connexion of Commerce and Religion explains the history of Africa from the beginning until now. Nomadism is a law of nature, and Asia,

Africa, Europe present different pictures of it. The architecture of each nation had its root in nature. How ample the materials show, when once we have the true Idea that explains all! Then the modern man, the geography, the ruins, the geology, the traditions as well as authentic history, recite and confirm the tale. I said above, Cause and Effect forever! in the thought that out of such incongruous patchwork, thoughtlessly put together as our histories are, nothing can come but incongruous impressions, obscure, unsatisfactory to the mind; but that views obtained by patient wisdom drudging amidst facts would give an analogous impression to the landscape. They say the sublime silent desert now testifies through the mouths of Bruce, Lyon, Caillaud, Burkhardt, to the truth of the calumniated Herodotus.

September 29.

I have a full quiver of facts under that Sapphic and Adonian text of "Every Dog," etc. We are ungrateful creatures. There is nothing we value and hunt and cultivate and strive to draw to us, but in some hour we turn and rend it. We sneer at ignorance and the life of the senses and the ridicule of never thinking, and then goes by a fine girl like M. R., a piece of life, gay because she is happy and making these very commonalities beautiful by the energy and heart with which she does them, and seeing this, straightway we admire and love her and them, say, "Lo! a genuine creature of the fair earth, not *blasé*, not *flétri* by books, philosophy, religion or care"; insinuating by these very words a treachery and contempt for all that we had so long loved and wrought in ourselves and others.

[Many quotations from the writings of Arnold L. Heeren on Asia and Africa occur in this Journal, some of which are used in "History" and other essays.]

As Nature enforces intercourse among men by putting salt and dates and gold and slaves in the desert, and corn in the fields, and hides on the mountains, and fishes in the sea, and these cannot be had but by going thither where they are, so various circles of society possess facts which cannot be had by the student without repairing to them, and they are people he does not like and cannot approach without preparation; Frenchmen, Italians, Germans, Talleyrand, Esterhazy, Metternich, merchants, lovers of art, owners of picture galleries at home, the physician and the master mechanics.

I once wrote that the most abstract truth is the most practical. See how quickly the whole community is touched by an academical discourse on theism. At an imagined assault of a cardinal truth, the very mud boils. Literary men amuse themselves with speculations which do not go into the abstract and absolute, but linger in the conditional and verbal. Wit, *old* poetry, *old* philosophy, mathematics are favorite amusements, for they have no claws, no dangers.

Censure and Praise.[1] — I hate to be defended in a newspaper. As long as all that is said is said *against* me, I feel a certain sublime assurance of success, but as soon as honied words of praise are spoken for me, I feel as one that lies unprotected before his enemies.

1 This passage is printed in " Compensation " (p. 118), but it is given here with those immediately preceding and following it, because this was a stormy period with a doubtful future to Mr. Emerson and his wife, for the " Divinity School Address " had excited a storm of criticism. It seemed a question whether Mr. Emerson's lectures would be attended. The attacks of Professor Andrews Norton and others drew out replies from George Ripley, Orestes Brownson, Theophilus Parsons, and James Freeman Clarke.

Blessed be the wife, that in the talk to-night shared no vulgar sentiment, but said, " In the gossip and excitement of the hour, be as one blind and deaf to it; know it not. Do as if nothing had befallen." And when it was said by the friend, " The end is not yet : wait till it is done," she said, " It is done in Eternity." Blessed be the wife! I, as always, venerate the oracular nature of woman. The sentiment which the man thinks he came unto gradually through the events of years, to his surprise he finds woman dwelling there in the same, as in her native home.

September 30.

Nearness and distinctness seem to be convertible. A noise, a jar, a rumble, is infinitely far off from my nature, though it be within a few inches of the tympanum, but a voice speaking the most intelligible of propositions is so near as to be already a part of myself.

It seems as if a man should learn to fish, to plant, or to hunt, that he might secure his subsistence if he were cast out from society and not be painful to his friends and fellow men.[1]

1 This was more than an abstract speculation to Mr. Emerson at this crisis.

Royal Education. — It would seem that in the
ancient Eastern kingdoms better views of an
education at court prevailed than in the kingdoms of modern Europe. "And the king spake
unto Ashpenaz, the master of his eunuchs, that
he should bring certain of the children of Israel
and of the king's seed and of the princes; children in whom was no blemish, but well favoured
and skilful in all wisdom, and cunning in knowledge, and understanding science, and such as
had ability in them, to stand in the king's palace, and whom they might teach the learning
and tongue of the Chaldeans." DANIEL, i, 3, 4.

Rich and Poor. — My grandfather, John Haskins, was wont to say, "that the poor ought to
pray for the prosperity of the rich, for, in that
lay their own." Not so thinks the Globe.

Every vice is only an exaggeration of a necessary and virtuous function.

We love to hear in the midst of society some
word that nothing but austerest solitude and
conversation with God, with love and death,
could ever have uttered. Such, too, is the sincerest joy of fine society to meet in its princes

and princesses some authentic token of the
Eternal Beauty.

October 4.

Letter to W. Silsbee. — I read in your letter
the expressions of an earnest character of faith,
of hope, with extreme interest; and if I can contribute any aid by sympathy or suggestion to
the solution of the great problems that occupy
you, I shall be glad. But I think it must be
done by degrees. I am not sufficiently master
of the little truth I see, to know how to state it
in forms so general as shall put every mind in
possession of my point of view. We generalize
and rectify our expressions by continual efforts
from day to day, from month to month, to reconcile our own sight with that of our companions. So shall two inquirers have the best mutual action on each other. But I should never
attempt a direct answer to such questions as
yours. I have no language that could shortly
present my state of mind in regard to each
of them with any fidelity; for my state of
mind on each is nowise final and detached, but
tentative, progressive, and strictly connected
with the whole circle of my thoughts. It seems
to me that to understand any man's thoughts
respecting the Supreme Being, we need an in-

sight into the general habit and tendency of his speculations : for, every man's idea of God is the last or most comprehensive generalization at which he has arrived. — But besides the extreme difficulty of stating our results on such questions in a few propositions, I think, my dear sir, that a certain religious feeling deters us from the attempt. I do not gladly utter any deep conviction of the soul in any company where I think it will be contested, no, nor unless I think it will be welcome. Truth has already ceased to be itself if polemically said; and if the soul would utter oracles, as every soul should, it must live for itself, keep itself right-minded, — observe with such awe its own law as to concern itself very little with the engrossing topics of the hour, unless they be its own. I believe that most of the speculative difficulties which infest us, we must thank ourselves for ; each mind, if true to itself, will, by living forthright, and not importing into it the doubts of other men, dissolve all difficulties, as the sun at midsummer burns up the clouds. Hence I think the aid we can give each other is only incidental, lateral, and sympathetic. If we are true and benevolent, we reënforce each other by every act and word. Your heroism stimulates mine ; your light kindles mine. And the end of all this is, that I thank you heartily for the confidence of your letter, and beg you to use your earliest leisure to come and see me. It is very possible that I shall not be able to give you one definition, but I will show you with joy what I strive after and what I worship, as far as I can. Meantime, I shall be very glad to hear from you by letter.

October 5.

Once I thought it a defect peculiar to me, that I was confounded by interrogatories and when put on my wits for a definition was unable to reply without injuring my own truth: but now, I believe it proper to man to be unable to answer in terms the great problems put by his fellow: it is enough if he can live his own definitions. A problem appears to me. I cannot solve it with all my wits: but leave it there; let it lie awhile: I can by patient, faithful truth live at last its uttermost darkness into light.

Books. — It seems meritorious to read: but from everything but history or the works of the old commanding writers I come back with a conviction that the slightest *wood-thought*, the least significant native emotion of my own, is more to me.

Compensation. — How soon the sunk spirits rise again, how quick the little wounds of fortune skin over and are forgotten. I am sensitive as a leaf to impressions from abroad, and under this night's beautiful heaven I have forgotten that ever I was reviewed. It is strange how superficial are our views of these matters, seeing we are all writers and philosophers. A man thinks it of importance what the great sheet or pamphlet of to-day proclaims of him to all the reading town; and if he sees graceful compliments, he relishes his dinner; and if he sees threatening paragraphs and odious nicknames, it becomes a solemn, depressing fact and sables his whole thoughts until bedtime. But in truth the effect of these paragraphs is mathematically measureable by their depth of thought. How much water do they draw? If they awaken you to think — if they lift you from your feet with the great voice of eloquence — then their effect is to be wide, slow, permanent over the minds of men: but if they instruct you not, they will die like flies in an hour.

October 9.

They put their finger on their lip, — the Powers above.[1]

1 The opening line of "Eros" (*Poems*, Appendix, p. 362).

I have intimations of my riches much more than possession, as is the lot of other heirs. Every object suggests to me in certain moods a dim anticipation of profound meaning, as if, by and by, it would appear to me why the apple-tree, why the meadow, why the stump stand there, and what they signify to me.

Van Burenism. — I passed by the shop and saw my spruce neighbor, the dictator of our rural Jacobins, teaching his little circle of villagers their political lessons. And here, thought I, is one who loves what I hate: here is one wholly reversing my code. I hate persons who are nothing but persons. I hate numbers. He cares for nothing but numbers and persons. All the qualities of man, all his accomplishments, affections, enterprises, except solely the ticket he votes for, are nothing to this philosopher. Numbers of majorities are all he sees in the newspaper. All of North or South, all in Georgia, Alabama, Pennsylvania or New England that this man considers is, What is the relation of Mr. Clay, or of Mr. Van Buren, to those mighty mountain chains, those vast, fruitful champaigns, those expanding nations of men. What an existence is this, to have no home, no heart, but to feed on the very refuse and old straw and chaff of man,—the numbers and names of voters!

One thing deserves the thought of the modern Jacobin. It seems the relations of society, the position of classes, irk and sting him.[1] . . .

In our vulgar politics the knowing men have a good deal to say about the "moral effect" of a victory and a defeat. The fact that the city of New York has gone for the Whigs, though only by a slender majority, is of the utmost importance to the Whig party about to vote in a distant state. Why? because it is a fact, a presentable fact. States of mind we care not for; we ignore them; but a mere fact, though proving a less favorable state of mind than we have a right to infer, we overvalue. A man writes a book which displeases somebody, who writes an angry paragraph about it in the next newspaper. That solitary paragraph, whilst it stands unanswered, seems the voice of the world. Hundreds of passive readers read it with such passiveness that it becomes their voice. The man that made

1 The rest of the passage thus beginning on "the Offence of Superiority in persons" is in "Aristocracy" (*Lectures and Biographical Sketches*, p. 35).

the book and his friends are superstitious about it. They cannot put it out of their heads. Their entire relations to society seem changed. What was yesterday a warm, convenient, hospitable world, soliciting all the talents of all its children, looks bleak and hostile, and our native tendency to complete any view we take carries the imagination out at once to images of persecution, hatred and want.

In debate, the last speaker always carries with him such a prevailing air that all seems to be over and the question settled when he concludes; so that, if a new man arise and state with nonchalance a new and opposite view, we draw our breath freely and hear with a marked surprise this suspension of fate.

An Election. — The fact of having been elected to a conspicuous office, as President, King, Governor, etc., even though we know the paltry machinery by which it was brought about, is, notwithstanding, a certificate of value to the person in *all* men's eyes, ever after.

The courage of men is shown in resisting this *fact* and preferring the *state of mind*.[1] The poet

1 Compare Thoreau's attitude. "Thoreau" (*Lectures and Biographical Sketches*, p. 471).

must set over against the lampoon his conviction of divine light, the patriot his deep devotion to the country against the mere hurra of the boys in the street.

Faces. — A domestic warning we have against degradation in the face of a man whilst he speaks his best and whilst he speaks his basest sentiment. Now, uttering his genuine life, he is strong as the world, and his face is manly, but instantly, on his expression of a mean thought, his countenance is changed to a pitiful, ridden, bestial portrait.

If a man live in the saddle, the saddle somehow will come to live in him. Tick, tack.

Any single fact considered by itself confounds, misleads us. Let it lie awhile. It will find its place, by and by, in God's chain; its golden brothers will come, one on the right hand and one on the left, and in an instant it will be the simplest, gladdest, friendliest of things.

Turns. — It is a beautiful fact that every spot of earth, every dog, pebble, and ash-heap, as well as every palace and every man, is whirled round in turn to the meridian.

Eloquence. — I thought I saw the sun and moon fall into his head, as seeds fall into the ground, that they might quicken and bring forth new worlds to fill nature.[1]

October 11.

It is not true that educated men desire truth. The medical committee decline proffered opportunities of witnessing experiments in animal magnetism.

Swedenborgianism is one of the many forms of Manichæism. It denies the omnipotence of God or pure spirit.

October 12.

If it were possible to speak to the virtue in each of our friends in perfect simplicity, then would society instantly attain its perfection. If I could say to the young man, the young girl whom I meet in company, "Your countenance, your behaviour please me: I discover in you the sparkles of a right royal virtue. I entreat you to revere its sublime intimations"; and this could be heard by the other party with a quiet, perfect trust, then instantly a league is struck between

1 See "Fragments on the Poet," etc. (*Poems*, Appendix v, p. 326), also the last sentence in "Man the Reformer" (*Nature, Addresses, and Lectures*).

two souls that makes life grand, and suffering and sorrow musical. Who would pine under the endurance of the many heavy hours of incapacity and mere waiting that creep over us? Who would decline a sacrifice, if once his soul had been accosted, his virtue recognized, and he was assured that a Watcher, a Holy One followed him ever with long, affectionate glances of inexhaustible love? What then if many simple souls, studious of science, of botany, of chemistry, natural history, lovers of all learning, and scorners of all seeming, should freely say to me, " God keep you, brother; let us worship virtue," — by what a heavenly guard I should feel myself environed! But the charm is that mere heathens should say this. They may be lovers of Christ, be sure, but they must love him heathenly. For if there be the least smoothness and passive reception in them, then all their talk is cant, and I quit the room if they speak to me.

But now I am not sure that the educated class ever ascend to the idea of virtue; or that they desire truth: they want safety, utility, decorum. In order to present the bare idea of virtue, it is necessary that we should go quite out of our circumstance and custom, else it will be instantly confounded with the poor decency and inanition,

the poor ghost that wears its name in good society. Therefore it is that we fly to the pagans
and use the name and relations of Socrates, of
Confucius, Menu, Zoroaster; not that these are
better or as good as Jesus and Paul (for they
have not uttered so deep moralities), but because
they are good algebraic terms, not liable to confusion of thought like those we habitually use.
So Michel Angelo's sonnets addressed to Vit-
toria Colonna, we see to be mere rhapsodies to
Virtue, and in him, a savage Artist, they are as
unsuspicious, uncanting, as if a Spartan or an
Arab spoke them.

It seems not unfit that the scholar should
deal plainly with society and tell them that he
saw well enough before he spoke the consequence of his speaking; that up there in his silent study, by his dim lamp, he fore-heard this
Babel of outcries. The nature of man he knew,
the insanity that comes of inaction and tradition, and knew well that when their dream and
routine were disturbed, like bats and owls and
nocturnal beasts they would howl and shriek
and fly at the torch-bearer. But he saw plainly
that under this their distressing disguise of bird-
form and beast form, the divine features of man

were hidden, and he felt that he would dare to be so much their friend as to do them this violence to drag them to the day and to the healthy air and water of God, that the unclean spirits that had possessed them might be exorcised and depart. The taunts and cries of hatred and anger, the very epithets you bestow on me, are so familiar long ago in my reading that they sound to me ridiculously old and stale. The same thing has happened so many times over (that is, with the appearance of every original observer) that, if people were not very ignorant of literary history, they would be struck with the exact coincidence. I, whilst I see this, that you must have been shocked and must cry out at what I have said, I see too that we cannot easily be reconciled, for I have a great deal more to say that will shock you out of all patience.

Every day I am struck with new particulars of the antagonism between your habits of thought and action, and the divine law of your being, and as fast as these become clear to me you may depend on my proclaiming them.

Succession, division, parts, particles, — this is the condition, this the tragedy of man. All things cohere and unite. Man studies the parts, strives to tear the part from its connexion, to magnify it, and make it a whole. He sides with the part against other parts; and fights for parts, fights for lies, and his whole mind becomes an *inflamed part*, an amputated member, a wound, an offence. Meantime within him is the soul of the whole, the wise silence, the Universal Beauty to which every part and particle is equally related, the eternal one. Speech is the sign of partiality, difference, ignorance, and the more perfect the understanding between men, the less need of words. And when I know all, I shall cease to commend any part. An ignorant man thinks the divine wisdom is conspicuously shown in some fact or creature: a wise man sees that every fact contains the same. I should think Water the best invention, if I were not acquainted with Fire and Earth and Air. But as we advance, every proposition, every action, every feeling, runs out into the infinite. If we go to affirm anything we are checked in our speech by the need of recognizing all other things, until speech presently becomes rambling, general, indefinite, and merely tautology. The only speech will at last be action, such as Confucius describes the speech of God.

October 12.

I wrote Margaret Fuller;— I begin to be proud of my contemporaries and wish to behold their whole course. Such pictures as you have sent me now and before exalt our interest in individual characters and suggest ideas of society how lofty and refined! but not now to be realized.[1] . . . I see my old gossip Montaigne is coming up again to honor in these prim, decorous days; who would think it? And are you not struck with a certain subterranean current of identical thought that bubbles up to daylight in very remote and dissimilar circles of thought and culture?

The physician tends always to invert man, to look upon the body as the cause of the soul, to look upon man as tyrannized over by his members.

October 13.

Do not be a night-chair, a warming-pan, at sick-beds and rheumatic souls. Do not let them make a convenience of you. Do not be a pastry-cook either and give parties.

1 Here follows the passage in " Friendship " about subtle antagonisms, etc. (*Essays*, First Series, p. 199).

October 14.

Measure your present habit of thought and action by all your external standards, if you will; by the remembrance of your dead; by the remembrance of the three or four great men who are yet alive; by the image of your distant friends; by the lives and precepts of the heroes and philosophers; these all are only shadows of the primary sentiment at home in your old soul.

The talent of the poet seems to consist in presence of mind, the ability to seize the fact and image which all others know very well, but cannot collect themselves sufficiently to use in the right time.

October 16.

Reform and potatoes seem to have a pretty strict understanding. Most venerable plant! thou sturdy republican, abolitionist, anti-money, teetotaller! Does a man hear of Temperance or Peace, or Embargo, or Slavery, or domestic hired Service, or the rise of the poor against the rich; of any revolution or project of perfection? — he thinks directly on blue-noses and long-reds.

Here came on Sunday morning (14th) Edward Palmer and departed today, a gentle, faithful, sensible, well-balanced man for an enthusiast. He has renounced, since a year ago last April, the use of money. When he travels, he stops at night at a house and asks if it would give them any satisfaction to lodge a traveller without money or price. If they do not give him a hospitable answer, he goes on, but generally finds the country people free and willing. When he goes away, he gives them his papers or tracts. He has sometimes found it necessary to go twenty-four hours without food, and all night without lodging. Once he found a wagon with a good buffalo under a shed, and had a very good nap. By the seashore he finds it difficult to travel, as they are inhospitable. He presents his views with great gentleness; and is not troubled if he cannot show the way in which the destruction of money is to be brought about; he feels no responsibility to show or know the details. It is enough for him that he is sure it must fall, and that he clears himself of the institution altogether.

Why should not I, if a man comes and asks me for a book, give it him? If he asks me to write a letter for him, write it? If he ask me to write a poem or a discourse which I can fitly write, why should I not? And if my neighbor is as skilful in making cloth, why should not all of us who have wool send it to him to make for the common benefit, and when we want ten yards or twenty yards go to him and ask for so much, and he, like a gentleman gives us exactly what we ask without hesitation, and so let every house keep a store-room in which they place their superfluity of what they produce, and open it with ready confidence to the wants of the neighborhood, and without an account of debtor and credit?[1] Edward Palmer asks if it would be a good plan for a family of brothers and sisters to keep an account of debtor and creditor of their good turns, and expect an exact balance? And is not the human race a family? Does not kindness disarm?

It is plain that if perfect confidence reigned, then it would be possible, and he asks how is confidence to be promoted but by reposing confidence? It seems to me that I have a perfect claim on the community for the supply of all my wants if I have worked hard all day, or if I have spent my day well, have done what I could, though no meat, shoes, cloth, or utensils, have been made by me; yet if I have spent my time in the best manner I could, I must have bene-

---

1 The above seems to be Mr. Emerson's abstract of Palmer's theory, considerately stated.

fitted the world in some manner that will appear and be felt somewhere. If we all do so, we shall all find ourselves able to ask and able to bestow with confidence. It seems, too, that we should be able to say to the lazy, "You are lazy; you should work and cure this disease. I will not give you all you ask, but only a part. Pinch yourself today and ask me for more when you have laboured more, as your brothers do, for them."

However, I incline to think that among angels the money or certificate system might have some important convenience, not for thy satisfaction of whom I borrow, but for my satisfaction that I have not exceeded carelessly any proper wants, — have not overdrawn.

The devil can quote texts. There is one rule that should regulate the appeal, often so indecorous and irrational, to Scripture: You may quote the example of Paul or Jesus to a better sentiment or practice than the one proposed, but never to a worse. Thus, if it is acknowledged or felt that there would be a superior purity in using water to using wine, — do not quote Jesus as using wine. If it would be nobler to appeal to the love of men when you want bread or shoes than to give them a pledge of restoring them (which money is) do not quote Jesus or Paul as paying taxes or living in "mine own hired home."

It was said in conversation at Mr. B's, that the world owes the world more than the world can pay, so that the world had better fail and settle up.

Edward Palmer said that it usually happened at farmhouses where he stopped, that, "when he came in conversation to unfold his views to the people, they were interested in his plan." Thus each reformer carries about in him a piece of me, and as soon as I know it, I am perforce his kinsman and brother. I must feel that he is pleading my cause and shall account myself serving myself in giving him what he lacketh.

October 18.

Sent a letter today to T. Carlyle, per *Royal William*.[1]

1 This is Letter XXVIII in the *Carlyle-Emerson Correspondence*, in which Mr. Emerson asks Carlyle to postpone his intended visit and the lecturing scheme in America until the storm which the "Divinity School Address" had raised up

Today came Washburn, Lippitt, Ellis, and Atkins to dine.[1]

October 19.

Let me add of quoting Scripture, to what was said above, that I hate to meet this slavish custom in a solemn expression of sentiment, like the late manifesto of the Peace Convention. It seems to deny, with the multitude, the omnipresence and the eternity of God. Once, he spoke through good men these special words. Now, if we have aught high and holy to do, we must wrench somehow their words to speak it in. We have none of our own. Humbly rather let us go and ask God's leave to use the Hour and Language that now is. Cannot you ransack the grave-yards and get your great-grandfather's clothes also? It is like the single coat in Sainte Lucie in which the islanders one by one paid their respects to the new governor. It is a poor-spirited age. The great army of cowards who bellow and bully from their bed-chamber windows have no confidence in truth or God.

should abate, for he felt that Carlyle's prospects would suffer thereby.

1 Edward A. Washburn, George Warren Lippitt, Rufus Ellis, and Benjamin F. Atkins ; the first three, having graduated at Harvard that year, were divinity students.

Truth will not maintain itself, they fancy, unless they bolster it up, and whip and stone the assailants; and the religion of God, the being of God, they seem to think dependent on what we say of it. The feminine vehemence with which the A. N.[1] of the Daily Advertiser beseeches the dear people to whip that naughty heretic is the natural feeling in the mind whose religion is external. It cannot subsist; it suffers shipwreck if its faith is not confirmed by all surrounding persons. A believer, a mind whose faith is consciousness, is never disturbed because other persons do not yet see the fact which he sees.

It is plain that there are two classes in our educated community: first, those who confine themselves to the facts in their consciousness; and secondly, those who superadd sundry propositions. The aim of a true teacher now would be to bring men back to a trust in God and destroy before their eyes these idolatrous propositions: to teach the doctrine of the perpetual revelation.

October 20.

All inquiry into antiquity, all curiosity re-

----

[1] Andrews Norton.

specting the Pyramids . . . is simply and at last the desire to do away this wild savage preposterous *Then*, introduce in its place the *Now*: it is to banish the *not me* and supply the *me*; it is to abolish *difference* and restore *unity*.[1] . . . And this is also the aim in all science, in the unprofitable abysses of entomology, in the gigantic masses of geology, and spaces of astronomy, simply to transport our consciousness of cause and effect into those remote and by us uninhabited members, and see that they all proceed from " causes now in operation," from one mind, and that ours.

Steady, steady! When this fog of good and evil affections falls, it is hard to see and walk straight.

One Mind. — The ancients exchanged their names with their friends, signifying that in their friend they loved their own soul.

What said my brave Asia[2] concerning the paragraph writers, today? that " this whole

1 Here occurs the paragraph so beginning in " History " (p. 11).

2 One of Mr. Emerson's names for his wife.

practice of self-justification and recrimination betwixt literary men seemed every whit as low as the quarrels of the Paddies."

Then said I, "But what will you say, excellent Asia, when my smart article comes out in the paper, in reply to Mr. A. and Dr. B.?" — "Why, then," answered she, "I shall feel the first emotion of fear and sorrow on your account." — "But do you know," I asked, "how many fine things I have thought of to say to these fighters? They are too good to be lost." — "Then," rejoined the queen, "there is some merit in being silent."

It is plain from all the noise that there is atheism somewhere ; the only question is now, Which is the atheist?

It is observable, as I have written before, that even the science of the day is introversive. The microscope is carried to perfection. And Geology looks no longer in written histories, but examines the earth that it may be its own chronicle.

"Please, papa, tell me a story," says the child of two years ; who will say then that the novel has not a foundation in nature?

Idols. — Men are not units but poor mixtures.
. . . They accept how weary a load of tradition
from their elders and more forcible neighbors.
By and by, as the divine effort of creation and
growth begins in them, new loves, new aversions, take effect, — the first radiation of their
own soul amidst things. Yet each of these outbursts of the central life is partial, and leaves
abundance of traditions still in force. Each
soul has its idols.[1] . . .

But the new expansion and upthrusting from
the centre shall classify our facts by new radiation and will show us idols in how many things
which now we esteem part and parcel of our
constitution and lot in nature. Property, Government, Books, Systems of Education and of
Religion, will successively detach themselves
from the growing spirit. I call an Idol anything which a man honors, which the constitution of his mind does not necessitate him to
honor.

TO MISS EMERSON

October 21.

Is the ideal society always to be only a dream,
a song, a luxury of thought, and never a step

1 Here follows the passage on the idol of Italy, of travelling,
etc. ("Self-Reliance," pp. 80, 81).

taken to realize the vision for living and indigent men without misgivings within and wildest ridicule abroad ? Between poetry and prose must the great gulf yawn ever, and they who try to bridge it over be lunatics or hypocrites ? And yet the too dark ground of history is starred over with solitary heroes who dared to believe better of their brothers, and who prevailed by actually executing the law (the high ideal) in their own life, and, though a hissing and an offence to their contemporaries, yet they became a celestial sign to all succeeding souls as they journeyed through nature. How shine the names of Abraham, Diogenes, Pythagoras, and the transcendent Jesus, in antiquity ! And now, in our turn, shall we esteem the elegant decorum of our world, and what is called greatness and splendor in it, of such a vast and outweighing worth, as to reckon all aspirations after the Better fanciful or pitiable, and all aspirants pert and loathsome? There is a limit, and (as in some hours we fancy) a pretty speedy limit, to the value of what is called success in life. The great world, too, always bears unexpected witness to the rhapsodies of the idealists. The fine and gay people are often disconcerted when the Reformer points out examples of his doctrine in the midst of what is finest and gayest. Thus always the Christian humility was aped by the protestations of courtesy, and always the great-hearted children of fortune, — the Cæsars, Cleopatras, Alcibiadeses, Essexes and Sidneys within their own proud pale have treated fortune and the popular estimates with a certain defiance and contempt. Irregular glimpses they had of the real Good and Fair which added a more than royal loftiness to their behavior and to their dealing with houses and lands.

Is it not droll, though, that these porcelain creatures should turn as quick as the fashionable mob on the poor cobblers, peasants and school-masters who preached the good and fair to mankind, and be willing to burn them up with the rays of aristocratic majesty?

I, for my part, am very well pleased to see the variety and velocity of the movements that all over our broad land, in spots and corners, agitate society. War, slavery, alcohol, animal food, domestic hired service, colleges, creeds, and now at last money, also, have their spirited and unweariable assailants, and must pass out of use or must learn a law.

Mine Asia [1] says, A human being should be-

[1] Mrs. Emerson.

ware how he laughs, for then he shows all his faults.

A great colossal soul, I fancy, was Swedenborg.[1] . . .

Edward Palmer asked me if I liked two services in a Sabbath. I told him, Not very well. If the sermon was good I wished to think of it; if it was bad, one was enough.

October 26.

Jones Very came hither, two days since, and gave occasion to many thoughts on his peculiar state of mind and his relation to society. His position accuses society as much as society names it false and morbid; and much of his discourse concerning society, the church, and the college was perfectly just.

Entertain every thought, every character, that goes by with the hospitality of your soul. Give him the freedom of your inner house. He shall make you wise to the extent of his own uttermost receivings.

1 Here occurs the passage beginning similarly in *Representative Men*, p. 102. It is followed by the passage in the same volume (p. 204) as to the effect of Shakspear's work on German thought.

Especially if one of these monotones, whereof, as my friends think, I have a savage society, like a menagerie of monsters, come to you, receive him. For the partial action of his mind in one direction is a telescope for the objects on which it is pointed. And as we know that every path we take is but a radius of our sphere, and we may dive as deep in every other direction as we have in that, a far insight of one evil suggests instantly the immense extent of that revolution that must be wrought before He whose right it is shall reign, the all in all.

Vocabularies. — In going through Italy I speak Italian, through Arabia, Arabic: I say the same *things*, but have altered my speech. But ignorant people think a foreigner speaking a foreign tongue a formidable, odious nature, alien to the backbone. So is it with our brothers. Our journey, the journey of the soul, is through different regions of thought, and to each its own vocabulary. As soon as we hear a new vocabulary from our own, at once we exaggerate the alarming differences, — account the man suspicious, a thief, a pagan, and set no bounds to our disgust or hatred, and, late in life, perhaps too late, we find he was loving and hating, doing and thinking the same *things* as we, under his own vocabulary.

Scholar. — Every word, every striking word that occurs in the pages of an original genius, will provoke attack and be the subject of twenty pamphlets and a hundred paragraphs. Should he be so duped as to stop and listen? Rather, let him know that the page he writes today will contain a new subject for the pamphleteers, and that which he writes tomorrow, more. Let him not be misled to give it any more than the notice due from him, viz., just that which it had in his first page, before the controversy. The exaggeration of the notice is right for them, false for him. Every word that he quite naturally writes is as prodigious and offensive. So write on, and, by and by, will come a reader and an age that will justify all your contest. Do not even look behind. Leave that bone for them to pick and welcome.

Let me study and work contentedly and faithfully; I do not remember my critics. I forget them, — I depart from them by every step I take. If I think then of them, it is a bad sign.

In my weak hours I look fondly to Europe

and think how gladly I would live in Florence
and Rome. In my manly hours, I defy these
leanings, these lingering looks *behind*, these
flesh-pots of Egypt, and feel that my duty is
my place and that the merrymen of circumstance should follow as they might. . . .

*Quand on a raison, on a souvent beaucoup plus
raison qu' on ne croit.* — GUIZOT.

We refer all things to time, as we refer the
immensely sundered stars to one concave sphere,
and so we say that the Judgment is near.[1] . . .

C. had a persuasion to win fate to his purpose ; make that which was seem to the beholders not to be, and his tongue did lick the
four elements away.

Converse with a soul which is grandly simple,
and literature looks like word-catching.[2] . . .

O, worthy Mr. Graham, poet of bran-bread
and pumpkins, there is a limit to the revolu-

[1] Here follows a long passage printed in " The Over-
Soul," beginning thus (*Essays*, First Series, p. 273).

[2] Here occurs the long passage so beginning in " The
Over-Soul " (pp. 291, 292).

tions of a pumpkin, project it along the ground with what force soever. It is not a winged orb like the Egyptian symbol of dominion, but an unfeathered, ridgy, yellow pumpkin, and will quickly come to a standstill.[1]

Literature is a heap of verbs and nouns enclosing an intuition or two, a few ideas and a few fables.

Literature is a subterfuge.

One man might have writ all the first rate pieces we call English literature.

Literature is eaves-dropping.

Literature is an amusement; virtue is the business of the universe.

We must use the language of facts, and not be superstitiously abstract.

October 27.

The ray of light passes invisible through space, and only when it falls on an object, is it seen. So your spiritual energy is barren and useless until it is directed on something outward: then is it a thought: the relation between

1 This apostrophe is to Mr. Sylvester Graham, the diet reformer, whose book, *Bread and Bread-Making*, had a great influence among dyspeptics and reformers in those days.

you and it first makes you, the value of you, apparent to me.

It is the tragedy of life that the highest gifts are not secure. What purer efflux of the Godhead than the ray of the moral sentiment? Yet it comes before me so pure as to consent in language to all the tests we can apply, and yet is it morbid, painful, unwise. My faith is perfect that what is from God shall be more wise, more fair, more gracious, more manifold, more rejoicing than aught the soul had already. How sad to behold aught coming in that name (self delighted too that it comes from him), which gives no light, which confounds only, which shines on nothing, affirming meantime that it is all light; which does nothing, affirming steadily that it does and is all.

Mrs. Ripley is superior to all she knows. She reminds one of a steam-mill of great activity and power which must be fed, and she grinds German, Italian, Greek, Chemistry, Metaphysics, Theology, with utter indifference which, — something she must have to keep the machine from tearing itself.

The influence of an original genius is matter

of literary history. It seems as if the Shakspear could not be admired, could not even be seen until his living, conversing and writing had diffused his spirit into the young and acquiring class so that he had multiplied himself into a thousand sons, a thousand Shakspears and so *understands himself*.

October 28.

Jones Very says it is with him a day of hate; that he discerns the bad element in every person whom he meets, which repels him : he even shrinks a little to give the hand, — that sign of receiving. The institutions, the cities which men have built the world over, look to him like a huge blot of ink. His own only guard in going to see men is that he goes to do them good, else they would injure him (spiritually). He lives in the sight that he who made him, made the things he sees.

He would as soon embrace a black Egyptian mummy as Socrates. He would obey, obey. He is not disposed to attack religions and charities, though false. The bruised reed he would not break ; the smoking flax he would not quench. To Lidian he says, " Your thought speaks there, and not your life." And he is very sensible of *interference* in thought and act. A very accurate

discernment of spirits belongs to his state, and
he detects at once the presence of an alien element, though he cannot tell whence, how, or
whereto it is. He thinks me covetous in my hold
of truth, of seeing truth separate, and of receiving or taking it, instead of merely obeying. The
Will is to him all, as to me (after my own showing)
Truth. He is sensible in me of a little colder
air than that he breathes. He says, " You do not
disobey because you do the wrong act; but you
do the wrong act, because you disobey ; and you
do not obey because you do the good action, but
you do the good action because you first obey."
He has nothing to do with time, because he
obeys. A man who is busy says he has no time ;
— he does not recognize that element. A man
who is idle says he does not know what to do
with his time. Obedience is in eternity. He says,
It is the necessity of the spirit to speak with authority. What led him to study Shakspear was
the fact that all young men say, Shakspear was
no saint, — yet see what genius ! He wished to
solve that problem.

He had the manners of a man, one, that is,
to whom life was more than meat, the body than
raiment. He felt it an honor, he said, to wash
his face, being, as it was, the temple of the spirit.

And he is gone into the multitude as solitary as
Jesus. In dismissing him I seem to have discharged an arrow into the heart of society.
Wherever that young enthusiast goes he will astonish and disconcert men by dividing for them
the cloud that covers the profound gulf that is
in man.

October 29.

We are wiser, I see well, than we know.[1] . . .

Travelling foolish. We imagine that in Germany is the aliment which the mind seeks, or in
this reading, or in that. But go to Germany, and
you shall not find it. They have sent it to America. It is not without, but within: it is not in
geography, but in the soul.

Sincerity is the highest compliment you can
pay. Jones Very charmed us all by telling us he
hated us all.

October 30.

And I am to seek to solve for my fellows the
problem of Human Life, in words, — for that is

1 Here follows the sentences in "The Over-Soul" about
not interfering with the thought, and the soul's being a separating sword (*Essays*, First Series, p. 280) ; and that on the
Divine thought demolishing centuries, witness Christ's teaching (p. 273).

the subject advertised for my lectures presently.
Well, boy, what canst thou say? Knowest thou
its law? its way? its equipoise? its endless end?
Seest thou the inevitable conditions which all
seek to dodge?[1] . . .

There is reason enough for the coincidences,
the signs, the presentiments which astonish every
person now and then in the course of his life.
For, as every spirit makes its own condition and
history, the reason of the event is always latent
in the life.

The correspondence of O'Connell and our
American Stevenson indicates a new step taken
in civilization. Our haughty, feudal Virginian
suddenly finds his rights to enter the society of
gentlemen questioned, and he obliged to mince
and shuffle and equivocate in his sentences, to
deny that he is a slave-breeder without denying
that he is a slave-owner. He finds that the eyes
of men have got so far opened that they must
see well the distinction between a cavalier and
the cavalier's negro-driver, a race abhorred.

1 Here follow the passages in "Compensation" thus beginning (p. 105), and on the price exacted for eminence, for
light, wealth, and fame (pp. 99, 100, 104).

The men you meet and seek to raise to higher thought know as well as you know that you are of them, and that you stand yet on the ground, whilst you say to them sincerely, let us arise, let us fly. But once fly yourself, and they will look up to you.

There is no terror like that of being known. The world lies in night of sin. It hears not the cock crowing : it sees not the grey streak in the East. At the first entering ray of light, society is shaken with fear and anger from side to side. Who opened that shutter? they cry, Wo to him! They belie it, they call it darkness that comes in, affirming that they were in light before. Before the man who has spoken to them the dread word, they tremble and flee. They flee to new topics, to their learning, to the solid institutions about them, to their great men, to their windows, and look-out on the road and passengers, to their very furniture, and meats, and drinks, — any-where, anyhow to escape the apparition. The wild horse has heard the whisper of the tamer : the maniac has caught the glance of the keeper. They try to forget the memory of the speaker, to put him down into the same obscure place he occupied in their minds before he spake to

them. It is all in vain. They even flatter themselves that they have killed and buried the enemy, when they have magisterially denied and
denounced him. But vain, vain, all vain. It was
but the first mutter of the distant storm they
heard, — it was the first cry of the Revolution,
— it was the touch, the palpitation that goes
before the earthquake. Even now society is
shaken because a thought or two have been
thrown into the midst. The sects, the colleges,
the church, the statesmen all have forebodings.
It now works only in a handful. What does
State Street and Wall Street and the Royal Exchange and the Bourse at Paris care for these
few thoughts and these few men? Very little;
truly; most truly. But the doom of State Street,
and Wall Street, of London, and France, of the
whole world, is advertised by those thoughts;
is in the procession of the Soul which comes
after those few thoughts.

Does a man wish to remain concealed? A few
questions (who does not see?) determine a man's
whole connexion and place. Does he read Wordsworth, Goethe, Swedenborg, Bentham or Spurzheim? Botany? Geology? Abolition? Diet?
Shakspear? Coleridge?

The tone a man takes indicates his right ascension.

Swedenborgianism introduces unnecessary machinery.

Young men rough and unmelodious.

The point of absolute rest in communion with God.

Nature is loved by what is best in us.[1] . . .

There are some men above grief and some men below it.

I ought not to omit recording the astonishment which seized all the company when our brave saint,[2] the other day, fronted the presiding preacher. The preacher began to tower and dogmatize with many words. Instantly I foresaw that his doom was fixed; and as quick as he ceased speaking, the saint set right and blew away all his words in an instant, — unhorsed him, I may say, and tumbled him along the ground in utter dismay, like my angel of Heliodorus. Never was discomfiture more complete. In tones of genuine pathos he "bid him wonder

1 The passage thus beginning occurs in "Nature" (*Essays*, Second Series, p. 178).

2 Jones Very.

at the Love which suffered him to speak there
in his chair, of things he knew nothing of; one
might expect to see the book taken from his
hands and him thrust out of the room, — and
yet he was allowed to sit and talk, whilst every
word he spoke was a step of departure from the
truth, and of this he commanded himself to
bear witness!"

October 31.

Yesterday evening L——'s *soirée*. As soon
as the party is broken up, I shrink and wince,
and try to forget it. . . .

When I look at life, and see the patches of
thought, the gleams of goodness here and there
amid the wide and wild madness, I seem to be
a god dreaming; and when shall I awake and
dissipate these fumes and phantoms?

November 2.

Heard I not that a fair girl said, She would
not be "charitable" as she wished to, because it
looked to her so like *feeding? Rem acu tetigisti.*
To all let us be men, and not pastry-cooks.

Culture thorough. — I see in the lip of the
speaker the presence or absence of Wordsworth,
Coleridge, Shakspear, and the mighty masters.

November 3.

The Trismegisti. — There is always a higher region of thought, — soar as high as you will; and in literature very few words are found *touching* the best thought; Laodamia; James Nayler's dying words; the Address of the parliamentary soldier to the army, in Coleridge's *Friend;* and Sampson Reed's oration; these are of the highest moral class.

Come on, ye angels who are to write with pens of flame the poetry of the new age. The old heathens who have written for us will not budge one step, — neither Plato nor Shakspear, — until a natural majesty equal to their own, and purer, and of a higher strain, shall appear. Goethe will die hard. Even Scott dares stand his ground.

Henry IV of France a nascent Napoleon and the first *European* king.

Weans and Wife. — That 's the true pathos and sublime of human life.

We owe a good many valuable observations to people who are not very acute or profound, and who say the thing without effort which we want and have been long toiling for in vain.[1] This and that other fact, that we kindle each other's interest so fast in what happen to be our present studies, and the rapid communication of results that is obviously possible between scholars of various pursuit, — lead me to think that acquisition would be increased by literary society : that I could read more, learn faster, by association with good scholars, than I do or can alone.

There are few scholars. The mob of so-called scholars are unapt peasants caught late, coated over merely with a thin varnish of Latin and reading-room literature, but unlearned and unintelligent : they sleep in the afternoons, read little, and cannot be said to have faith or hope. For this reason, I think the reading of Sir William Jones's Life, or the life of Gibbon, or the letters of Goethe, might serve the purpose of shaming us into an emulating industry.

I should not dare to tell all my story. A great deal of it I do not yet understand. How much of it is incomplete. In my strait and decorous way of living, native to my family and to my country, and more strictly proper to me, is no-

[1] This sentence is printed in " The Over-Soul."

thing extravagant or flowing. I content myself
with moderate, languid actions, and never trans-
gress the staidness of village manners. Herein I
consult the poorness of my powers. More culture would come out of great virtues and vices
perhaps, but I am not up to that. Should I
obey an irregular impulse, and establish every
new relation that my fancy prompted with the
men and women I see, I should not be followed
by my faculties; they would play me false in making good their very suggestions. They delight in
inceptions, but they warrant nothing else. I see
very well the beauty of sincerity, and tend that
way, but if I should obey the impulse so far as
to say to my fashionable acquaintance, "you are
a coxcomb, — I dislike your manners — I pray
you avoid my sight," — I should not serve him
nor me, and still less the truth; I should act quite
unworthy of the truth, for I could not carry out
the declaration with a sustained, even-minded
frankness and love, which alone could save such
a speech from rant and absurdity.

We must tend ever to the good life.

I told Jones Very that I had never suffered,
that I could scarce bring myself to feel a concern
for the safety and life of my nearest friends that

would satisfy them; that I saw clearly that if my wife, my child, my mother, should be taken from me, I should still remain whole, with the same capacity of cheap enjoyment from all things. I should not grieve enough, although I love them. But could I make them feel what I feel, — the boundless resources of the soul, — remaining entire when particular threads of relation are snapped, — I should then dismiss forever the little remains of uneasiness I have in regard to them.

November 4.

I wish society to be a Congress of Sovereigns without the pride, but with the power. Therefore I do not like to see a worthy woman resemble those flowers that cannot bear transportation, and when I behold her in a foreign house perceive instantly that she has lost an inch or two of height — her manners not so *tall* as they were at home. A woman should always challenge our respect, and never move our compassion. If they be great only on their own ground, and demure and restless in a new house, they have all to learn. If people were all true, we should feel that all persons were infinitely deep natures. But now in an evening party you have no variety of persons, but only one person. For, say what you will, to whom you will, — they shall all render one and the same answer, without thought, without heart, — a conversation of the lips. . . .

Chaucer. — The religion of the early English wits is anomalous; so devout, and so blasphemous, in the same breath. The merriest tale concludes —

> Thus endeth here my tale of Januarie, —
> God blesse us, and his moder, Seinte Marie.
>   CHAUCER.

Chaucer's canon had such wit and art, that he could turn upside down all the ground between here and Canterbury, and pave it with silver and gold, yet was "his overest sloppe not worth a mite."

> He is too wise, in faith, as I believe;
> Thing that is overdone, it will not preve
> Aright, as clerkés say; it is a vice.
> Wherefore in that I hold him lewd and nice;
> For, when a man hath over great a wit,
> Full oft it happeth to misusen it.

We do not justice to ourselves in conversation. An agreeable instance of this I have repeatedly remarked, — when a man warmly opposes in conversation your opinion, even to an extreme, and afterwards, in his public discourse, tempers his opposition so freely with your thought that it is scarcely opposition.

Religion. — Our religion stands on numbers of believers. A very bad sign. Whenever the appeal is made, no matter how indirectly, to numbers, — proclamation is then and there made that religion is not. He that finds God a sweet, enveloping thought to him, never counts his company.

Insanity. — Swedenborg said insanity was a screen; so I think are the active trades and professions that employ and educate and *restrain* so many thousands of unbelievers. We are screened from premature ideas.

One of the tests of sanity is repose. I demand of a great spirit entire self-command. He must be free and detached, and take the world up into him, and not suggest the idea of a restless soul bestridden alway by an invisible rider. He must not be feverish, but free.

A divine man, be assured, will not be impudent. An angel may indeed come to Heliodorus all wrath, but its terror will be beautiful.[1]

1 Mr. Emerson took great delight in the head of the avenging angel in Raphael's stanza in the Vatican.

I am very sensible to beauty in the human form, in children, in boys, in girls, in old men, and old women. No trait of beauty I think escapes me. So am I to beauty in nature: a clump of flags in a stream, a hill, a wood, a path running into the woods, captivate me as I pass. If you please to tell me that I have no just relish for the beauty of man or of nature, it would not disturb me certainly. I do not know but it may be so, and that you have so much juster, deeper, richer knowledge, as that I, when I come to know it, shall say the same thing. But now your telling me that I do not love nature will not in the least annoy me. I should still have a perfect conviction that, love it, or love it not, every bough that waved, every cloud that floated, every water ripple is and must remain a minister to me of mysterious joy. But I hear occasionally young people dwelling with emphasis on beauties of nature, which may be there or may not, but which I do not catch, and blind, at the same time, to the objects which give me most pleasure. I am quite unable to tell the difference, only I see that they are less easily satisfied than I; that they talk where I would be silent, and clamorously demand my delight where it is not spontaneous. I fancy the love of nature of such persons is rhetorical.

If, however, I tell them, as I am moved to do, that I think they are not susceptible of this pleasure, straightway they are offended, and set themselves at once to prove to me with many words that they always had a remarkable delight in solitude and in nature. They even affirm it with tears. Then can I not resist the belief that the sense of joy from every pebble, stake, and dry leaf is not yet opened in them.

"Hope, the master element of a commanding genius." — COLERIDGE, "Macbeth."

I doubt the statement. There is somewhat low in hope. Faith or Trust, yes, Trust, the conviction that all is well, that Good and God is at the centre, will always rest as basis to the intellectual and outward activity of a great man, but this may coexist with great despondence and apathy as to the present order of things and of persons.

November 7.

Freedom. — I will, I think, no longer do things unfit for me. Why should I act the part of the silly women who send out invitations to many persons, and receive each billet of acceptance as if it were a pistol-shot? Why should I read lectures with care and pain and afflict myself with all the meanness of ticket-mongering, when I might sit, as God in his goodness has enabled me, a free, poor man with wholesome bread and warm clothes, though without cakes or gew-gaws, and write and speak the beautiful and formidable words of a free man? If you cannot be free, be as free as you can.

November 8.

The Asylums of the Mind. — I have said on a former page that natural science always stands open to us as any asylum, and that, in the conflict with the common cares, we throw an occasional affectionate glance at lichen and fungus, barometer and microscope, as cities of refuge to which we can one day flee, if the worst come to the worst. Another asylum is in the exercise of the fancy. Puck and Oberon, Tam O'Shanter and Lili's Park, the Troubadours and old ballads are bowers of joy that beguile us of our woes, catch us up into short heavens and drown all remembrance, and that too without a death-tramp of Eumenides being heard close behind, as behind other revels. Better still it is to soar into the heaven of invention, and coin fancies of our own, — weave a web of dreams as gay and beautiful as any of these our brothers have done, and learn by bold attempt our own riches. As the body is rested and refreshed by riding in the saddle after walking, and by walking again after the saddle, or as new muscles are called into play in climbing a hill, and then in descending, or walking on the plain, an analogous joy and strength flows from this exercise. Let no man despise these entertainments as if it were mere luxury and the drunkard's bowl. These airy realms of perpetual joy are also in nature, and what they are may well move the deep wonder and inquisition of the coldest and surliest philosopher.

So is music an asylum. It takes us out of the actual and whispers to us dim secrets that startle our wonder as to who we are, and for what, whence, and whereto. All the great interrogatories, like questioning angels, float in on its waves of sound. "Away, away," said Richter to it, "thou speakest to me of things which in all my endless being I have found not and shall not find."

So is Beauty an asylum.

Asylums; Books, Natural Science, Fancy, Music, Beauty.

Everything must have its flower or effort at the beautiful, finer or coarser according to its stuff. The architect not only makes sewers and offices, but halls and chapels. The carpenter of a village farmhouse expends his taste and ornament on the front door; the cook rejoices in his dinner, the laborer has his Sunday clothes, the poorest Irish scullion has her ribbon and tags of finery. And in society the senses, the appetites, the life of the actual world, has also its virtues or seemings. Thus, in the Planting States, where the whole culture is a culture of appearance, exists what is called a romantic state of society, and the wine-bibber and drabber is yet required to meet blow with blow, and pistol with pistol. . . .

It makes little difference, the circumstance.[1] Obedience or disobedience is all. We read Lear and hate the unkind daughters. But meantime perhaps our fathers and mothers find *us* hard and forgetful. We swell the cry of horror at the slave-holder, and we treat our laborer or grocer or farmer as a thing, and so hold slaves ourselves.

Not always shall we need to avoid society. When many men have been bred with God they are able to know God in each other. Yea, who-

1 This is preceded by several sentences used in the first few pages of " History."

ever has come to a steady communion with Him can well come into society. Remember Hampden's letter to Eliot.

Let me never fall into the vulgar mistake of dreaming that I am persecuted whenever I am contradicted. No man, I think, had ever a greater well-being with a less desert than I. I can very well afford to be accounted bad or foolish by a few dozen or a few hundred persons, — I who see myself greeted by the good expectation of so many friends far beyond any power of thought or communication of thought residing in me. Besides, I own, I am often inclined to take part with those who say I am bad or foolish, for I fear I am both. I believe and know there must be a perfect compensation. I know too well my own dark spots. Not having myself attained, not satisfied myself, far from a holy obedience, — how can I expect to satisfy others, to command their love? A few sour faces, a few biting paragraphs, — is but a cheap expiation for all these short-comings of mine.

November 9.

With the vision of this world the fugitive measures of Time and Space shall vanish. Spirits

Can crowd eternity into an hour,
Or stretch an hour to eternity.[1]

This superstition about magnitude and duration is a classification for beginners introductory to the real classification of cause and effect, as the Linnæan botany gives way to the natural classes of Jussieu. Why should that complex fact we call Assyria, with its hundreds of years, its thousands of miles, its millions of souls, be to me more than a violet which I pluck out of the grass? It stands for about so much; it awakens perchance not so much emotion and thought. I surely shall not cumber myself to make it more. Everything passes for what it is worth.

Shakspear. — Read Lear yesterday and Hamlet today with new wonder, and mused much on the great soul whose authentic signs flashed on my sight in the broad continuous *daylight* of these poems. Especially I wonder at the perfect reception this wit and immense knowledge of iife and intellectual superiority find in us all in connexion with our utter incapacity to produce anything like it. The superior tone of Hamlet

1 The editors have not been able to find the source of this quotation which occurs also in "The Over-Soul."

in all the conversations how perfectly preserved, without any mediocrity, much less any dulness in the other speakers.

How real the loftiness! an inborn gentleman; and above that, an exalted intellect. What incessant growth and plenitude of thought, pausing on itself never an instant; and each sally of wit sufficient to save the play. How true then and unerring the *earnest* of the dialogue, as when Hamlet talks with the Queen! How terrible his discourse!

What less can be said of the perfect mastery, as by a superior being, of the conduct of the drama, as the free introduction of this capital advice to the players; the commanding good sense which never retreats except before the godhead which inspires certain passages, — the more I think of it, the more I wonder. I will think nothing impossible to man. No Parthenon, no sculpture, no picture, no architecture can be named beside this. All this is perfectly visible to me and to many, — the wonderful truth and mastery of this work, of these works, — yet for our lives could not I, or any man, or all men, produce anything comparable to one scene in Hamlet or Lear. With all my admiration of this life-like picture, — set me to producing a match for it, and I should instantly depart into mouthing rhetoric.

Now why is this, that we know so much better than we do? that we do not yet possess ourselves, and know at the same time that we are much more?[1] . . .

One other fact Shakspear presents us; that not by books are great poets made. Somewhat, and much he unquestionably owes to his books; but you could not find in his circumstances the history of his poem. It was made without hands in his invisible world. A mightier magic than any learning, the deep logic of cause and effect he studied: its roots were cast so deep, therefore it flung out its branches so high.

I find no good lives. I would live well, I seem to be free to do so, yet I think with very little respect of my way of living; it is weak, partial, not full and not progressive. But I do not see any other that suits me better. The scholars are shiftless and the merchants are dull.

Expression of Faces.— In many faces we are

[1] The rest of the passage is printed in "The Over-Soul," as to Jove nodding to Jove, and the Arab Sheiks (*Essays*, First Series, p. 278).

struck with the fact that magnitude is nothing, —proportion is all. A brow may be so formed that in its few square inches I may receive the impression of vast spaces : what amplitude ! what fields of magnanimity ! of trust ! of humanity !

November 10.

[The opening entry of this date is the passage in "History" (page 6) as to our reading as superior beings and in the grandest strokes of the author feeling most at home. Also about our sympathy with riches and character. This is followed by the passage in "Intellect" as to our being draughtsmen in dreams (*Essays*, First Series, p. 337).]

Shakspear fills us with wonder the first time we approach him. We go away and work and think, for years, and come again,—he astonishes us anew. Then having drank deeply and saturated us with his genius, we lose sight of him for another period of years. By and by we return, and there he stands immeasurable as at first. We have grown wiser, but only that we should see him wiser than ever. He resembles a high mountain which the traveller sees in the morning and thinks he shall quickly near it and pass it and leave it behind. But he journeys all day till noon, till night. There still is the dim mountain close by him, having scarce altered its bearings since the morning light.

My brave Henry Thoreau walked with me to Walden this afternoon and complained of the proprietors who compelled him, to whom, as much as to any, the whole world belonged, to walk in a strip of road and crowded him out of all the rest of God's earth. He must not get over the fence: but to the building of that fence he was no party. Suppose, he said, some great proprietor, before he was born, had bought up the whole globe. So had he been hustled out of nature. Not having been privy to any of these arrangements, he does not feel called on to consent to them, and so cuts fishpoles in the woods without asking who has a better title to the wood than he. I defended, of course, the good institution as a scheme, not good, but the best that could be hit on for making the woods and waters and fields available to wit and worth, and for restraining the bold, bad man. At all events, I begged him, having this maggot of Freedom and Humanity in his brain, to write it out into good poetry and so clear himself of it. He replied, that he feared that that was not the best way, that in doing justice to the thought, the man did not always do justice to himself, the poem ought to sing itself: if the man took too much pains with the expression, he was not any longer the Idea himself. I acceded and confessed that this was the tragedy of Art that the artist was at the expense of the man; and hence, in the first age, as they tell, the sons of God printed no epics, carved no stone, painted no pictures, built no railroad; for the sculpture, the poetry, the music, and architecture, were in the man. And truly Bolts and Bars do not seem to me the most exalted or exalting of our institutions. And what other spirit reigns in our intellectual works? We have literary property. The very recording of a thought betrays a distrust that there is any more, or much more, as good for us. If we felt that the universe was ours, that we dwelled in eternity, and advance into all wisdom, we should be less covetous of these sparks and cinders. Why should we covetously build a Saint Peter's, if we had the seeing Eye which beheld all the radiance of beauty and majesty in the matted grass and the overarching boughs? Why should a man spend years upon the carving an Apollo, who looked

Apollos into the landscape with every glance he threw?[1]

Always pay, for first or last you must pay your entire expense.[2] . . .

Should not the will be dramatised in a man who, put him where you would, commanded, and who saw what he willed come to pass?[3] . . . A supreme commander over all his passions and affections as much as Hampden, yet the secret of his power is higher than that. It is God in the hands. Men and women are his game : where they are, he cannot be without resource. Shall I introduce you to Mr. R? to Madame B? "No," he replies, "introduction is for dolls : I have business with A and with B."

1 This walk with Thoreau seems to have suggested the conversation in "The Conservative," between the protesting youth and the men of the established order (*Nature, Addresses, and Lectures,* pp. 306, 307).

2 Here follows the sentence thus beginning in "Compensation" (p. 113). It is immediately followed by the concluding sentences in "Self-Reliance," as to easy days being deceptive, peace only to come from yourself.

3 Here follows the long passage about Cæsar and men of that stamp in "Eloquence" (*Society and Solitude,* pp. 78, 79).

Will never consults the law, or prudence, or uses any paltry expedient, like that falsely ascribed to Saint Paul about the unknown God. Tricks, saith Will, for little folks. I am dearer to you than your laws, for which neither you nor I care a pin. He is a cool fellow. Everybody in the street reminds us of somewhat else. Will or Reality reminds you of nothing else. It takes place of the whole creation.

> " He'd harpit a fish out of saut water,
>   Or water out of a stone,
>   Or milk out of a maiden's breast
>   That bairn had never none." [1]

The counterpart to this master in my Drama should be a maiden, one of those natural magnets who make place and a court where they are. She should serve in menial office and they who saw her should not know it, for what she touched she decorated, and what she did the stars and moon do stoop to see. But this magnetism should not be meant for him and he should only honor it as he went by. It is to work on others, on another as a balance to him, or, if I may refine so far, another Richmond,[2] a

1 " Glenkindie," in Child's *English and Scottish Ballads.*
2 "I think there be six Richmonds in the field."
    SHAKSPEAR, *Richard III*, last scene.

transmuted will infused into *form* and now *unconscious*, yet omnipotent as before and in a sweeter way.

November 12.

I could forgive your want of faith if you had any knowledge of the uttermost that man could be and do, if arithmetic could predict the last possibilities of instinct. But men are not made like boxes, a hundred or thousand to order, and all exactly alike, of known dimension, and all their properties known; but no, they come into nature through a nine months' astonishment, and of a character, each one, incalculable, and of extravagant possibilities. Out of darkness and out of the awful Cause they come to be caught up into this vision of a seeing, partaking, acting and suffering life, not foreknown, not fore-estimable, but slowly or speedily they unfold new, unknown, mighty traits : not boxes, but these machines are alive, agitated, fearing, sorrowing.

Great Men. — I like the rare, extravagant spirits who disclose to me new facts in nature. Always, I doubt not, men of God have, from time to time, walked among men and made their commission felt in the heart and soul of the commonest hearer. Hence evidently the tripod, the priest, the inspired priestess with the divine afflatus. They saw it was not of the common, natural life; they felt its consonance with the inmost constitution of man and revered it, without the attempt to reconcile it to the actual life.

Swedenborg is now scarce yet appreciable. Shakspear has for the first time in our time found adequate criticism, if indeed ye have yet found it. Coleridge, Lamb, Schlegel, Goethe, Very, Herder.

The great facts of history are four or five names: Homer, Phidias, Jesus, Shakspear,— one or two names more I will not add, but see what these names stand for. All civil history and all philosophy consists of endeavors more or less vain to explain these persons.

November 13.

Yesterday H. G. O. Blake[1] spent with me; and departed this morning. We walked in the woods to the Cliff, to the spring, and had social music.

Ah, Memory, dear daughter of God! Thy

---

1 Harrison Gray Otis Blake of Worcester, Thoreau's friend and correspondent, and the editor of some of his works. He was a man of great sincerity, modesty, refinement, and personal charm.

blessing is million-fold. The poor, short, lone fact that dies at the birth, thou catchest up and bathest in immortal waters. Then a thousand times over it lives and acts again, each time transfigured, ennobled. Then in solitude and darkness, I walk over again my sunny walks; in streets behold again the shadows of my grey birches in the still river; hear the joyful voices of my brothers, a thousand times over; and vibrate anew to the tenderness and dainty music of the early poetry I fed upon in boyhood. As fair to me the clump of flags that bent over the water, as if to see its own beauty below, one evening last summer, as any plants that are growing there today. At this hour, the stream is flowing, though I hear it not; the plants are drinking their accustomed life, and repaying it with their beautiful forms, but I need not wander thither. It flows for me, and they grow for me in the returning images of former summers.

"Fire," Aunt Mary said, "was a great deal of company"; and so is there company, I find, in water. It animates the solitude. Then somewhat nearer to human society is in the hermit birds that harbor in the wood. I can do well for weeks with no other society than the partridge and the jay, my daily company.

"The miraculous," said Sampson Reed, "is the measure of our alienation from God." It is so in persons as much as in facts. . . .

The child is a realization of a remembrance, and our love of the child is an acknowledgment of the beauty of human nature. The soul sub-tends the same angle in the child and in the man. The proportion of each is the same, and the central power and magnitude, whether of space or time, disappears in the eye of God.

Gladly I would solve, if I could, this prob-lem of a vocabulary which, like some treach-erous, wide shoal, waylays the tall bark, the goodly soul, and there it founders and suffers shipwreck. In common life, every man is led by the nose by a verb. Even the great and gifted do not escape, but with great talents and partial inspiration have local cramps, withered arms and mortification. Proportion is not. Every man is lobsided, and even holding in his hands some authentic token and gift of God, holds it awry. It must be from everlasting and from the infinitude of God, that when God speaketh, he should then and there exist; should fill the world with his voice, should scatter forth light, nature, time, souls, from the centre of the present thought; and new date and new create the whole.[1] . . .

The present hour is the descending God, and all things obey: all the past exists to it as subordinate: all the future is contained in it. All things are made sacred by relation to it, one thing as much as another. It smooths down the mountainous differences of appearance, and breathes one life through creation from side to side. . . . If a man interposes betwixt you and your Maker, himself or some other person or persons, believe him not: God has better things for you. This should be plain enough; yet see how great and vivacious souls, with grand truths in their keeping, do fail in faith to see God face to face, to see Time pass away and be no more, and to utter directly from him that which he would give them to say; but rather imprison it in the old Hebrew language, mimick David, Jeremiah and Paul and disbelieve that God, who maketh the stars and stones sing, can speak our English tongue in Massachusetts and give as deep and glad a melody to it as shall make the whole world and all coming ages ring with

[1] The passage thus beginning occupies most of p. 66, of "Self-Reliance." Sentences not there given are retained.

the sound. Be assured we shall not always set so great a price on a few texts, on a few lives.[1] . . .

November 14.

This palsy of tradition goes so far that when a soul in which the intellectual activity is a balance for the veneration (whose excess seems to generate this love of the old word) renounces the superstition out of love for the primary teaching in his heart, the doctors of the church are not glad, as they ought to be, that a new and original confirmation comes to the truth, but they curse and swear because he scorns their idolatry of the nouns and verbs, the vellum and ink, in which the same teaching was anciently conveyed.[2] . . .

I said, in the wood, to the Soul, that I received thankfully the *reprieve* which kind and candid opinions make to the dark and steep and painful road which truth must travel, and it seemed to me the while that man never appears to such advantage as in the act of acknowledgment with melting eye and plaintive voice.

1 Here follows a long passage to be found in " Self-Reliance " (pp. 67, 68).

2 The rest of the passage, on the highest truth of this subject, is mainly to be found in " Self-Reliance " (p. 68).

What is the hardest task in the world? To think.[1] . . .

Musical Eyes. — I think sometimes that my lack of musical ear is made good to me through my eyes. That which others hear, I *see*. All the soothing, plaintive, brisk or romantic moods which corresponding melodies waken in them, I find in the carpet of the wood, in the margin of the pond, in the shade of the hemlock grove, or in the infinite variety and rapid dance of the treetops as I hurry along.

Knowledge of Character. — We are all born discerners of spirits.[2] . . .

November 15.

A pathetic thing it is, that we allow men of talents, and characters in which we are interested, to which we are naturally allied, to go by us without heed and the tribute of our sympathy, because of our momentary preoccupation with some nearer object. Use hospitality to *thoughts*.

One Wise Word. — A single remark indicating wisdom characterizes the person who made

1 See "Intellect" (*Essays*, First Series, p. 331).

2 For the rest of the passage, see "The Over-Soul" (pp. 285, 286).

it. All we know of him is these dozen words; yet patiently, with a good assurance, we wait until he shall make good that pledge in a whole orbit as grand as that curve.

November 16.

All we are responsible for is the will. But your will cannot always make you appear well. In the presence of a man or woman of elegance and fashionable manners, you do not play a quite manly part. Where is your wisdom? Why falters the word of truth on your tongue, and comes so lamely and inarticulately off? Why do you defer to such persons? Have you not been taught of God that all things are yours? Why should you decline from the state of truth, and vail your manly supremacy to a woman or a fine gentleman? It is in vain these questions are asked: you have asked them yourself. You cannot do otherwise. Admit your weakness. Do not be disturbed by it. Keep your will true and erect, and, by and by, this rebellious blood, this painful suppleness, this epilepsy of the wit, will pass away imperceptibly, and the whole man shall be the faithful organ of the wisdom which is no respecter of persons.

Books. — You are wrong in demanding of the

Bible more than can be in a book. Its only defect is that it is a book, and not alive.

"Seek ye first the kingdom of God, and all these things shall be added unto you." What! Art? Hamlets? Ballads?

The life is more than meat and the body than raiment.

The Soul. — He judgeth every man, yet is judged of no man.

November 17.

The Traveller. — It occurs to me that, in remembrance of my own extreme needs when I was in Europe, I ought to keep by me a blank-book to be called "The Traveller," and from time to time insert in it the names and places of such objects as a student of Art or of natural Beauty or of History should especially visit. So shall I have a useful gift for those who, having eyes, cross the ocean. I am reminded of this project by the notice of Giotto's frescoes at Pisa in Coleridge's *Table-Talk*, vol. i, pp. 123, 124. See also *ibidem*, p. 138.

"Poets are guardians of admiration in the hearts of the people." Fine offices are discharged by the men of literary and poetic faculty everywhere. Each has certain opinions, tastes, shades of thought, which go at large in the great common world of men, of books, selecting every connate fact, particle, word, relation, work of art, until, by and by, that which was or might seem a mere whimsy or trifle not worth the entertainment of a thought has grown to some size and is ready to be born.

Jones Very said to me in the woods, One might forget here that the world was desart and empty, all the people wicked, . . . and [ignored?] the whole refreshment or consolatory aspect of the natural sciences, of the telescope and barometer. In Coleridge's *Table-Talk*, vol. i, p. 129, I find the following : "John Thelwall had something very good in him. We were once sitting in a beautiful recess in the Quantocks, when I said to him, 'Citizen John, this is a fine place to talk treason in!' 'Nay, citizen Samuel,' replied he, 'it is rather a place to make a man forget that there is any necessity for treason!'"

November 18.

The infallible index of true progress is found in the tone the man takes.[1] . . .

[1] The rest of this passage occurs in "The Over-Soul" (pp. 286, 287).

The Swedenborgian violates the old law of rhetoric and philosophy, *Nec deus intersit dignus nisi vindice nodus*, in its forcible interposing of a squadron of angels for the transmission of thought from God to man. I say, I think, or I receive, in proportion to my obedience, truth from God; I put myself aside, and let him be. The New Churchman says: No; that would kill you, if God should directly shine into you: there is an immense continuity of mediation. As if that bridged the gulf from the infinite to the finite by so much as one plank. Would he not kill the highest angel into whom he shone just as quick?

November 25.

At Portsmouth Mr. Haven described the passage to the guillotine of Manuel and General Houchard, as he saw it in Paris.

Alfred Haven remarked (when I said that Universalism certainly covered a truth) that never a soul was without hope of life everlasting, and of course no soul was ever fully convinced that it deserved hell, and of course God would justify his act to the soul of the sinner.

I remember that when I preached my first sermon in Concord, "On Showing Piety at

Home," Dr. Ripley remarked on the frequent occurrence of the word *Virtue* in it, and said his people would not understand it, for the largest part of them, when Virtue was spoken of, understood *Chastity*. I do not imagine, however, that the people thought any such thing. It was an old-school preacher's contractedness.

The great distinction between teachers sacred or literary; between poets like Herbert and poets like Warton; between philosophers like Coleridge and philosophers like Mackintosh; between talkers like Reed and Very and talkers like Walker and Ripley, is, that, one class speak *ab intra*, and the other class, *ab extra*. It is of no use to preach to me *ab extra*. I can do that myself. Jesus preaches always *ab intra*, and so infinitely distinguishes himself from all others. In that is the miracle. That includes the miracle. My soul believes beforehand that it ought so to be. That is what I mean when I say I look for a Teacher, as all men do say. If however you preach *ab extra*, at least confess it.[1]

1 All of the above entry is, in substance, in "The Over-Soul" (p. 287), but is here given because of the difference in the authors named, and because of its relation to what follows.

Say, " Come let us do thus and so," and not affect to say, " Come thou up hither." For thy pretension deceives nobody. Thy body, I can see well enough, stands above me in a pulpit: but thy soul, I can see as well, stands down on my own, or even a lower level.

That is the essential distinction of genius, the charm of its every syllable, — that they are an emanation of that very thing or reality they tell of, and not merely an echo or picture of it. See these lines of Edward Powell to Fletcher :

> " Fletcher, whose wit
> Was not an accident to the soul, but It ;
> Only diffused ; thus we the same Sun call
> Moving i' the sphere or shining on a wall."

How incalculable and potent seem to me the strokes and glances of a few mystics, saints and philosophers whom I have seen and reverenced, living within the veil of their sanctuaries ! How feeble and calculable the uttermost that modish divines, writers, and readers can say ! This is the reason why you must respect all your private impressions. A few anecdotes, a few traits of character, manners, face, — a few incidents, have an emphasis in your memory out of all proportion to their apparent significance, if you measure them by the ordinary standards of history. Do not, for this, a moment doubt their value to you. They relate to you, to your peculiar gift. Let them have all their weight, and do not reject them and cast about for illustration and facts more usual in English literature.

Swedenborg taught *ab intra;* and in music Beethoven, and whosoever like him grandly renounces all forms, societies and laws as impediments and lives in, on, and for his genius and guiding Idea. How great the influence of such! how it rebukes, how it invites and raises me! My soul answers them saying, "So it is, even as I have heard: it is no dream: God is; and there is a heaven for his saints; and that heaven is obedience to him. I hear ye what ye say, great servants of my Lord! I also believe; Lord, help mine unbelief!" The fine account I read of Beethoven was translated from Bettina von Arnim's correspondence with Goethe, in a notice of that book in the (London) *Gentleman's Magazine* for October, 1838.

A man of letters who goes into fashionable society on their terms and not on his own makes a fool of himself. Why I should be given up to that shame so many times after so much considered experience, I cannot tell. Heaven has good purposes in these often mortifications, perchance.

It is strange to me how sensible I am to circumstances. I know not how it is, but in the streets I feel mean. If a man should accost me in Washington Street and call me base fellow! I should not be sure that I could make him feel by my answer and behaviour that my ends were worthy and noble.[1] If the same thing should occur in the country I should feel no doubt at all that I could justify myself to his conscience.

Sir Thomas Browne. — George Haven, at Portsmouth, read me noble passages in Sir Thomas Browne's writings. How inward he is! What a true example of the noble daring of a thinker who sees that the soul alone is real, and that it is a true wisdom to launch abroad into its deep, and push his way as far as any glimmer of light is given, though the element and

1 Compare what is said of Saadi (used in that place for the ideal poet) in the verse beginning, "God only knew how Saadi dined." See *Poems*, Appendix, "Fragments on the Poet and the Poetic Gift," v, p. 325.

the path be in wild contradiction to any use or
practice of this world.

Boys and Girls. — The strong bent of nature
is very prettily seen in the winning, half-artful,
half-artless ways of young girls in the middle
classes who go into the shops to buy a skein of
silk or a sheet of paper and talk half an hour
about nothing with the broad-faced, good-natured shop-boy.[1] . . .

November 26.

Impotent creatures that we are! Stung by
this desire for thought, we run up and down
into booksellers' shops, into colleges, into Athe-
næums, into the studies of learned men. The
moment we receive a new thought, it is the
identical thing we had before with a new mask,
and therefore, though hailed as authentic, yet
as soon as we have received it, we desire another new one, we are not really enriched. But
when we receive it we are beatified for the time.
We seem to be capable of all thought. We are
on a level then with all Intelligences. We cast
all books and teachers behind us. What have
I to do with means, when I am in the presence

1 Here occurs the passage in "Love" (p. 173), on
wholesome village boy and girl relations.

of the Infinite Light? And yet, familiar as that state of mind is, the books of Bacon and Leibnitz still retain their value from age to age. So impassable is, at last, that thin, imperceptible boundary between perfect understanding of the author, perfect fellowship with him, *quasi* consciousness of the same gifts, — and the faculty of subordinating that rapture to the Will in such degree as to be able ourselves to conjoin and record our states of mind. I have written above that the price of the picture indicates the odds that exist against the appearance of a genius pure as Raphael or Angelo. So is the glory of the name of Shakspear, Bacon, Milton, an index of the exceeding difficulty with which the reader who perfectly understands what they say, and sees no reason why he should not continue the sentence, — overleaps that invisible barrier and continues the sentence. Whilst he reads, the drawbridge is down. Nothing hinders that he should pass with the author. When he assays to write — lo suddenly! the draw is up, and will not down.[1]

[1] The latter part of this entry occurred in the third lecture of the course on "Human Life," called "School." See Abstracts in Cabot's Memoir, Appendix F, 1838.

November 27.

The brilliant young student full of philosophy and happy in the faculty of unfolding and illustrating his theories, should dread his own theories. They are snares for his own feet. We put our love where we have put our labor. Having done so well, having won so much praise by them, and so many opinions, how can he turn his back on them and follow the great light of truth to which these were only porches? Yet must you leave your theory, as Joseph his coat in the hand of the harlot, and flee.

I have no less disgust than any other at the cant of spiritualism. I had rather hear a round volley of Ann Street oaths than the affectation of that which is divine on the foolish lips of coxcombs.

The man who fears and is therefore intolerant indicates at once that he is not yet grounded in the soul: for lack of his natural root, he clings by tendrils of affection to society, mayhap to what is best and greatest in it, and in calm times it will not appear that he is adrift and not moored; but let any disorder take place in society, any revolution of custom, of law, of opinion, and instantly his whole type of permanence is rudely shaken. In the disorder of society, universal disorder seems to him to take place, Chaos is come again, and his despair takes at first the form of rage and hatred against the act or actor which has broken the seeming peace of nature, but the fact is, he was already a driving wreck before the wind arose, which merely revealed to him his vagabond state. If a man is at one with the soul and in all things obeyeth it, society becomes to him at once a fair show and reflection of that which he knoweth beforehand in himself. If anyone affirm a strange doctrine, or do a wild deed, or if any perversity or profligacy appears in the whole society, he will see it for what it is, and grieve for it as a man and member of society, but it will not touch him with resentment, it will not cast one shadow over the lofty brow of the soul. The soul will not grieve. The soul sits behind there in a serene peace; no jot or tittle of its convictions can either be shaken or confirmed. It sees already in the ebullition of sin the simultaneous remedy arising. This is the city which hath foundations whose builder and maker is God.

Phrenology and animal magnetism are studied a little in the spirit in which alchemy and witchcraft or the black art were, namely, for power. That vitiates and besmirches them and makes them black arts. All separation of the soul's things from the soul is suicidal. So are phrenology and animal magnetism damned.[1]

Extremes meet: the sublime of war in the Iliad meets the doctrine of *one mind.* Hector says to Ajax: —

> Exchange some gift, that Greece and Troy may say,
> Not hate, but glory, made these chiefs contend
> And each brave foe was in his soul a friend.
>
> *Iliad,* Book VII.

The test of a religion or philosophy is the number of things it can explain: so true is it. But the religion of our churches explains neither art nor society nor history, but itself needs explanation.

Whence this fact that the natural history of man has never been written?[2] . . . Whence, but because God inhabits man and cannot be known but by God?

The ancients affirmed the incorruptibility of

1 Compare "Demonology" (*Lectures and Biographical Sketches,* p. 25).

2 Compare "The Over-Soul" (*Essays,* First Series, p. 367).

the world: modern geology teaches the same doctrine in the perpetual renewing of what is perpetually consumed. Races pass and perish; cities rise and fall, like the perpetual succession of shells on the beach; and the sound of the waters and the colors of the flower, cloud, and the voice of man are as new and affecting today as at any moment in the vast Past.

[On December 5, Mr. Emerson began his course of ten lectures in Boston, one a week, the subject being "Human Life," as follows: —

I, Doctrine of the Soul (parts of this were printed later in "The Over-Soul"); II, Home; III, School; IV, Love; V, Genius; VI, The Protest; VII, Tragedy; VIII, Comedy; IX, Duty; X, Demonology.]

AUTHORS OR BOOKS QUOTED OR REFERRED TO
IN JOURNAL FOR 1838

[As has been mentioned in a previous volume, certain standard authors, and the favorites of Mr. Emerson, most frequently referred to in the Journals, will be omitted from the lists; viz., Homer, Plato, Plutarch, Cicero, Virgil, Horace, Juvenal, Montaigne, Bacon, Shakspear, Ben Jonson, Beaumont and Fletcher, Donne, Herrick, Herbert, Sir Thomas Browne, Jeremy Taylor, Pascal, Newton, Fénelon, Young, Pope, Pitt, Johnson, Swedenborg, Gibbon, De Staël, Wordsworth, Scott, Landor, Coleridge, Byron.

In spite of the frequent mention of Plotinus, Proclus, and the other neo-platonists, and of the Oriental Scriptures and poets, these names will appear in the list, as shedding light on the question when Mr. Emerson was reading them. Goethe and Carlyle will also be mentioned.

The names of the books, which appear year by year, charged to Mr. Emerson in the record of the Boston Athenæum Library are also given.

It must be borne in mind that often the authors are not quoted directly, but Mr. Emerson came upon some passage from their works in another writer's book.]

Menu, *Institutes of*; Buddha; Zoroaster; Confucius;

Xenophanes; Pindar; Herodotus; Thucydides; Polybius; Terence; Plautus;

Pliny the Elder; Martial; Epictetus; Seneca; Galen; Hermes Trismegistus; Synesius; Proclus;

Roger Bacon; Dante, *Purgatorio*; Chaucer, *Griselda*; Erasmus; Michel Angelo, *Sonnets*; Sir Thomas More; Troubadours; Ballads;

Luther; Richard Edwards; Calvin; Giordano Bruno;

Richard Hooker; Sir Philip Sidney; Kepler; Boehmen, *Aurora;* Thomas Hobbes; John Hampden, *Letters to Eliot;* Cudworth;

Marvell; Charles Cotton; Dryden; Pepys, *Diary;*

Newton; Leibnitz; Rousseau; Voltaire; Spence, *Anecdotes;* Linnæus; Winckelmann, *History of Art;*

Warton; Lessing; James Bruce, *Travels;* Spinoza; Niebuhr; Horne Tooke (John Horne); Herschel; Herder;

Sir William Jones, *Translations of Asiatic Poetry;* Bentham; Goethe, *William Meister, Farbenlehre, Faust, Iphigenia;* Thomas Taylor; Burns, *Tam O'Shanter;* Heeren, *Leading Peoples of the Ancient World;* Fichte; Schleiermacher; Humboldt; Schlegel; Bettina von Arnim, *Letters to Goethe;*

Charles Lamb; O'Connell, *Correspondence with Stevenson;*

Miss Jane Porter, *Novels;* Spurzheim; Davy, *Chemistry;*

Belzoni, *Discoveries in the Pyramids;* Sir Charles Bell, *On the Hand;*

Dr. William Ellery Channing; Jane Taylor,

Poems; Daniel Webster; Southey, *Kehama;* O'Meara, *Napoleon;* Andrews Norton; Sprague, *Centennial Ode;* Guizot; Caillaud, *Travels;*

Miss Catherine M. Sedgwick, *Novels;* Cousin; Sylvester Graham, *Bread and Bread-Making;*

Jouffroy; Jussieu; George B. Emerson; Carlyle; Hugh Williamson; Tennyson; Dickens, *Oliver Twist;* Jones Very; Sampson Reed; Henry D. Thoreau, *Poems;* W. Ellery Channing, *Poems;*

North American and *Edinburgh Reviews, Foreign Quarterly, London Quarterly, Fraser's* and *Blackwood's Magazines.*

JOURNAL

BOSTON LECTURES

SYMPOSIA

VISITORS

JONES VERY. EDWARD PALMER

THE WHITE MOUNTAINS

JOURNAL XXX

1839

(From Journals D and E)

For Virtue's whole sum is to know and dare.

DONNE.

Still lives the song, though Regnar dies, —
Fill high the cups again!

STERLING.

[THE course of lectures on "Human Life," begun in December, 1838, lasted until the latter part of February. It was interfered with by the sleeplessness of which Mr. Emerson speaks, and, later, by weakening colds. These made the course seem unsatisfactory to him, and he told his audience that he had meant to round out the series by two more lectures, one on the limitations of human activity by the laws of the world, and one on the intrinsic powers and resources of our nature. Yet Mr. Alcott, on returning from the sixth lecture ("The Protest"), wrote in his journal: "Emerson has triumphed, . . . the large hall in the Temple was filled; and the audience, the choicest that could be gathered in New England." Of the closing lecture he wrote: "The peroration was grand. He dwelt for a moment on the spirit in which his word had been conceived and uttered; on the inscrutability of the soul, its marvellous fact; the feeble insight which he had been suffered to get of it. The audience was larger than on any former evening."]

(From D)

January 1, 1839.

Adjourned the promised lecture on Genius until Wednesday week, on account of my unaccountable vigils now for four or five nights, which destroy all power of concentration by day.

Sunday, *January* 6.

It seemed to me at church today that the Communion service, as it is now and here celebrated, is a document of the dulness of the race. Then presently, when I thought of the divine soul of my Nazarene whose name is used here, and considered how these my good neighbors, the bending deacons with their cups and plates, would have straightened themselves to sturdiness if the proposition came before them to honor thus a known fellow-man, I was constrained to feel the force of Genius that, hallowing once those Hebrew lips, should propagate its influences thus far and not be quite utterly lost in these ultimate shoals and shores of our Concord congregation.

January 12.

Set your own rate.[1] . . .

Let us call Goose Pond the Drop, or God's Pond. Henry Thoreau says, " No; that will shock the people; call it Satan's Pond and they will like it, or still better, Tom Wyman's Pond." Alas! say I, for the personality that eats us up.

" Seekest thou great things? Seek them not." — JEREMIAH, xiv, 5.

February 3.

Returned last night from Plymouth, where on Thursday evening, 31 January, I read a lecture on Genius; on Friday afternoon, one on Home; and in the evening, one on Being and Seeming.

February 7.

The drunkard retires on a keg and locks himself up for a three days' debauch. When I am sick, I please myself not less in retiring on a

---

1 The sentence thus beginning is in "Spiritual Laws" (*Essays*, First Series, p. 151), and is immediately followed by that about *soul* in dealing with a child (" The Over-Soul," p. 279).

Salamander stove, heaping the chamber with fuel, and inundating lungs, liver, head and feet with floods of caloric, heats on heats. It is dainty to be sick, if you have leisure and convenience for it. How bland the aspect of all things! One sees the colors of the carpet and the paper-hangings. All the housemates have a softer, fainter look to the debilitated retina.

Yesterday I saw pencil sketches done by Stewart Newton whilst confined in the Insane Asylum a little before his death. They seemed to betray the richest invention, so rich as almost to say, Why draw any line, since you can draw all? Genius has given you the freedom of the universe, why then come within any walls? [Written to James Freeman Clarke.]

As soon as you once come up against a man's limitations, it is all over with him;[1] . . .

Public speaking, not Realism.—We see it advertised that Mr. A. will deliver an oration on the Fourth of July.[2] . . .

---

1 The passage thus beginning occurs in "Circles" (*Essays*, First Series, p. 308).

2 The passage following is printed in "Spiritual Laws" (*Essays*, First Series, p. 152).

As soon as a child has left the room his strown toys become affecting.

Falling.—" It is as easy as falling."—In nature nothing is done but in the cheapest way. When the fruit is ripe, it *falls*. When the fruit is despatched, the leaf *falls*. The circuit of the waters is mere falling: the walking of man and all animals is a falling forward. All our manual labor and works of strength, as prying, splitting, digging, rowing, etc., are done by dint of continual falling; and the globe and the globes, earth, moon, sun, comet, star, fall forever and ever. Nature works by short ways.

February 8.

Memory is

The deaf man's hearing and the blind man's sight.
PLUTARCH's *Morals*, vol. iv, p. 47.

February 14.

Demonology seems to me to be the intensation of the individual nature, the extension of this beyond its due bounds and into the domain of the infinite and universal. The faith in a Genius; in a family Destiny; in a ghost; in an amulet, is the projection of that instinctive care which the individual takes of his individuality beyond what is meet and into the region where the individuality is forever bounded by generic, cosmic and universal laws.

Yet I find traces of this usurpation in very high places, in Christianity, for example. Christianity, as it figures now in the history of ages, intrudes the element of a limited personality into the high place which nothing but spiritual energy can fill, representing that Jesus can come in where a will is an intrusion, into growth, repentance, reformation.

The divine will, or, *the eternal tendency to the good of the whole, active in every atom, every moment,* is the only will that can be supposed predominant a single hairbreadth beyond the lines of individual action and influence, as known to the experience; but a ghost, a Jupiter, a fairy, a devil, and not less a saint, an angel, and the God of popular religion, as of Calvinism, and Romanism, is an aggrandized and monstrous individual will. The divine will, such as I describe it, is Spiritual. These other things, though called spiritual, are not so, but only demonological; and fictions.

February 15.

Walking. — In the morning a man walks with his whole body; in the evening, only with his legs; the trunk is carried along almost motionless.

What fine traits Plutarch gives Epaminondas in his essay on the Demon of Socrates, representing him as taking no part in a bold attempt upon Archias and the tyrants because his nature was averse to it; and, "He loves to be silent, said his father; he is very cautious how he proposeth anything, but will hear eternally, and is never weary of an instructive story."

Ellen was never alone. I could not imagine her poor and solitary. She was like a tree in flower, so much soft, budding, informing beauty was society for itself, and she taught the eye that beheld her why Beauty was ever painted with loves and graces attending her steps.

February 22.

I closed on Wednesday evening, 21 February, my course of lectures at the Masonic Temple in Boston, on Human Life.

The pathetic lies usually not in miseries, but petty losses and disappointments, as when the poor family have spent their little utmost upon a wedding or a christening festival, and their feast is dishonoured by some insult or petty disaster, — the falling of the salver, or the spoiling of a carpet. When I was a boy I was sent by my mother with a dollar bill, to buy me a pair of shoes at Mr. Baxter's shop, and I lost the bill; and remember being sent out by my disappointed mother to look among the fallen leaves under the poplar trees opposite the house for the lost bank note.

My Ambition. — When I was in college, Robert Barnwell, the first scholar in my class, put his hand on the back of my head to feel for the bump of ambition and pronounced that it was very, very small.

Would you know if the man is just, ask of the tax-gatherer.

Bambino. — "Where's the cover that lives in this box?" asks little Waldo. When he saw the dead bird, he said, "He was gone by-by"; then he said, "He was broke." When Dr. Jackson smoked a cigar, Waldo said, "See the cobwebs go up out of the gentleman's mouth."

February 25.

Yesterday morning, 24 February at 8 o'clock, a daughter was born to me, a soft, quiet, swarthy little creature, apparently perfect and healthy. My sacred child! Blessings on thy head, little winter bud! And comest thou to try thy luck in this world, and know if the things of God are things for thee? Well assured, and very soft and still, the little maiden expresses great contentment with all she finds, and her delicate but fixed determination to stay where she is, and grow. So be it, my fair child! Lidian, who magnanimously makes my gods her gods, calls the babe Ellen. I can hardly ask more for thee, my babe, than that name implies. Be that vision, and remain with us, and after us.[1]

March 3.

The memory plays a great part in settling the intellectual rank of men. A seneschal of Parnassus is Mnemosyne. Thus, am I a better scholar than one of my neighbors who visited me? I see how it is. We read the same books a year, two years, ten years ago; we read the same books this month. Well, that fact which struck us both, then, with equal force, I still contemplate. He has lost it. He and the world have only *this* fact. I have that *and* this.

A fine voice in a choir seems to inundate the

1 It was the fortune of Ellen to be a joy and comfort to her father and mother in the home through all the years, and to take care of them in their last days.

house with spouts and jets and streams of sound, and to float the old hulk of the choir itself, insinuating itself under all the droning groans and shrill screams and hurrying them all away, the spoils of its own stream.

[On March 5, The Symposium met at Mr. Morse's, the subject of the evening being "Wonder and Worship." The next day Mr. Emerson gave a discourse, "Intellectual Integrity," before the Mechanics' Apprentices' Association. Again, on March 11, The Symposium gathered at Mr. Morse's and conversed on "Innocence and Guilt."]

Vanity. — We all wish to be of importance in one way or another. The child coughs with might and main, since it has no other claims on the company.

No Age in Talk. — I make no allowance for youth in talking with my friends. If a youth or maiden converses with me I forget they are not as old as I am.

Young Love. — The rude village boy teases the girls about the schoolhouse door.[1] . . .

1 Here follows the passage thus beginning in "Love" (*Essays*, First Series, p. 172).

Mountain Heads. — Brant's head in Stone's *Life of Brant* reminded me instantly of a mountain head, and the furrows of the brow suggest the strata of the summit. Gladly I perceive this fine resemblance, for we like to reconcile man and the world in all ways. Then I went to Boston and saw Allston's "Sisters" at Alexander's room. There again were human forms more related to the lights of morning and evening than to human society as we know it.

Gentleman. — When I consider how much it is to be a gentleman, how deep the elements of the gentleman lie in nature, I doubt if I should find anywhere among the privileged classes, and the select even of these, anyone who would not in some point of behaviour suggest vulgarity and imperfect breeding. *Non è nel mondo se non volgo.*

[On the last day of January and the first of February Mr. Emerson by invitation gave three lectures at Plymouth : " Genius," " Home," and " Being and Seeming."

In February his friend James Freeman Clarke, then a young minister in Louisville, Kentucky, asked for some verses for his newspaper *The Western Messenger*, and Mr. Emerson sent him

"Good-bye," written in 1823, and "Each and All," founded on a boyish experience recorded in the Journal, May 16, 1834, and turned into verse later.]

March 9.

The Indo-American war of Brant and Gansevoort, etc., illustrate as well as any other the uninventive, the inventive. All sit still in the fort, persuaded that the militia cannot meet the British regulars and the dreadful Indians. At last comes a restless, creative man, some General Herkimer, or Captain Willett, and makes a sally to the woods to a distant fort, engages the Indians, beats them, and shows the stupidity of the former sitting. Instantly "they conquer who believe they can." God invents: God advances. The world, the flesh, and the devil sit and rot. Not less is all society an optical illusion to the young adventurer.[1] . . . Stay at home in God, and the whole population will do homage with cap and knee.

General Gates behaved with great delicacy to General Burgoyne when he capitulated, in 1777, at Saratoga. Burgoyne mentions in a letter to

[1] The rest of this passage is found in the first paragraph of "Politics" (*Essays*, First Series).

the Earl of Derby, that when the British soldiers had marched out of their camp to the place where they were to pile their arms, not a man of the American troops was to be seen. (See Stone's *Life of Brant*.)

Books. — " What's Hecuba to him ? "

Byron says of Jack Bunting, " He knew not what to say, and so he swore." I may say it of our preposterous use of books, He knew not what to do, and so *he read*.[1] . . .

March 10.

I charge the church with a want of respect to the soul of the worshipper. The question every worshipper should ask of the preacher is, " What is that to me ? What have I to do with thee ? What with thy fact ; what with thy history ; thy person ; thine alleged inclinations, and aversions ? I am here. Behold thy tribunal. Come with thy persons and facts to judgment." And the church, the preacher should say, " Soul of my brother, methinks I have glad tidings for thee. Methinks I have found something of thine spoken by one Jesus, by one Zoroaster, by

1 The rest of the paragraph is printed in " Spiritual Laws " (*Essays*, First Series, p. 164).

one Penn. Hear and judge.—But now we are a mob; man does not stand in awe of man;[1] . . ."

I suppose that my desire to retain a church visible grows out of the present state of society, and that, in a right state, every meeting for practical, intellectual, or civic purposes would be predominated by the sentiment of holiness, and would yield the precise satisfactions I have in view, when I ask more Sabbath than the eternal Sabbath of action.

Vanity.—Do not be so troublesome modest, you vain fellow. Real modesty still puts the thing forward and postpones the person, nor worries me with endless apologies.

"*Another State.*"—I am weary of hearing at church of another state. When shall I hear the prophet of the present state?

Also the preacher admonishes his man not to bring a dishonor on religion by his misconduct. Why not ask him not to shut his eyes for fear of putting out the sunshine?

Isolation must precede society. I like the

1 The substance of what follows is in "Self-Reliance" (p. 71).

silent church before the service begins better than any preaching.[1] . . .

At church in the afternoon I doubted whether that dislocation, disunion, reflex life, second thought, that mars all our simplicity, be not an universal disease, and whether all literary pictures of Nathan the Wise, or whatever calm, placid philosopher, be not false and overcharged. Howbeit, I thought it best to seek one peace by fidelity; and at least I would write my procrastinated letters. . . . Then again it seemed wise to sit at home contented with my work and word, and never rove into other men's acres more. Why this needless visiting? If you can really serve them, they will visit you.

One thing more. It is not by running after Napoleon that the corresponding element, the Napoleonism in you, is stimulated and matured; but by withdrawing from him, from all, back on the deeps of Home. All history is in us.

March 13.

Conversation.— The office of conversation is to give me self-possession. I lie torpid as a clod.

[1] The rest of the passage is found in " Self-Reliance " (pp. 71, 72).

Virtue, wisdom, sound to me fabulous,—all cant. I am an unbeliever. Then comes by a safe and gentle spirit who spreads out in order before me his own life and aims, not as experience, but as the good and desirable. Straightway I feel the presence of a new and yet old, a genial, a native element. I am like a Southerner, who, having spent the winter in a polar climate, feels at last the south wind blow, the rigid fibres relax, and his whole frame expands to the welcome heats. In this bland, flowing atmosphere, I regain, one by one, my faculties, my organs; life returns to a finger, a hand, a foot. A new nimbleness,—almost wings, unfold at my side,—and I see my right to the heaven as well as to the farthest fields of the earth. The effect of the conversation resembles the effect of a beautiful voice in a church choir as I have noted it above, which insinuates itself as water into all chinks and cracks and presently floats the whole discordant choir and holds it in solution in its melody. Well, I too am a ship aground, and the bard directs a river to my shoals, relieves me of these perilous rubs and strains, and at last fairly uplifts me on the waters, and I put forth my sails, and turn my head to the sea. Alcott is the only majestic converser I now meet.

He gives me leave to be, more than all others.
Alcott is so apprehensive that he does not need
to be learned.

Institutions are optical illusions. All concentrates; let us not rove. A few sounds, a few
sights, suffice and outvalue a multitude. Kings
make their own scale and new write the tariff of
prices. Let us mind our business with a great
heart and never vex ourselves with institutions
or consequences. The great man knew not that
he was great.[1] . . .

Painting seems to be to the eye what dancing
is to the body.[2] . . .

March 19.

Such is my confidence in the compensations
of nature that I no longer wish to find silver
dollars in the road, nor to have the best of the
bargain in my dealings with people, nor that my
property should be increased, — knowing that
all such gains are apparent, and not real; for
they pay the sure tax. But the perception that

[1] The rest of this passage occurs in "Spiritual Laws"
(p. 155).

[2] The rest of this long passage occurs in "Art" (*Essays,*
First Series, p. 336).

it is not desirable to find the dollar, I enjoy without any alloy. This is an abiding good: this is so much accession of Godhead.

Popularity is for dolls; a hero cannot be popular.

I meet men whose faces instantly assure me they are where I left them; no new thoughts, new books, new facts, but facts old and decrepit by the inaction of the soul. Others I know, who are new men, in new regions, with faint memory of their own words and deeds on past occasions.

"*It is in bad taste*," is the most formidable word an Englishman can pronounce.

Peepers and Listeners. — There is other peeping beside setting the eye to chinks and keyholes; Reading Goethe's letters, or the History of the Saracens, for example.[1]

March 23.

Art. — Each work of art excludes the world, concentrates attention on itself. For the time it

1 Mr. Emerson refers here to a previous page in which he had spoken of "the preposterous use of books," also the continuation of the subject in "Spiritual Laws" (p. 164).

is the only thing worth doing, to do just that; be it a sonnet, a statue, a landscape, an outline head of Cæsar, or an oration.[1] . . .

A man must consider what a rich realm he abdicates when he becomes a conformist.[2] . . .

March 26.

A good man is contented. I love and honor Epaminondas, but I do not wish to be Epaminondas.[3] . . . We are always ducking with our unseasonable apologies. Shall the priest or priestess on the tripod, full of the God, baulk the inquirer with nonsense of modesty?

To Him who Said it Before. — I see my thought standing, growing, walking, working, out there in nature. Look where I will, I see it. Yet when I seek to say it, all men say, "No: it is not. These are whimsies and dreams!" Then I think they look at one thing, and I at others. My

1 The substance of what follows is printed in " Art " (p. 353).

2 Here follows the passage in " Self-Reliance " about the preacher hampered by being an attorney for his sect (pp. 54, 55).

3 Here occurs the long passage so beginning, which is printed in " Spiritual Laws " (pp. 162, 163).

thoughts, though not false, are far, as yet, from simple truth, and I am rebuked by their disapprobation, nor think of questioning it. Society is yet too great for me. But I go back to my library and open my books and lo I read this word spoken out of immemorial time, " God is the unity of men." Behold, I say, my very thought! This is what I am rebuked for saying; and here it is and has been for centuries in this book which circulates among men without reproof, nay, with honor. But behold again here in another book, " Man is good, but men are bad." Why, I have said no more. And here again, read these words, " *Ne te quaesiveris extra.*" What then! I have not been talking nonsense. These lines of Greek and Latin, which pass now current in all literatures as proverbs of old, wise men, are expressions of the very facts which the sky, the sea, the plant, the ox, the man, the picture, said daily unto me, and which I repeated to you. I see that I was right; that not only I was right, which I could not doubt, but my language was right : that the soul has always said these things, and that you ought to hear it and say the same. And thou, good ancient brother, who to ancient nations, to earlier modes of life and politics and religion, didst utter this my perception of today, I greet thee with reverence, and give thee joy of that which thou so long hast held and which today, a perfect blessing, one and indivisible, yields itself to me also, yields itself all to me, without making the possession less.

The perception of identity is a good mercury of the progress of the mind. I talk with very accomplished persons who betray instantly that they are strangers in nature. The cloud, the tree, the sod, the cat, are not theirs, have nothing of them. They are visitors in the world, and all the proceedings and events are alien, immeasureable, and across a great gulf. The poet, the true naturalist, for example, domesticates himself in nature with a sense of strict consanguinity. His own blood is in the rose and the apple-tree. The Cause of him is Cause of all. The volcano has its analogies in him. He is in the chain of magnetic, electric, geologic, meteorologic phenomena, and so he comes to live in nature and extend his being through all: then is true science.

April 6.

I have regard to appearance still. So am I no hero. Do what you are doing with a single mind and utter disregard of eyes, and then what you have done before will justify you now.[1] . . .

Cousins. — Would it not dissipate the maiden's romance if she foresaw, in the hour of wedding, the arrival of young cousins three, four years hence at her door, without any work in their hands, or word in their mouths, dropped out of the stage-coach like eggs not yet alive, to spend a fortnight?

" The learning to write and to read was better than the Latin lessons in poetry whereby I was constrained to lay up the follies of I know not what Æneas, whilst I forgot mine own, and to bewail Dido dead because she killed herself for love, whilst in the meantime I, most miserable creature, did endure myself with dry eyes to depart and die from thee, O my God, and my life." (St. AUGUSTINE's *Confessions*, Book I, chap. xiii.) See what I have written above.[2]

April 7.

Popular Christianity is far below, in its tone of teaching, the poorest moral philosophy that

1 The rest of the passage with similar beginning is in "Self-Reliance" (p. 59).

2 Mr. Emerson again alludes to what he wrote, on March 9, of the "preposterous use of books."

has been originally taught. The pulpit concedes that judgment is not executed in this world; that the wicked are successful; that the good are miserable;[1] . . . that is to say, these last are to have their full swing of wine and peaches another day. . . . You sin now, we shall sin by and by. Or we would sin now if we could; not being successful, we expect our revenge tomorrow.

Of course such teaching degrades the disciple. Can they wonder that every pure, generous and intelligent man and woman rejects what they call their gospel? Every pure mind has always rejected the popular estimate of men and things, and made its own. It has not called bread happiness. It has said, "I am in heaven when I am true. Poor wanderers, comfort, flatter each other that you are happy because you have flocks and herds, gardens and cellars, piles of wood and piles of coin; you are not happy; I know it; you know it in my presence. All literature, all grandeur of spirit, testifies for me, if testimony I needed; but I need none, I affirm, I *am*, the fact; and you need none, — confront us, and you confess!"

[1] Here follows in nearly the same words the account of the sermon which disgusted him, that is printed on the second page of "Compensation."

The teaching that shows this would be spiritual; the teaching that shows the omnipotence of the will, that Heaven proceeds forever *from* me outward to all things, and not *to* me from coffee and custard. The teaching that concedes success to sensual good, the teaching of Calvinistic and Unitarian pulpits, is carnal.

An opium pill does not teach the doctrine of the Soul, but the preponderance of structure.

In the prints of Rogers's Italy I am struck in certain figures which are handsome and unblameable, with the quite conventional character. They are not original. Every outline, however coarse, from the Phidian marbles, and every drawing in that book of Salvator Rosa's, is as original as a man, and strong as a tree or a stone; but these pretty English pictures look thin and superficial.

Whatever we travel to see was domestic, and not the product of travelling; as the Pyramids, the Parthenon, its marbles; Raphael's and Michael Angelo's pictures; Venice, and the residence of Dante, Shakspear, Burns. We shall never find God out there in the world. Always he abides fast at home.

[It appears from the letter to Carlyle that, in April, Mr. Emerson began to put his papers together in preparation for his first book of Essays.]

April 9.

Housekeeping. — Unroof any house, and you must find there confusion. Order is too precious and divine a thing to dwell with such fools and sinners as we all are.[1] . . . Incredible is it to me that in any family the work can be despatched from Monday to Monday again, all the year round, with sense and system. Then if the house is well kept, are the relations of the keepers, the men and women and children well and reverently observed, or are persons made things? On the whole, I am sure there is no house well kept: there go too many things to it.

April 11.

"The large utterance of the early gods."

It is the best part of each writer which has nothing private in it. That is the best part of each which he does not know ; that which flowed out of his constitution.[2] . . .

1 Here follows the passage on the disproportion in the sacrifice of higher things in homes to good housekeeping, printed in "Domestic Life" (*Society and Solitude,* p. 112).

2 Here occurs the passage thus beginning, printed in "Compensation" (p. 108).

"The large utterance of the early gods." I
believe, not only in Omnipotence, but in Eternity. And these are not words, but things.
I believe in the omnipresence; that is, that the
All is in each particle; that entire nature reap-
pears in every leaf and moss. I believe in Eternity; that is, I can find Greece and Palestine
and Italy and England and the Islands, — the
genius and creative principle of each and of all
eras, in my own mind.[1] The primeval world,
the Foreworld, as the Germans say, I can dive
to it in myself as well as grope for it with re-
searching fingers in catacombs, libraries, and the
broken reliefs and torsos of ruined villas.[2]

There is, at this moment, there is for me an
utterance undoubtedly bare and grand as that
of the colossal chisel of Phidias, or trowel of
the Egyptians, or pen of Moses or Dante, but
different from all these. Not possibly will the
soul deign to repeat itself, but if I can hear what
these patriarchs say, surely I can reply to them
on the same pitch of voice. Dwell up there in
the simple and noble regions of thy life, act
thy heart, and skulk no longer nor respect thy

1 This sentence occurs in "History" (*Essays*, First Series,
p. 9).

2 Printed in "History" (p. 23).

fears, and thou shalt reproduce the Foreworld again.

Realism. — Of Fletcher, William Cartwright writes, —

> Where, in a worthy scorn, he dares refuse
> All other gods, and makes the thing his muse.

>   Fletcher, whose wit
> Was not an accident to the soul, but It;
> Only diffused; thus we the same sun call
> Moving i' the sphere and shining on a wall.
>   EDWARD POWELL.

> Nor were thy plays the lotteries of wit,
> But like to Dürer's pencil, which first knew
> The laws of faces, and then faces drew.
>   WILLIAM CARTWRIGHT.

April 13.

Fletcher's *Bonduca* is a play whose tune goes manly. Let the professors and reviewers who prate of strong Saxon speech read this, and write so. It is short of Shakspear's *dire* style (as in Hamlet's dialogue with his mother), but only of that. Caratach is right great, especially in the first scene, and the hard knocks which Junius and Petilius give each other recruit the ear and heart. These men are not mush.

Then I read *The Coxcombs*, a play which is a just encomium of woman. The situations and sentiments of Viola are genuinely pathetic and true. And the true nature of woman in her, when she asks Valerio, —

> Pray what is love? for I am full of that
> I do not know, —

contrasts with that violated nature which Valerio considers when he says, —

> Thy thoughts would be,
> Like a thrice married widow, full of ends.

In *Bonduca*, Caratach [showing the impossibility of peace] paints the Romans out of Tacitus: —

And with those swords that know no end of battle;
Those men beside themselves allow no neighbor;
Those minds, that, where the day is, claim inheritance;
And where the sun makes ripe the fruits, their harvest;
And where they march but measure out more ground
To add to Rome, and here in the bowels on us, —
It must not be.

April 14.

Yesterday, I read Beaumont and Fletcher's tragedy, *The False One*, which, instead of taking its name from Septimius, ought to have been *Cleopatra*. A singular fortune is that of the man

Cæsar, to have given name, as he has, to all that is heroic ambition in the imaginations of painters and poets. Cæsar must still be the speaking-trumpet through which this large, wild, commanding spirit must always be poured.

The poet would be a great man. His power is intellectual. Instantly he seizes these hollow puppets of Cæsar, of Tamerlane, of Boadicea, of Belisarius, and inflates them with his own vital air. If he can verily ascend to grandeur,—if his soul is grand, behold his puppets attest his might, they are no more puppets, but instant vehicles of the wine of God ; they shine and overflow with the streams of that universal energy that beamed from Cæsar's eye, poised itself in Hector's spear, purer sat with Epaminondas, with Socrates, purest with thee, thou holy child, Jesus!

The poet has used these names and conventions as he would use a flute or a pencil to convey his sense. He does not therefore defer to the nature of these accidental men, these stock heroes.[1] . . . The great names cannot stead him ; if he have not life himself. Let a man believe in God, and not in names and places and persons. . . .

[1]   The rest of the passage thus beginning forms the concluding pages of " Spiritual Laws."

We are the photometers, we the irritable gold-leaf and tinfoil that measure the accumulations of the subtle element. We know the authentic effects of the true fire through every one of its million disguises.[1] Does it raise and astonish the spirits, does it soar above all custom and use, and work new in every stroke, yet quietly and lawfully as rosebuds open, and constrain thee to greet in its newest and strangest works a friendly and domestic power, kind to thee as was thy mother's milk, — then we know the sign of God. Always it stays at home; never is gadding.

Isolation you must have, but it must not be mechanical, but spiritual, that is, Elevation.[2] The whole world seems to be in conspiracy to invade you, to vanquish you with emphatic details, to break you into crumbs, to fritter your time. Friend, wife, child, mother, fear, want, charity, all knock at the student's door at the critical moment, ring larums in his ear, scare away the Muse, and spoil the poem. Do not spill

1 The sentence above, with which " Spiritual Laws " ends, is given for the sake of its conclusion in the Journal, which is omitted there.

2 This passage occurs in " Self-Reliance " (p. 72), but is given here to show its original form and different ending.

thy soul, do not all descend, but keep thy state; stay at home in thine own heaven and let fingers do the fingers' work. Unite and break not.

Music Masses. — The philosopher has a good deal of knowledge which cannot be abstractly imparted, which needs the combinations and complexity of social action to paint it out, as many emotions in the soul of Handel and Mozart are thousand-voiced and utterly incapable of being told in a simpler air on a lute, but must ride on the mingling whirlwinds and rivers and storms of sound of the great orchestra of organ, pipe, sackbut, dulcimer, and all kinds of music. As the musician avails himself of the concert, so the philosopher avails himself of the drama, the epic, the novel, and becomes a poet; for these complex forms allow of the utterance of his knowledge of life by *indirections* as well as in the didactic way, and can therefore express the fluxional quantities and values which the thesis or dissertation could never give. There is the courage of the cabinet as of the field. There is the courage of painting and of poetry as well as of siege and stake.

April 15.

My books are my picture-gallery. Every man has his fine recreations and elegancies allowed him by the liberal God, as well as his chores. These noble English poems, so rich, so sincere, so coloured in the grain, proceeding out of a depth of nature answering to the good Saxon heart in us, these are the Pitti Palace and Vatican of me and my friends. Why should I grudge the Grand Duke of Tuscany his gallery? The citizen of old Thebes needed not inquire after the young artists of Athens or Ionia as he stood in his gigantic palaces in the shadow of a sphinx. The Hindoo at Elephanta dwelt also with his own national ornaments. To each his own the liberal God supplies. Only accept your own. Drink deep of this enjoyment. Know your books, and brilliant souls that soared and sang, yet kept their own law, and so tell of great Nature to you. Your native, proper muses, your own cousins and college,—they are the wild flowers that fringe your sod; but go sometimes, of a morning or evening, into this garden of delight.

Artificial Memory. Value of a Catalogue. — The simple knot of Now and Then will give an immeasureable value to any sort of catalogue or journal kept with common sense for a year or two. See in the merchant's counting-room, for his peddling of cotton and indigo, the value that comes to be attached to any Blotting book or Ledger; and if your aims and deeds are superior, how can any record of yours (suppose, of the books you wish to read, of the pictures you would see, of the facts you would scrutinize), any record that you are genuinely moved to begin and continue, not have a value proportionately superior? It converts the heights you have reached into table-land. That book or literary fact which had the whole emphasis of attention a month ago stands here along with one which was as important in preceding months, and with that of yesterday; and, next month, there will be another. Here they all occupy but four lines, and I cannot read these together without juster views of each than when I read them singly.

To know One you must know All. — Nature hates finites and cripples. It is of no use to say, because the world is represented in each particle as in a moss or an apple, Come, I will dedicate myself to the study of botany, in one thing; I will explore the dandelions. A dandelion shall be my meat and drink, house and home, and through that alone will I achieve nature. It is all in vain, for the way Nature tells her secrets is by exposing one function in one flower, and another function in a different plant. If the spiral vessels are seen in bulbs, the vesicles are seen in others, *stomata* in another, *pila* in another, and *chromule* in a fifth; and to show all the parts of the one plant, she leads you all round the garden.

Self-Reliance. — Ask nothing of men, and in the endless mutation, thou, only firm column, must presently appear on a throne, the king of all men.

April 17.

Am I a hypocrite, who am disgusted by vanity everywhere and preach self-trust every day?

We give you leave to prefer your work to the whole world, so long as you remain in it; but when, uninvited, you come to visit me, what was the praise of God sounds in my ear like self-praise.

I will assume that a stranger is judicious and benevolent. If he is, I will thereby keep him so. If he is not, it will tend to instruct him.

The author appeals to the judicious reader; but if he has prevailed so far with any reader that he is influenced with a desire to behold and converse with this master, the author is shy, suspicious and disdainful. Let him go into his closet and pray the Divinity to make him so great as to be good-natured.

Philosophy teaches how to be personal without being unparliamentary.

In life it is a great matter to live with the people you are used to. Go where there is real affinity and the highest relations for you, and it serves very well for the short time that thought and poetry flow, but as soon as the tea-tray comes in, we feel the yoke of foreigners, and wish we were at home with our stupid familiars.

April 21.

How great it is to do a little, as, for instance, to deserve the praise of good nature, or of humility, or of punctuality; but to say, This was a man; he lived wisely; he lived well,—outgoes all probability. I dare not believe it of my fellow.

Many thoughts lately on truth of character, but they are fugitive; so let not the volitions be, or rather, the preceding instructions of the soul! I thought how slowly we learn to be single and meek. If you visit your friend, why need

you apologize for not having visited him and
waste his time and deface your own act? Visit
him now.[1] . . .

In Landor's noble book, *Pericles and Aspasia*,
is honor and elegance enough to polish a nation
for an age. All the elements of the gentleman
are there, except holiness. Religion in a high
degree he does not know.

What is the substance of elegance but the
will to serve all? How does a benevolent person who has helped, helps, and will help men,
sitting by your side, rise out of all considerations of fashion of the times, of costume, of
birth, decorated only by this primary nobility!

[In the last days of April, Mr. Alcott and
Mr. John S. Dwight, Mr. Emerson's successor
as preacher in East Lexington, came to visit
him. He told them of an engagement at noon
to marry some young people at the Middlesex
Tavern. The bridegroom was Samuel Staples,
then bar-tender, and the bride the landlord's
daughter. This good man, three years later, in
his official capacity, arrested for refusal to pay

1 For the rest of the passage, see "Spiritual Laws" (pp.
160, 161).

taxes Alcott, Thoreau, and Charles Lane, the English friend of the former, and held two of them in jail until ransomed by friends. It should be said that he offered to pay Thoreau's tax himself, but this Thoreau would not allow. Having come to Concord a boy, with a few pence in his pocket, and begun as hostler, Mr. Staples rose through the grades of bar-tender, clerk, constable and jailer, deputy-sheriff, representative to the General Court, auctioneer, real-estate agent, and gentleman-farmer, to be one of the most valued and respected fathers of the village-family. In Mr. Emerson's last years, Mr. Staples was his next neighbor and good friend, and came affectionately to bid him good-bye in the last hours of his life. He once was commenting to a friend of the family on the number of visitors that came, some of them from beyond the seas, and added, "Well, I suppose there's a great many things that Mr. Emerson knows that I couldn't understand; but I *know* that there's a damn sight of things that I know that he don't know anything about."

On May 1, Mr. Emerson read "Comedy" at the Concord Lyceum, and after the lecture several of the friends and neighbors came to his home and the talk ran on Conversation. The next evening Mr. Alcott had a "Conversation" at the house of Mr. Thoreau.]

May 4.

In reference to the philanthropies of the day, it seems better to use than to flout them. Shall it be said of the hero that he opposed all the contemporary good because it was not grand? I think it better to get their humble good and to catch the golden boon of purity and temperance and mercy from these poor ——s and ——s and ——s.

[May 8, The Symposium met at Rev. Cyrus Bartol's. The company were Alcott, Hedge, George Ripley, Theodore Parker, Dr. LeBaron Russell, Rev. Caleb Stetson, Rev. Mr. Osgood, and Emerson. The subjects were, The Journals, Property, and Harvard College.]

May 10.

The best conversation equally, I think, with the worst, makes me say, I will not seek society. At least I wish to hear the thoughts of men which differ widely in some important respect from my own. I would hear an artist, or a wise mechanic, or agriculturist, or statesman, or historian, or wit, or poet, or scholar, great in a peculiar department of learning, but not one who only gives me in a varied garb my own daily thoughts. I think it is better to sever and scatter men of kindred genius than to unite them.

I hate to quote my friend, who, with all his superiority, still thinks like me. In quoting him, I am presently reduced to defend his opinion. Then I find it not only hard, but impossible, to separate his view from mine, and I am admonished to preach another time from God and not from a man. Hence comes the *Pereant qui ante nos nostra dixerunt.*

May 11.

Two letters from Carlyle, dated 13 and 17 April.

Beasts belong to the hour: they are the literature of the present moment. Men are the result or value of the Past. Prophecy alone records the Eternal.

May 12.

Does it not seem imperative that the soul should find an articulate utterance, in these days, on man and religion? All or almost all that I hear at church is mythological; and of the few books or preachers or talkers who pretend to have made some progress, the most are in a transition state, Janus-faced, and speak alternately to the old and the new.

It is manifest in every word the man says whether he speaks with truth or tradition. You can tell by his pronunciation of God whether he is Theist or Atheist.

Our aim in our writings ought to be to make daylight shine through them.

Once I supposed that only my manner of living was superficial; that all other men's was solid. Now I find we are all alike shallow.

May 19.

The Epochs of Life.—God loveth not size: whale and minnow are of like dimension. But we call the poet inactive because he is not a governor, a president, a merchant or a porter. But real action is in silent moments. The epochs of our life are not in the visible facts of our choice of a calling.[1] . . .

Propriety.— The propriety which distinguishes the great writer is more excellent than any one profound thought or sublime image, for it

1 Here follows the rest of this long passage in "Spiritual Laws" (pp. 161, 162).

is truth or beauty *domesticated*, and not now a sally of the soul, a single wild peal of music, but so habitual that it modulates every thought and movement. A plateau or table-land is a vast collection of mountains with no valleys between the peaks.

I am struck with the propriety of Shakspear, Taylor, Burke, Saint Augustine.

Add the *humanity* of the great writers and their spontaneity.

I think I gain more from one picture than from a gallery. One picture gives me, in the first place, all the agreeable stimulus of color, — itself a tonic, — that a gallery can. This makes me brisk, gay, and thoughtful. Then, I see freely the forms, and dream pleasantly of what they would say ; — I carry the picture out far and wide on every side, and I highly enjoy the unity of the hour: for the picture, of course, excludes all other things ; and for a long time afterwards I can well remember the day. I conspire with the painter, lend myself willingly to him, see more than he has done, see what he meant to do. But the gallery will not permit this. The eye glances from picture to picture. Each interferes with the other. Each can only now stand for what it really is, no more. And the artist is lowered, not exalted, by the beholder. At least thus thought I at Allston's gallery, where I recognized in almost all the pictures that they gained nothing by Juxtaposition.

It is somewhat so with men. They are less together than they are apart. They are somewhat wronged, discrowned and disgraced by being put many together in one apartment.

At church today I felt how unequal is this match of words against things. Cease, O thou unauthorized talker, to prate of consolation, and resignation, and spiritual joys, in neat and balanced sentences. For I know these men who sit below, and on the hearing of these words look up. Hush, quickly: for care and calamity are *things* to them. There is Mr. T——, the shoemaker, whose daughter is gone mad, and he is looking up through his spectacles to hear what you can offer for his case. Here is my friend, whose scholars are all leaving him, and he knows not what to turn his hand to, next. Here is my wife, who has come to church in hope of being soothed and strengthened after being wounded by the sharp tongue of a slut in her house. Here is the stage-driver who has the jaundice, and cannot get well. Here is B., who failed last week, and he is looking up. O speak things, then, or hold thy tongue.

There is no such thing as concealment: every element hangs out its flag. Health is a quality that cannot lie; so is disease. The wild exotic which no man can tell of, at last puts out its flower, its fruit, and the secret can be kept no longer. Ali may keep the secret of his gold, but a bit will stick to the wax at the bottom of the peck measure. You cannot wipe out the foot-track, you cannot draw up the ladder, so as to leave no trace and no inlet. To those who have crimes to conceal the simplest laws and elements of nature, fire, water, snow, wind, gravitation, become penalties, and the sun and the moon are the frowns of God and lanthorns of his police.[1]

In fable, again, there is the vindictive circumstance in the old age of the immortal Tithon.

In society let this be thy aim, to put men in tune. Untune nobody. If, O Doctor Prose! the faces of thy friends do lengthen and quiver

[1] Some sentences of this paragraph are in "Compensation" (p. 116).

and gape, canst thou not retreat to thine own
lexicons and grammars, to thy spade and poultry-yard? The narrowest life is very wide; as
wide as the largest.

[On May 22, The Symposium met at Mr.
George Ripley's, and the talk was on the Genius
and Claims of Jesus. Present, Hedge, Bartol,
Emerson, Alcott (Rev. Ephraim?), Peabody,
Stetson and Rev. Convers Francis.]

May 23.

The poor madman, whipped through the
world by his thoughts!

Fear is an instructor who has a great talent.
You may learn one thing of him passing well,
this, namely, that there is certainly rottenness
where he appears.[1] . . . If you do not feel pleasantly toward your workman or workwoman, your
kinsman or townsman, you have not dealt justly.

Landor's *Pericles and Aspasia* has little religion, but it speaks to your taste, your honor, and
your wit; then it charms me that he never stoops
to explanation, nor uses seven words where one
will do.

1 Here follows the passage thus beginning in " Compensation " (pp. 111, 112).

In that old rotten country of Germany it seems as if spontaneous character — fresh outbursts of dear Nature — were less rare than in this country, called new and free. We are the most timid, crippled old uncles and aunts that ever hobbled along the highway without daring to quit the sidewalk. I have no better sponsors however at this moment in mind than Beethoven and Bettina.

A College.— My College should have Allston, Greenough, Bryant, Irving, Webster, Alcott, summoned for its domestic professors. And if I must send abroad (and, if we send for dancers and singers and actors, why not at the same prices for scholars?), Carlyle, Hallam, Campbell, should come and read lectures on History, Poetry, Letters. I would bid my men come for the love of God and man, promising them an open field and a boundless opportunity, and they should make their own terms. Then I would open my lecture rooms to the wide nation; and they should pay, each man, a fee that should give my professor a remuneration fit and noble. Then I should see the lecture-room, the college, filled with life and hope. Students would come from far; for who would not ride a hundred miles to hear some one of these men giving his selectest thoughts to those who received them with joy? I should see living learning; the Muse once more in the eye and cheek of the youth.

"If I love you what is that to you?" etc.[1]

Character. — What we value in a man is that he should give us a sense of mass. Society is frivolous; cuts up its day into shreds.[2] . . .

Two persons lately, very young children of the most high God, have admonished me by their silent being.[3] . . .

The wise man not only leaves out of his thought the multitude when he converses on poetry or on virtue, but also the few.

Tell me not that you are sufficient to yourself but have nothing to impart. I know and am assured that whoever is sufficient to himself will, if only by existing, suffice me also.

1 See "Love" (*Essays*, First Series, p. 180).

2 The entry thus beginning is from a loose sheet in Journal D. The rest of the passage occurs in "Character" (*Essays*, Second Series, p. 99).

3 This passage also is from the same loose sheet, and is printed in "Experience" (pp. 105, 106).

May 26.

At Waltham I repeated, with somewhat more emphasis perhaps than was needed, the impression the Allston gallery makes on me; that whilst Homer, Phidias, Dante, Shakspear, Michel Angelo, Milton, Raphael, make a positive impression, Allston does not. It is an eyeless face. It is an altar without fire. Beautiful drawing there is,—a rare merit,—taste there is; the blandest, selectest forms and circumstance; a highly cultivated mind; a beneficent genial atmosphere; but no man. And this it does not seem unreasonable or ungrateful to demand, that the artist should pierce the soul; should command; should not sit aloof and circumambient merely, but should come and take me by the hand and lead me somewhither.[1] . . .

Allston's pictures are Elysian; fair, serene, but unreal.

I extend the remark to all the American geniuses. Irving, Bryant, Greenough, Everett, Channing, even Webster in his recorded Eloquence, all lack nerve and dagger.

[1] The rest of the passage is printed in "Art" (*Essays*, First Series, bottom of p. 355).

If, as Hedge thinks, I overlook great facts in stating the absolute laws of the soul; if, as he seems to represent it, the world is not a dualism, is not a bipolar unity, but is *two*, is Me and It, then is there the alien, the unknown, and all we have believed and chanted out of our deep instinctive hope is a pretty dream.

The poor mind does not seem to itself to be anything unless it have an outside oddity, some Graham diet, or Quaker coat, or Calvinistic prayer-meeting, or Abolition effort, or anyhow some wild, contrasting action, to testify that it is somewhat. The rich mind lies in the sun and sleeps, and is Nature. Or why need you rail, or need a biting criticism on the church and the college to demonstrate your holiness and your intellectual aims? Let others draw that inference which damns the institutions, if they will. Be thyself too great for enmity and fault-finding.

May 27.

The compensations of calamity are not to be found by the understanding suddenly, but require years of time to make them sensible. The death of a dear friend, wife, brother, lover, seems

an unmixed loss.[1] . . . What loss like the loss of
a bridegroom to a bride? The wise and the unwise have but one sentiment. There seems no
atonement. Yet, come years after, and see self-
reliance where was frailty and tenderness alone;
come and see character where was only confid-
ing love; see sweetness and wisdom and endless
benevolent actions instead of a girl's tears. See,
instead of the mother of children, the friend
and lover and high counsellor of all young
maidens, exercising a better than maternal influence over the fine endowments and good aspirations of a large circle, encouraging, refining,
and hallowing many worthy young persons,—
you may reconcile yourself better to the early
bereavement.

A great genius must come and preach self-
reliance. Our people are timid, desponding,
recreant whimperers. If they fail in their first
enterprises they lose all heart. If the young
merchant fails, men say he is RUINED.[2] . . .

1 The passage thus beginning forms the conclusion of
"Compensation."

2 Here follows the long passage printed in "Self-Reliance"
(p. 79), of which a few sentences are here given as showing that
they were inspired by the manly young Thoreau.

My brave Henry here who is content to live now, and feels no shame in not studying any profession, for he does not postpone his life, but lives already, — pours contempt on these cry-babies of routine and Boston. He has not one chance but a hundred chances. Now let a stern preacher arise who shall reveal the resources of man, and tell men they are not leaning willows. . . .

A great act of much import to the new philosophical opinions is the garden discovery that a potato, put into a hole, in six weeks becomes ten. This is the miracle of the multiplication of loaves.

May 28.

There is no history. There is only Biography. The attempt to perpetrate, to fix a thought or principle, fails continually. You can only live for yourself; your action is good only whilst it is alive, — whilst it is in you. The awkward imitation of it by your child or your disciple is not a repetition of it, is not the same thing, but another thing. The new individual must work out the whole problem of science, letters and theology for himself ; can owe his fathers nothing. There is no history ; only biography.

We are idolaters of the old. We do not believe in the omnipotence of the Soul: we do not
believe there is any force in Today, to rival or
recreate that beautiful yesterday. We linger in
the ruins of the old tent.[1] . . .

In proper Eternity there are few believers, that
is, in omnipresence and omnipotence, few.

The finite is the foam of the infinite. We stand
on a shore and see the froth and shells which the
sea has just thrown up, and we call the sea by
the name of that boundary, as, the German
Ocean, the English Channel, the Mediterranean
Sea. We do the like with the Soul. We see the
world which it once has made, and we call that
God, though it was only one moment's production, and there have been a thousand moments
and a thousand productions since. But we are to
learn to transfer our view to the Sea instead of
the Shore, the living sea instead of the changing
shore, the energy instead of the limitation, the
Creator instead of the world.

1 Here follows the passage so beginning in "Compensation" (p. 125), which is here immediately followed by that
about the shell-fish crawling out of its beautiful case when out-
grown (pp. 124, 125).

Nature will not have us fret or fume. When we come out of the Caucus or the Abolition Convention or the Temperance Meeting, she says to us, "So hot, my little Sir!" [1] I fear the criticism of the sun and moon.

How can I hope for a friend to me who have never been one?

May 29.

The laws, literature, religion, at certain times appear but a sad travestie and caricature of nature, and so do our modes of living.

I think we ought to have manual labor, each man. Why else this rapid impoverishing which brings every man continually to the presence of the fact that bread is by the sweat of the face, and why this continual necessity in which we all stand of bodily labor, by walking, riding, fencing, pitching, shooting, or billiards, if not by ploughing and mowing. And why this sentiment of honor and independence which cannot receive

1 Printed in "Spiritual Laws" (*Essays*, First Series, p. 135). This passage is followed by the one on holding a man amenable for choosing an evil occupation (p. 140), and that on travelling being a fool's paradise. (See "Self-Reliance," p. 81.)

a pecuniary benefit until the man has suffered
a fatal slackness on his springs. I suppose his
needs of labor are such to the health of his organization, his life, and his thought, that these
hints are so broad. Labor makes solitude and
makes society. It kills foppery, shattered nerves,
and all kinds of emptiness. It makes life solid.
It puts Pericles and Jack upon a firm ground of
sweet and manly fellowship. But its degeneracy
comes from the too much, the exclusive life of
the senses. It is only human when tempered by
the touches of thought and love.

I think that the heroism which at this day
would make on me the impression of Epaminondas and Phocion must be that of a domestic
conqueror.[1] . . .

May 30.

'T is pity we should leave with the children
all the romance, all that is daintiest in life, and
reserve for ourselves as we grow old only the
prose. Goethe fell in love in his old age, and I
would never lose the capacity of delicate and
noble sentiments.

1 The rest of the passage forms the conclusion of "Domestic Life" (*Society and Solitude*, p. 133).

The Lotus-eaters. — Reform always has this damper, viz., that a new simplicity can be preached with equal emphasis (and who shall deny that it is preached with equal reason too?) on the simplicity it preaches. Thus, when we have come to live on the fruits of our own gardens, and begin to boast that we lead a man's life, then shall come some audacious upstart to upbraid us with our false and foreign taste, which steadily plucks up everything which Nature puts in our soil; and laboriously plants everything not intended to grow there. Behold, shall that man of the weeds say, the perpetual broad hint that Nature gives you. Every day these plants you destroyed yesterday, appear again; and see a frost, a rain, drought, has killed this exotic corn and wheat and beans and beets, which luxurious man would substitute for his native and allowed table. Then too will arise the Society for preventing the murder of worms. And it will be asked with indignation what right have we to tear our small fellow citizens out of the sod and put them to death for eating a morsel of corn, or a melon leaf, or a bit of apple, whilst it can be proved to any jury by a surgical examination of their jaws and forceps and stomachs, that this is the natural food of this eater. In the same age a man will be reproached with simony and sacrilege because he took money of the bookseller for his poem or history.

We see all persons who are not natural with a certain commiseration. We see that the avengers are on their track and that certain crises and purgatories they must pass through.

Compression. — There is a wide difference between compression and an elliptical style. The dense writer has yet ample room and choice of phrase, and even a gamesome mood often, between his noble words. There is no disagreeable contraction in his sentence any more than there is a human face, where in a square space of a few inches is found room for command and love and frolic and wisdom and for the expression even of great amplitude of surface.

Language is made up of the spoils of all actions, trades, arts, games, of men. Every word is a metaphor borrowed from some natural or mechanical, agricultural or nautical process. The poorest speaker is like the Indian dressed in a robe furnished by half a dozen animals. It is like our marble foot-slab made up of countless shells and exuviæ of a foreign world.

June 3.

Our young scholars read newspapers, smoke, and sleep in the afternoons. Goethe, Gibbon, Bentley might provoke them to industry. Undoubtedly the reason why our men are not learned, why G——, for instance, is not, is because the genius or the age does not tend that way. This old learning of Bentley and Gibbon was the natural fruit of the Traditional age in philosophy and religion. Ours is the Revolutionary age, when man is coming back to Consciousness, and from afar this mind begets a disrelish for lexicons. Alcott, therefore, and Very, who have this spirit in great exaltation, abhor books. But at least it behooves those who reject the new ideas, the sticklers of tradition, to be learned. But they are not.

The Sabbath is painfully consecrated because the other days are not, and we make prayers in the morning because we sin all day. And if we pray not aloud and in form, we are constrained to excuse ourselves to others with words. O son of man, thou should'st not excuse thyself with words. Thy doing or thy abstaining should preclude words, and make every contrary act from thine show false and ugly.

June 6.

I suppose the number of reforms preached
to this age exceeds the usual measure, and indicates the depth and universality of the movement which betrays itself by such variety of
symptom. Anti-money, anti-war, anti-slavery,
anti-government, anti-Christianity, anti-college;
and, the rights of Woman.

Our conventional style of writing is now so
trite and poor, so little idiomatic, that we have
several foreigners who write in our journals in
a style not to be distinguished from their native
colleagues. As Dr. Follen, Maroncelli, Dr.
Lieber, Græter. But whatever draws on the
language of conversation will not be so easily
imitated, but will speak as the stream flows.

My life is a May game, I will live as I like.
I defy your strait - laced, weary, social ways
and modes. Blue is the sky, green the fields
and groves, fresh the springs, glad the rivers,
and hospitable the splendor of sun and star. I
will play my game out. And if any shall say
me nay, shall come out with swords and staves
against me to prick me to death for their foolish laws, — come and welcome. I will not look

grave for such a fool's matter. I cannot lose my cheer for such trumpery. Life is a May game still.

Love is thaumaturgic. It converts a chair, a box, a scrap of paper, or a line carelessly drawn on it, a lock of hair, a faded weed, into amulets worth the world's fee. If we see out of what straws and nothings he builds his Elysium, we shall read nothing miraculous in the New Testament.

June 7.

If a great man turn his attention to inferior natures, he will show the divine in them. . . . The stars to which loving and hoping men have added such moral splendor are white points to the dull.

June 8.

I remembered in the wood the profuse Nature which scatters from her hand all sorts of creatures. At Dartmouth College, last July, was a good sheriff-like gentleman with a loud voice, a pompous air, and a fine coat, whose aid, it seemed, the College annually called in, to marshal their procession. He was in his element; he commanded us all with such despotic condescension, as put all dignities and talents but his own quite aside. He marched before, the College followed him like a tame dog.

June 9.

Guido's Aurora for a morning prayer; so wills and so loves us Thomas Carlyle.[1]

June 10.

Analysis, too, is legitimate to the poetic soul. I find analysis not less poetical than synthesis, but it must be analysis into elements, and not mechanical division. If I can detect Nature converting water into hydrogen and oxygen, two beautiful and perfect wholes, I see not that it is less grand than when she recomposes water, a new whole. Mechanical analysis picks the lock: right analysis produces the key.

June 11.

Two Absolutions. — You may fulfil acceptably your circle of duties by clearing yourself in the direct or in the reflex way.[2]

1 Carlyle had sent to Mrs. Emerson the engraving of the Rospigliosi Aurora, which always thereafter hung in the Emersons' parlor. On it he wrote, "Will the lady of Concord hang this Italian sun-chariot in her drawing-room and, seeing it, think of a household which has good reason to remember hers?"

2 The rest of this paragraph is in "Self-Reliance" (p. 74).

Iteration. — Walked to the two ponds yesterday with C. S. A beautiful afternoon in the woodlands and waters and aerial waters above. I thought how charming is always an analogy, as, for example, the iteration which delights us in so many parts of nature, the reflection of the shore and the trees in water; in architecture, in the repetition of posts in a fence, or windows or doors or rosettes in the wall, or, still finer, the pillars of a colonnade; in poetry, rhymes, and better, the iteration of the sense, as in Milton's

> "though fallen on evil days,
> On evil days though fallen and evil tongues," —

and the sublime death of Sisera.[1] . . .

June 12.

I know no means of calming the fret and perturbation into which too much sitting, too much talking, brings me, so perfect as labor. I have no animal spirits; therefore, when surprised by company and kept in a chair for many hours, my heart sinks, my brow is clouded and I think I will run for Acton woods, and live with the squirrels henceforward. But my garden is nearer,

1 (In the song of Deborah and Barak, *Judges,* v, 27.) "At her feet he bowed, he fell, he lay down: at her feet he bowed, he fell: where he bowed, there he fell down dead."

and my good hoe, as it bites the ground, revenges my wrongs, and I have less lust to bite my enemies. I confess I work at first with a little venom, lay to a little unnecessary strength. But by smoothing the rough hillocks, I smooth my temper; by extracting the long roots of the piper-grass, I draw out my own splinters; and in a short time I can hear the bobolink's song and see the blessed deluge of light and colour that rolls around me.

In Allston's Lorenzo and Jessica, there is moonlight, but no moon. In the Jeremiah, the receiving Baruch is the successful figure. His best figures read and hear: and always his genius seems feminine and not masculine.

I said, all History becomes subjective and repeats itself, Parthia, Macedon, Rome and Netherlands, in each man's life. And now Alcott with his hatred of labor and commanding contemplation, a haughty beneficiary, makes good to the Nineteenth Century Simeon the Stylite and the Thebaid, and the first Capuchins.[1]

1 Compare in "History" (p. 28) the passage beginning, "I have seen the first monks and anchorets without crossing the seas."

The prayer of the farmer.[1] . . .

June 14.

Shall I not call God the Beautiful, who daily showeth himself so to me in his gifts?[2]

June 16.

Was not the motto of the Welsh bards, "Those whom truth had made free before the world"? Certainly the progress of character and of art teaches to treat all persons with an infinite freedom. What are persons but certain good or evil thoughts masquerading before me in curious frocks of flesh and blood? I were a fool to mind the color or figure of the frock, and slight the deep, aboriginal thought which so arrays itself. In this sense you cannot overestimate persons. And now in my house, as I see them pass, or hear their step on the stair, it seems to me the step of Ages and Nations.

And truly these walls do not lack variety in the few individuals they hold. Here is Simeon the Stylite, or John of Patmos in the shape of Jones Very, religion for religion's sake, religion

1 See "Self-Reliance" (pp. 77, 78).

2 The long passage in "Friendship" follows, there beginning, "I awoke this morning with dumb thanksgiving for my friends, the old and new" (*Essays*, First Series, p. 194).

divorced, detached from man, from the world, from science and art; grim, unmarried, insulated, accusing; yet true in itself, and speaking things in every word. The lie is in the detachment; and when he is in the room with other persons, speech stops as if there were a corpse in the apartment. Then here is mine Asia, not without a deep tinge herself of the same old land, and exaggerated and detached pietism, and so she serves as bridge between Very and the Americans. Then comes the lofty maiden who represents the Hope of these modern days, whom the "limits of earthly existence, the highest knowledge, the fairest blessings, cannot in the slightest degree satisfy," and whose beautiful impatience of these *dregs of Romulus* predicts to us a fairer future. And here are the two babes not yet descended into our sympathy or the world where we work, not yet therefore individualized and rigid, but a common property to all, which each can blend with his own ideas.

June 18.

Yesterday departed Jones Very from my house. In the afternoon departed also C. S. In the evening came and departed George B. Emerson and Mr. Adam of Calcutta.

Goethe unlocks the faculties of the artist more than any writer. He teaches us to treat all subjects with greater freedom, and to skip over all obstruction, time, place, name, usage, and come full and strong on the emphasis of the fact.

The Savant is formed at the expense of the man. The naturalists whom I know are disproportioned persons and have nowise learned to ally their facts to themselves, to see unity. The office of the naturalist should certainly be poetic. He should domesticate me in nature. He should make me feel my kindred to the tree and bring the rock nearer to my spirit. C. S. rightly says she cannot draw a child by studying the outlines but by watching for a time his motions and plays.[1] . . .

Be sacred. Do not let any man crowd upon you by peeping into him. No man can come near me unless I cumber myself about him. He comes too near by my act, not otherwise. Remember the great sentiment, "What we love that we have, but by Desire we bereave ourselves of the

1 The rest of the passage occurs in "History" (*Essays*, First Series, p. 16).

love," which Schiller said, or said the like. I must be myself.[1] . . .

I do with my friends as I do with books.[2] . . .

Idealism. — There are degrees in idealism. We learn first to play with it academically.[3] . . .

There is no history, only biography. The private soul ascends to transcendental virtue. Like Very, he works hard without moving hand or foot; like Agathon, he loves the goddess and not the woman; like Alcott, he refuses to pay a debt without injustice; but this liberty is not transferable to any disciple, no, nor to the man himself, when he falls out of his trance and comes down from the tripod.

I will surrender to the Divine, — to nothing less: not to Jove, not to ephod or cross.

Beauty. — I seek beauty in the arts and in song and in emotion for itself, and suddenly I

---

1 The rest of this passage is in " Self-Reliance " (p. 73).

2 The long passage thus beginning is found in " Friendship " (pp. 215, 216).

3 For the rest of the passage, see " Circles " (*Essays*, First Series, p. 309).

find it to be sword and shield. For dwelling there in its depths I find myself above the region of Fear, and unassailable, like a god at the Olympian tables.

June 21.

It may be said in defence of this practice of *Composition*, which seems to young persons so mechanical and so *un*inspired, that to men working in Time all literary effort must be more or less of this kind, — to Byron, to Goethe, to De Staël not less than to Scott and Southey. Succession, moments, parts, are their destiny, and not wholes and worlds and eternity. But you say that so moving and moved on thoughts and verses, gathered in different parts of a long life, you sail no straight line, but are perpetually distracted by new and counter currents, and go a little way north, then a little way northeast, then a little northwest, then a little north again, and so on.

Be it so; Is any motion different? The curve line is not a curve, but an infinite polygon. The voyage of the best ship is a zigzag line on a hundred tacks. This is only microscopic criticism. See the line from a sufficient distance, and it straightens itself to the average tendency. All these verses and thoughts were as spontaneous at some time to that man as any one was. Being so, they were not his own, but above him the voice of simple, necessary, aboriginal nature, and, coming from so narrow experience as one mortal, they must be strictly related, even the farthest ends of his life, and, seen at the perspective of a few ages, will appear harmonious and univocal.

June 22.

It is one of the signs of our time, the ill health of all people. All the young people are near-sighted in the towns.

That which we are shall certainly teach, not voluntarily but involuntarily.[1] . . . Men imagine that they communicate their virtue or vice only by overt actions, and do not see that virtue or vice emit an aroma every moment.

I told Elizabeth Hoar last night that rhyme resembled music in this advantage, that it has a privilege of speaking truth which all Philistia is unable to challenge.[2]

1 For the rest of the passage, see "The Over-Soul" (p. 286).

2 For the rest of this passage, see "Poetry and Imagination" (*Letters and Social Aims*, pp. 51, 52).

It seems to me often as if a little concentration, perchance within the power of circumstances, — mountains, war, danger, or love, might give me that faculty of daring rhyme. I would gladly exchange my languid life for this drum-beat. Yet I will not decline a languid life, since also that seems to be the only pattern fashionable today.

As I read Ben Jonson the other eve, it seemed to me, as before, that there is a striking resemblance between the poetry of his age and the painting of the old masters in the depth of the style. With all the frolic and freedom, the poetry is not superficial, and with all the weight of thought, it is not solemn. The beauty is necessary, and the shadows are transparent.

As I looked into the river, the other afternoon, it struck me that the Rembrandts and Salvators who paint the dark pictures probably copied the *reflection* of the landscape in water. Certainly its charm is indescribable, and as I think, not to be painted.

June 27.

Rhyme. — Rhyme ; not tinkling rhyme, but grand Pindaric strokes, as firm as the tread of a horse. Rhyme that vindicates itself as an art, the stroke of the bell of a cathedral. Rhyme which knocks at prose and dullness with the stroke of a cannon ball. Rhyme which builds out into Chaos and old night a splendid architecture to bridge the impassable, and call aloud on all the children of morning that the Creation is recommencing.[1] I wish to write such rhymes as shall not suggest a restraint, but contrariwise the wildest freedom.

" No noble virtue ever was alone."

Religion does not seem to me to tend now to a *cultus*, as heretofore, but to a heroic life. We find extreme difficulty in conceiving any church, any liturgy, any rite, that would be genuine. But all things point at the house and

[1] Mr. Emerson's juvenile verses were modelled on the poets of the eighteenth century; smooth in rhythm, trite in imagery, the virtues, vices, and motives personified. His emancipation from tradition and formalism showed in his verses of the middle period, when he felt that the thought or image must be roughly hammered out while hot, so to speak. The wild and irregular song of the Norseman, or of the Welsh bards, seemed stronger and truer to nature. He softened as little as possible his first rhapsody for a poem that came to him in the woods. The verses of the third period were long kept by him and smoothed and ripened like wine.

the hearth. Let us learn to lead a clean and manly life. Write your poem, brave man, first in the earth with a man's hoe, and eat the bread of your own spade. I have no hope of any good in this piece of reform from those who only wish to reform one thing. A partial reform, like Palmer's, or Graham's, or the praiser of the country life, is always an extravaganza. A farm is a poor place to get a living by, in the common expectation. A Boston doll who comes out into the country and takes the hoe that he may have a good table and a showy parlor may easily be disappointed. But who takes hold of this great subject of reform in a generous spirit with the intent to lead a man's life will find the farm a proper place. He must join with it simple diet, and the annihilation by one stroke of his will of the whole nonsense of living for show; and he must take Ideas instead of customs. He must make the life more than meat, and see to it that " the intellectual world meets men everywhere," in his dwelling, in his mode of living. He must take his life in his hand too. I do not think this peaceful reform is to be effected by cowards. He is to front a corrupt society and speak rude truth, and emergencies may easily be where collision and suffering must ensue.

But all the objections to the great projects of
philanthropy are met and answered by a deep
and universal reform. Thus, it is said that, if
money is given up, and a system of universal
trust and largess adopted, the indolent will
prey on the good. Consider that our doctrine
is that the labor of society ought to be shared
by all, and that in a community where labor
was the point of honor, the coxcombs would
labor ; that a mountain of chagrins, inconveniences, diseases and sins would sink into the
sea with the uprise of this one doctrine of Labor.
Domestic hired service would go over the dam.
Slavery would fall into the pit. Dyspepsia would
die out. Morning calls would end. *Redeunt
Saturnia regna.*

Athenæum Gallery.— How rich the world is !
I said on reading a letter of M. M. E.; I say
the same when I hear a new verse of a new
poet. I said the same when I walked about
the Athenæum Gallery the other day and saw
these pictures called Rembrandt, Poussin,
Rubens, etc., painted by God knows who,
— obscure nameless persons yet with such
skill and mastery as to bring connoisseurs in
doubt.

Belief. — The man I saw believed that his suspenders would hold up his pantaloons and that his straps would hold them down. His creed went little farther.

Progress of the species! why the world is a treadmill.

A friend looks to the past and the future.[1] . . .

June 30.

You dare not say "I think," "I am," but quote St. Paul, or Jesus, or Bacon, or Locke. Yonder roses make no reference to former roses or to better ones. They exist with God today.[2]

It is proposed to form a very large society to devise and execute means for propping in some secure and permanent manner this planet. It has long filled the minds of the benevolent and anxious part of the community with lively emotion, the consideration of the exposed state of the globe; the danger of its falling and being

1 The passage thus beginning is in "Friendship" (p. 214).

2 The passage is differently expressed in "Self-Reliance" (p. 67).

swamped in absolute space; the danger of its being drawn too near the sun and roasting the race of mankind, and the daily danger of its being overturned, and, if a stage-coach overset costs valuable lives, what will not ensue on the upset of this omnibus? It has been thought that by a strenuous and very extensive concert aided by a committee of masterbuilders and blacksmiths, a system of booms and chains might be set round the exterior surface and that it might be underpinned in such a manner as to enable the aged and women and children to sleep and eat with greater security henceforward. It is true that there is not a perfect unanimity on this subject at present, and it is much to be regretted. A pert and flippant orator remarked to the meeting last Sunday that the world could stand without linch-pins, and that even if you should cut all the ropes and knock away the whole underpinning, it would swing and poise perfectly, for the poise was in the globe itself. But this is Transcendentalism.

July 3.

In Boston yesterday and the day before, and saw the Allston Gallery, and the Athenæum, and met Margaret Fuller, Miss Clarke, Dwight, and young Ward on that ground; and Alcott on the broader platform. In the Allston Gallery, the Polish Jews are an offence to me; they degrade and animalize. As soon as a beard becomes anything but an accident, we have, not a man, but a Turk, a Jew, a satyr, a dandy, a goat. So we paint angels, and Jesus, and Apollo, beardless, and the Greek and the Mohawk; leave them to Muftis and Monks.

The landscapes pleased me well. I like them all: he is a fine pastoral poet and invites us to come again and again. The drawing also of the figures is always pleasing, but they lack fire, and the impression of the gallery, though bland, is faint in the memory. Nothing haunts the memory from it. It never quickens a pulse of virtue, it never causes an emulous throb. Herein perhaps it resembles the genius of Spenser; and is, as I have said, Elysian.

When I went to Europe, I fancied the great pictures were great strangers; some new unexperienced pomp and show; a foreign wonder; "barbaric pearl and gold." [1] . . .

I now require this of all pictures, that they domesticate me, not that they dazzle me. All-

1 Here follows the long passage printed in "Art" (*Essays*, First Series, pp. 360–362).

ston's St. Peter is not yet human enough for
me. It is too picturesque, and like a bronzed
cast of the Socrates or Venus.

July 4.

Once the doctrine of hatred must be preached
as the counteraction of the doctrine of love,
when that pules and whines.[1] . . . I have no
duties so peremptory as my intellectual duties.

July 5.

Edward Palmer[2] left my house yesterday morning after staying here four days. His mind has
grown since he was here last fall. He said he
did not think it necessary for him to write anything, for, he thought he could do everything
that came into his mind and so not need any
record.

Why should we write dramas, and epics, and
sonnets, and novels in two volumes? Why not

1 Here follows the long passage about "*Whim,*" and the
"wicked dollar" in "Self-Reliance" (pp. 51, 52).

2 This was the young and eager apostle of doing away with
money, as a chief cause of mischief in the world. Mr. Emerson tells of him and his reforming schemes in "Life and Letters in New England" (*Lectures and Biographical Sketches,*
p. 345).

write as variously as we dress and think? A lecture is a new literature, which leaves aside all tradition, time, place, circumstance, and addresses an assembly as mere human beings, no more. It has never yet been done well. It is an organ of sublime power, a panharmonicon for variety of note. But only then is the orator successful when he is himself agitated, and is as much a hearer as any of the assembly. In that office you may and shall (please God!) yet see the electricity part from the cloud and shine from one part of heaven to the other.

July 7.

Reform. — The objection to conforming to usages that have become dead to you is, that it scatters your force.[1] . . .

I owe much to these beneficent reformers of all colors and qualities. Each one shows me that there is somewhat I can spare. Shows me thus how rich I am. Within my trench there is a wall; if the town be taken, there is yet a citadel. If the tower be stormed, there is still the invincible me. I thank Edward Palmer for this demonstration, and for one other recorded on the last page.

1 The passage is printed in "Self-Reliance" (p. 55).

In regard to his money movement, however, discussion always shows that the principle now and always takes effect, and that it would not much alter things to take money out of society, but it would alter things much to put the love in. Great men have always played with property, and used it as though they used it not. Spirit is all, acts indifferent. The sublime is always the true.

Palmer had somewhat great in him, a certain negligence of statement and extreme carelessness whether he was understood or not. He makes it felt also how surely a sincere person is raised by a partial into an universal reform.

There is no time to roses.[1] . . . So shall man one day live with living nature, happy and strong in the deep present. There is no time to just men. The profuse roses blow.

Men are made as drunk by party as by rum. In this county they have let a proven defaulter be chosen to Congress over an affectionate, honest, able gentleman, because, as the lovely philanthropists say, the only question they ask is, "What is his relation to the slave?" Thus you cease to be a man that you may be an Abolitionist.

[1] For the rest of this passage, see "Self-Reliance" (p. 67).

There is no art where society is unbelieving, honeycombed and hollow; but when it tingles and trembles with earnest, will beauty be born.

Be hospitable to the soul as well as to the body of thy guest, thou tart hater.

Miracles. — The miracle is always spiritual, always within the man, affecting his senses from the soul, so that the lover walks in miracles, and the man beside him sees nothing. The believer sees nothing as he ever saw it before; the unbeliever looks at the same facts and reads the old dull story. The true disciple never therefore magnifies the sensible miracle; he ignores it also; he says, "I knew a man once, whether in the body or out of the body I cannot tell, God knoweth."

Mass. — Extempore speaking can be good, and written discourses can be good. A tent is a very good thing, but so is a cathedral.

Reform. — The past has baked my loaf, and in the strength of its bread I break up the old oven.

A lady, it seems, has painted the auxiliary verbs, — Do, Ought, Might, Cannot. I gave C. S. for a subject, The Age, to be represented in a series of heads; Conservatism, State Street, Christian Register; Revolt; Protest; Fair Perplexity; Dyspepsia; Warren Chapel.

What Possibilities! — In the country church, I see the cousins of Napoleon, of Wellington, of Wilberforce, of Bentham, of Humboldt. A little air and sunshine, an hour of need, a provoking society, would call out the right fire from these slumbering peasants.

I went to the woods and heard the woodthrush sing, *Ah Willie Willie; He Willio, willio!*

We want all the elements of our being. High culture cannot spare one. We want the Exact and the Vast; we want our Dreams, and our Mathematics; we want our Folly and Guilt.

Yet a majestic soul never unfolds all these in speech, they lie at the base of what is said, and colour the word, but are reserved. You may be Goethe, but not Bettina.

July 9.

Wonderful Bettina! The rich, inventive genius of the painter must all be smothered and lost for want of the power of drawing; and when I walk in Walden wood, as on 4 July, I seem to myself an inexhaustible poet, if only I could once break through the fence of silence, and vent myself in adequate rhyme.

Nature is two - headed. Invoked, or uninvoked, God will be there. *Et vocatus et non vocatus Deus aderit.* It is even capable of a sublimer extension,—that the unhappiness of hell is overpowered by a happiness. All which liveth tendeth to good. It cannot be otherwise.

I like my boy, with his endless, sweet soliloquies and iterations, and his utter inability to conceive why I should not leave all my nonsense business and writing, and come to tie up his toy horse, as if there was or could be any end to nature beyond his horse. And he is wiser than we when threatens his whole threat, " I will not love you."

Nature delights in punishing stupid people. The very strawberry vines are more than a match for them with all their appetites, and all their fumbling fingers. The little, defenceless vine coolly hides the best berry, now under this leaf, then under that, and keeps the treasure for yonder darling boy with the bright eyes when Booby is gone.

July 14.

I desire that my housekeeping should be clean and sweet and that it should not shame or annoy me. I desire that it should appear in all its arrangements that human culture is the end to which that house is built and garnished. I wish my house to be a college, open as the air to all to whom I spiritually belong, and who belong to me. But it is not open to others, or for other purposes. I do not wish that it should be a confectioner's shop wherein eaters and drinkers may get strawberries and champagne. I do not wish that it should be a playground or house of entertainment for boys. They do well to play; I like that they should, but not with me, or in these precincts.[1] . . .

July 16.

The "*abandon*" of a scatter-brain, the "*abandon*" of a woman, are no better than calculation; but the "*abandon*" of a self-commanding and reserved mind is like the fire of troops when the enemy is at the end of the bayonet.

[1] Portions of this paragraph occur in slightly different form in "Domestic Life."

July 17.

Manners Demonological. — Beauty dwells also in the will. You plant a tree for your son, or for mankind in the next age. Decline also the low suggestion, stablish the lofty purpose in the moment when it flits so evanescently by, and you plant bodily beauty for the next age. Who saw you do the mean act? Ah brother! Your manners saw you, and they shall always report it to men.

People do not distinguish between perception and notion.[1]

July 20.

Night in this enchanting season is not night, but a miscellany of lights. The journeying twilight, the half-moon, the kindling Venus, the beaming Jove, — Saturn and Mars something less bright, and, fainter still, " the common people of the sky," as Crashaw said : then, below, the meadows and thickets flashing with the fireflies, and all around the farms the steadier lamps of men compose the softest, warmest illumination.

A poet is a Namer. His success is a new nomenclature.

1 This passage may be found in " Self-Reliance " (p. 65).

August 1.

Last night came to me a beautiful poem from Henry Thoreau, "Sympathy." The purest strain, and the loftiest, I think, that has yet pealed from this unpoetic American forest. I hear his verses with as much triumph as I point to my Guido when they praise half-poets and half-painters.[1]

I have no right of nomination in the choice of my friends. Sir, I should be happy to oblige you, but my friends must elect themselves.[2]

A thought is a prison also.[3] . . .

August 14.

The way in which the doctrine of the immortality of the soul is taught and heard is false. It is Duration, but there is no warrant for teaching this. There is no promise to Aaron and Abner that Aaron and Abner shall live. It is only the soul that, in rare awakenings, saith through

1 This was the poem beginning, —
        "Lately, alas! I knew a gentle boy,"
in which disguise Thoreau expressed his disappointment in love. Guido's Aurora was Carlyle's gift.

2 See "Friendship" (p. 209).

3 The rest of the passage is in "Intellect" (*Essays*, First Series, p. 339).

all her being, I AM, and Time is below me; and the awkward Understanding translates the rapture into English prose, and saith, That voice came out of a mortal man, and he said that he should live a good many thousand years.

It will not serve any good purpose to avail ourselves of the healing formula with which our wives and the kind-hearted mediate between the truth - speaker and the churchman, and affirming that the difference is merely in terms, that we misunderstand each other, etc., etc., and inferring that our discrepancy is only on the threshold of speculation; that after we have stated our whimsy of Instinct, of the One Mind, of the potential infinitude of every man, and the like, our doctrines then become identical with all orthodoxy, and differences vanish. But it is not so. It is the peculiarity of Truth that it must *live* every moment in the beginning, in the middle, and onward forever in every stage of statement. I cannot accept without qualification the most indisputable of your axioms. I see that they are not quite true.

August 16.

Conversation is an evanescent relation, — no more.[1] . . .

1 For the rest of the passage, see " Friendship " (p. 208).

With those devouring eyes, with that portraying hand, Carlyle has seen Webster.[1]

August 19.

This old complaint of the Unitarians, that the Calvinists deny them fellowship and access to the communion table, is a plain confession that their religion is nought, that they have no vision. Whoso has, never begs allowance; he commands and awes men. Fox and Penn, Swedenborg and Very, never complain of not being admitted, but complain that none come and ask admittance.

[On August 23, Mr. Emerson set forth for the hill-country of New Hampshire with a companion, probably his friend, Mr. George P. Bradford. The following notes remain on a loose sheet of paper.]

Centre Harbor, N. H., *August* 25.

Burke is a rhetoric, a robe to be always admired for the beauty with which he drapes facts, as we love light, or rather colour, which clothes

1 Mr. Emerson rejoiced that Carlyle had seen the idol of his youth. (See the *Carlyle-Emerson Correspondence*, vol. i, pp. 247, 248 and 255, 256 ; also pp. 16 and 19.)

all things. What rich temperance, what costly textures, what flowing variety!

Manners need somewhat negligent and even slow in the perceptions, as Business requires quick perceptions. Manners must have an ignoring eye, a languid, graceful hand; a sluggard knight who does not see the annoyances, inconveniences, shifts, that cloud the brow and smother the voice of the sensitive.[1] The popular men and women are often externally sluggish, lazy natures, not using superlatives, nor staking their all on every peppercorn.

August 27.

Yesterday ascended Red Hill and saw our lake and Squam Lake, Ossipee, Conway, Gunstock, and one dim summit which stood to us for the White Hills. Mrs. Cook lives on this Red Mountain, half a mile from the top and a mile from the bottom. We asked her what brought her here fifty-one years ago. She said, "Poverty brought and poverty kept her here." For our parts, we thought that a poor man could not afford to live here, that it was to in-

1 Mr. Emerson would never notice any awkwardnesses in service or mischances at table, but kept perfect serenity unless a servant were reproved; that always troubled him.

crease poverty tenfold, to set one's cabin at this helpless height. Her son makes 1000 pounds of maple sugar in a year. They use the coffee-bean for coffee, and the fever-bush for tea. The Hedysarum, which they call wild-bean, was the principal food of the cows when they first came here until grass grew.

There is no man in mountain or valley, but only abortions of such, and a degree of absurdity seems to attach to nature. On Sunday we heard sulphurous Calvinism. The preacher railed at Lord Byron. I thought Lord Byron's vice better than Rev. Mr. M.'s virtue. He told us of a man he had seen on Lake Michigan who saw his ship in danger and said, "If the Almighty would only stand neuter for six months, it was all he asked." In his horror at this sentiment, the preacher did not perceive that it was the legitimate inference from his own distorting creed; that it was the *reductio ad absurdum* of Calvinism.

CONCORD, *September* 4.

In the journey to the White Mountains from which I returned Monday evening, 2d September, I found few striking experiences. Nature seems ashamed of man and stands away from him, even while he lives from her bounty. The men and women whom we see, live in their sensations, and repeat in memory and talk their paltriest satisfactions. The Profile Mountain was a pleasing wonder. I admire the great and grave expression of this Mountain Bust (where Nature herself has done what Lysippus (?) and Michel Angelo projected) which sternly gazes eastward to the sea. Black eagles were wheeling over the summit when I saw it. But I believe the most agreeable circumstance in the tour was the echo of the horn blown at the door of the White Mountain Hotel [Fabyan's] which turned the mountains into an Æolian harp, and instantly explained the whole Attic mythology of Diana and all divine hunters and huntresses. How lofty, how haughtily beautiful is a musical note![1]

[Mr. Emerson had been, thus far in the year, below his standard of health, and went to the mountains for strength. On his return, he wrote to his brother William that he had gained little: "I am as usual neither sick nor well, but, for aught I see, as capable of work as ever, let once my subject stand, like a good ghost, palpable

[1] This experience is mentioned in "Nature" (*Essays*, Second Series, p. 175).

before me. But, since I came home, I do not write much, and writing is always my meter of health — writing, which a sane philosopher would say, was the surest index of a diseased mind."

A depressing circumstance moreover was that he saw the necessity of preparing another course of Boston lectures, because of the strain on his finances due to the advances for the publication here of his friend Carlyle's books. (See Cabot's Memoir, vol. ii, pp. 392, 393.)]

September 5.

How tedious is the perpetual self-preservation of the traveller! His whole road is a comparison of what he sees and does at home with what he sees and does now. Not a blessed moment does he forget himself and, yielding to the new world of facts that environ him, utter without memory that which they say. Could he once abandon himself to the wonder of the landscape, he would cease to find it strange. In New Hampshire the dignity of the landscape made more obvious the meanness of the tavern-haunting men.[1]

I do not know that I can recall the thought of last Thursday which made the mountains greater.

1 Compare the poem " Monadnoc."

Margaret Fuller and Frederic Henry Hedge must have talent in their associates. And so they find that they forgive many defects. They do not require simplicity. I require genius and, if I find that, I do not need talent: and talent without genius gives me no pleasure. George Bradford's verdict on a poem or a man I should value more than theirs, for Hedge would like Moore, and George Bradford not.

I am enlarged by the access of a great sentiment, of a virtuous impulse. It is the direct income of God. I am not enlarged by a prodigy, a raising of Lazarus, a turning water into wine: open my eyes by new virtue, and I shall see miracles enough in this current moment of time. You prefer to see a dove descending visibly on Jesus; I acknowledge his baptism by the spirit of God. And which is greater and more affecting, — to see some wonderful bird descending out of the sky, or to see the rays of a heavenly majesty of the mind and heart emitted from the countenance of a man?

Good Reading is an art also. I would read the great action and great passiveness of Fabius, his perfect equanimity under the popular odium and general calamity, as the exhortation which the great God gives me for this day's bread. As Bonaparte organized victory in the French armies, I would organize the old eternal heroism in mine. Society thinks of nothing less than of appropriating the fine sentiments which are repeated in it. They are merely ornaments for show-days, as when a very wealthy and hard aristocrat declaims with fine tones, —

" Let such, such only, tread this sacred floor,
　As dare to love their country and be poor."

The true conciseness of style would be such a writing as no dictionaries, but events and character only could illustrate.

September 12.

How to spend a day nobly is the problem to be solved, beside which all the great reforms which are preached seem to me trivial. If any day has not the privilege of a great action, then, at least, raise it by a wise passion. If thou canst not do, at least abstain. Now the memory of the few past little days so works in me that I hardly dare front a new day when I leave my bed. When shall I come to the end of these shameful days and organize honour in every day?

September 14.

Yesterday Mr. Mann's Address on Education. It was full of the modern gloomy view of our democratical institutions, and hence the inference to the importance of schools. But as far as it betrayed distrust, it seemed to pray, as do all our pulpits, for the consolation of Stoicism. A Life in Plutarch would be a perfect rebuke to such a sad discourse. If Christianity is effete, let us try the doctrine of power to endure.

Education. — Sad it was to see the death-cold convention yesterday morning, as they sat shivering, a handful of pale men and women in a large church, for it seems the Law has touched the business of Education with the point of its pen, and instantly it has frozen stiff in the universal congelation of society. An education in things is not. We all are involved in the condemnation of words, an age of words. We are shut up in schools and college recitation rooms for ten or fifteen years, and come out at last with a bellyful of words and do not know a thing.[1] We

1 Although the remainder of the paragraph is printed in " New England Reformers," it is given here because of its connection with the voyage of John and Henry Thoreau on the Concord and Merrimac rivers, referred to on next page;

cannot use our hands, or our legs, or our eyes, or our arms. We do not know an edible root in the woods. We cannot tell our course by the stars, nor the hour of the day by the sun. It is well if we can swim and skate. We are afraid of a horse, of a cow, of a dog, of a cat, of a spider. Far better was the Roman rule to teach a boy nothing that he could not learn standing.

Now here are my wise young neighbors[1] who, instead of getting, like the woodmen, into a railroad-car, where they have not even the activity of holding the reins, have got into a boat which they have built with their own hands, with sails which they have contrived to serve as a tent by night, and gone up the Merrimack to live by their wits on the fish of the stream and the berries of the wood. My worthy neighbor Dr. Bartlett expressed a true parental instinct when he desired to send his boy with them to learn something. The farm, the farm, is the right school. The reason of my deep respect for the farmer is that he is a realist, and not a dictionary. The farm is a piece of the world, the school-house is not.

also because of its harmony with the educational trend advocated by many to-day.

1 John and Henry Thoreau. (See *A Week on the Concord and Merrimack Rivers.*)

The farm, by training the physical, rectifies and invigorates the metaphysical and moral nature.

Now so bad we are that the world is stripped of love and of terror. Here came the other night an Aurora so wonderful, a curtain of red and blue and silver glory, that in any other age or nation it would have moved the awe and words of men and mingled with the profoundest sentiments of religion and love, — and we all saw it with cold, arithmetical eyes, we knew how many colors shone, how many degrees it extended, how many hours it lasted, and of this heavenly flower we beheld nothing more: a primrose by the brim of the river of time.

Shall we not wish back again the Seven Whistlers, the Flying Dutchman, the lucky and unlucky days, and the terrors of the Day of Doom?

I lament that I find in me no enthusiasm, no resources for the instruction and guidance of the people, when they shall discover that their present guides are blind. This convention of Education is cold, but I should perhaps affect a hope I do not feel, if I were bidden to counsel it. I hate preaching, whether in pulpits or in teachers' meetings. Preaching is a pledge, and I wish to say what I think and feel today, with the proviso that tomorrow perhaps I shall contradict it all. Freedom boundless I wish. I will not pledge myself not to drink wine, not to drink ink, not to lie, and not to commit adultery, lest I hanker tomorrow to do these very things by reason of my having tied my hands. Besides, man is so poor he cannot afford to part with any advantages, or bereave himself of the functions even of one hair. I do not like to speak to the Peace Society, if so I am to restrain me in so extreme a privilege as the use of the sword and bullet. For the peace of the man who has forsworn the use of the bullet seems to me not quite peace, but a canting impotence: but with knife and pistol in my hands, if I, from greater bravery and honor, cast them aside; then I know the glory of peace.

It was a fine corollary of Stoicism that Aristotle said that the honour of chastity consisted in self-sufficiency.

The mob are always interesting. We hate editors, preachers and all manner of scholars, and fashionists. A blacksmith, a truckman, a farmer, we follow into the bar-room and watch with eagerness what they shall say, for such as they do not speak because they are expected to, but because they have somewhat to say.

How sad a spectacle, so frequent nowadays, to see a young man after ten years of college education come out, ready for his voyage of life, — and to see that the entire ship is made of rotten timber, of rotten, honeycombed, traditional timber without so much as an inch of new plank in the hull.

It seems as if the present age of words should naturally be followed by an age of silence, when men shall speak only through facts, and so regain their health. We die of words. We are hanged, drawn and quartered by dictionaries. We walk in the vale of shadows. It is an age of hobgoblins. . . . When shall we attain to be real, and be born into the new heaven and earth of nature and truth?

It is not good sense to repeat an old story to the same child. Yet the pulpit thinks there is some piquancy or rag of meat in his paragraph about the traitor Judas or the good Samaritan.

Things versus Men. — How many men can measure themselves with a ton of coals? Over a thing power and awe hang inseparably. In every moment and change it represents nature, but these transformed men are an impotent canting.

September 18.

The teamsters write on their teams, "No monopoly. Old Union Line, Fitchburg, Groton," etc. On the guide-boards they paint, "Free trade and teamster's rights."[1]

With the Past, as past, I have nothing to do; nor with the Future, as future. I live now, and will verify all past history in my own moments.

I heard with great pleasure lately the songs of Jane Tuckerman. The tone of her voice is not in the first hearing quite pure and agreeable. The tone of Abby Warren's voice is much more pure and noble;[2] but the wonderful talent of Miss Tuckerman, her perfect taste, the sweetness of all her tones, and the rich variety and the extreme tenuity with which she spins the thread of sound

1 This seems to have been due to the alarm of the coming railroad.

2 This was the voice in the village choir that he has praised before. The lady, as Mrs. Belden, later sang in Park Street Church.

to a point as fine as a ray of light, makes the ear listen to her with the most delicious confidence. Her songs were better with every repetition. I found my way about in the hollows and alleys of their music better each time. Yet still her music was a phenomenon to me. I admired it as a beautiful curiosity, as a piece of *virtu*. It does not marry itself to the mind and become a part of it. She composes me by the serenity of her manners.

All conversation among literary men is muddy. I derive from literary meetings no satisfaction. Yet it is pity that meetings for conversation should end as quickly as they ordinarily do. They end as soon as the blood is up, and we are about to say daring and extraordinary things. They adjourn for a fortnight, and when we are reassembled we have forgot all we had to say.[1]

1 Under date of September 18, Mr. Alcott wrote in his Journal: "Symposium met again at Bartol's, Chestnut Street. We discussed the subject of a journal designed as the organ of views more in accordance with the Soul. Present, Francis, Alcott, Hedge, Bartol, W. Channing [William Henry Channing], Dwight, Ripley, Parker, Bartlett, Russell, Robbins, Morison, Shattuck, Miss Fuller. A good deal was said about our journal, but no definite action taken upon it. Its idea and plan are not defined."

The rich man will presently come to be ashamed of his riches, when he sees he has any accidental advantage which takes away all the praise of every good thing he does. The race is won by no skill or strength of his, but by the sinews of his good horse. The serene and beneficent life he leads solves the problem of life for nobody but the rich. His wealth, then, if not the earning of his own sweat, is his backbiter and enemy in all men's ears.

It is no easy matter to write a dialogue. Cooper, Sterling, Dickens, and Hawthorne cannot.

Water is more agreeable to the imagination as an article of diet than any other, because it is a kind of material absolute.

The common household tasks are agreeable to the imagination: they are the subjects of all the Greek gems.

How trifling to insist on *ex tempore* speech, or spontaneous conversation, and decry the written poem or dissertation, or the debating club. A man's deep conviction lies too far down in nature to be much affected by these trifles. Do what

we can, your genius will speak from you, and
mine from me.

September 20.

It is only by doing without Shakspear that
we can do without his book. Be Shakspear, and
we shall value it no longer. So it is with the holy
men whose life is recorded in the religious books
of the nations.

Children like the story that makes them weep
better than the one that makes them laugh. Men
love the play, or the fight, or the news that
scares or agitates them. And the great man loves
the conversation or the book that convicts him;
not that which soothes and flatters him. For this
opens to him a new and great career, fills him
with hope. Therefore a great man always keeps
before him the transcendent, and humbles himself in its presence. Losing this he is no longer
great.

Temperance that knows itself is not temperance. That you cease to drink wine or coffee or
tea is no true temperance if you still desire them
and think of them; there is nothing angelic there.
It is thus far only prudence.

The only condition on which I can expect a better sight is, that I put off all that is foreign. I am still busy in that initial endeavor, I have not yet arrived at virtue. I burn in purgatory still.[1]

"*These Men.*" — In Massachusetts a number of young and adult persons are at this moment the subject of a revolution. They are not organized into any conspiracy: they do not vote, or print, or meet together. They do not know each other's faces or names. They are united only in a common love of truth and love of its work. They are of all conditions and natures. They are, some of them, mean in attire, and some mean in station, and some mean in body, having inherited from their parents faces and forms scrawled with the traits of every vice. Not in churches, or in courts, or in large assemblies; not in solemn holidays, where men were met in festal dress, have these pledged themselves to new life, but in lonely and obscure places, in

[1] The tone of the Journals of this and the next two or three years seems to show that the widespread awakening and manifold protests of the period had stirred Mr. Emerson out of the serenity of the immediately preceding years. The new lights must be tested as guides to action. It required time and more solitude than his many visitors left him to regain his equipoise.

servitude, in solitude, in solitary compunctions and shames and fears, in disappointments, in diseases, trudging beside the team in the dusty road, or drudging, a hireling in other men's cornfields, schoolmasters who teach a few children rudiments for a pittance, ministers of small parishes of the obscurer sects, lone women in dependent condition, matrons and young maidens, rich and poor, beautiful and hard-favoured, without conceit or proclamation of any kind, have silently given in their several adherence to a new hope.

September 24.

Friendship. — I do not wish to treat friendships daintily.[1] . . . I have the most romantic relations precisely with my oldest friends. . . . Who is rich, who is fashionable, who is highbred, has great hindrances to success [in friendships]. Very hardly will he attain to mastery with all these ribbons, laces and plumes, in a tug where all the hap depends on eternal facts, on intrinsic nobleness and the contempt of trifles. Genius and Virtue, like diamonds, are best plain set, — set in lead, set in poverty. And the highest Beauty should be plain set.

1 Here follow several sentences which are printed in "Friendship" (pp. 201, 202).

Those only can sleep who do not care to sleep, and those only can act or write well who do not respect the writing or the act.

I have read *Oliver Twist* in obedience to the opinions of so many intelligent people as have praised it. The author has an acute eye for costume; he sees the expression of dress, of form, of gait, of personal deformities; of furniture, of the outside and inside of houses; but his eye rests always on surfaces; he has no insight into character. For want of key to the moral powers the author is fain to strain all his stage trick of grimace, of bodily terror, of murder, and the most approved performances of Remorse. It all avails nothing, there is nothing memorable in the book except the *flash*, which is got at a police office, and the dancing of the madman which strikes a momentary terror. Like Cooper and Hawthorne he has no dramatic talent. The moment he attempts dialogue the improbability of life hardens to wood and stone. And the book begins and ends without a poetic ray, and so perishes in the reading.

Children are all foreigners. We treat them as such. We cannot understand their speech or the mode of life, and so our Education is remote and accidental and not closely applied to the facts.

Day and Night are vests only of Things.

[Here follows a page or more of anecdotes of Cromwell.]

I have been reading all this in no bigger book than a volume of *Lardner's Cabinet Cyclopædia*, by Forster. The man is great, though his historian is small. Cromwell is a droll, and always has a design under his dulness or his horseplay. It is odd indeed, his talk to the Parliament. He talks like a porter with his endless expletives and circumstantial statement of nothings, and affirmations that he is telling the truth. He is a new combination, and suggests, as every strong nature does, how easily those qualities may be combined in the next babe that is born, which we commonly pronounce incompatible, — the inspiration of holiness, for example, with the shrewdest selfishness. We love force and we care very little how it is exhibited. State is a great game which is fit for young natures to play at, though not for the strongest, for these selfish fellows never can, in my judgment, compete with

the Artist. He draws out of the invisible his material, his counters, and then plays his game by
a skill not taught or quickened by his appetites.
The Cromwells and Cæsars are a mob beside him.

Histories are written, like this Forster's, in ridiculous deference to all the lowest prejudices.
The simple fact of being the potentate of England seems to the good scribe a thing so incredible and venerable that he can never allude to it
without new astonishment and never records a
victory without new bows and duckings and *em-
pressements*, like a Catholic priest kneeling whenever he passes the crucifix in crossing the church.
A gentleman sees empire and victory in every
right action, and makes no ado about the circumstances.

" These applications of the wit and mind are
tender things; they do not fancy the sun and
the cloud, but delight in shade and retirement.
Like noble and delicate maidens, they must
rather be kept safe at home, than brought forth
into engagements and perils." — *Milton to
Cromwell.*

Woods. *A Prose Sonnet*

Wise are ye, O ancient woods! wiser than
man. Whoso goeth in your paths or into your

thickets where no paths are, readeth the same cheerful lesson whether he be a young child, or a hundred years old, comes he in good fortune, or bad, — ye say the same things, and from age to age. Ever the needles of the pine grow and fall, the acorns on the oak, the maples redden in autumn, and at all times of the year the ground pine and the pyrola bud and root under foot. What is called fortune and what is called Time by men — ye know them not. Men have not language to describe one moment of your eternal life. This I would ask of you, O sacred woods, when ye shall next give me somewhat to say, give me also the tune wherein to say it. Give me a tune of your own, like your winds or rains or brooks or birds; for the songs of men grow old when they have been often repeated, but yours, though a man have heard them for seventy years, are never the same, but always new, like time itself, or like love.

September 28.

Usefulness is always handsome, uselessness always vulgar. Hint a little service of the household, — a lady will instantly do it, a nurse will toss her foolish head with, " Lor! I 'll call someone."

The life of Raffaelle is the catalogue of his works. The life of a great artist always is thus inward, a life on no events. Shakespear has no biography worth speaking. Dante, by how much he had a biography, is by so much the worst artist. For Dante is a person of strong understanding and shares the vulgar pride of noblemen and fashionists, and seldom a seer.

I love the Sunday morning. I hail it from afar. I walk with gladness and a holiday feeling always on that day. The church is ever my desk. If I did not go thither I should not write so many of these wayward pages. The better place, the better deed.

Mr. Dewey said to me that W. C. promised to be a great man twenty years hence. Mr. Felt, then one of the parish committee in the First Church in New York, observed, "Yes, but we want a minister ready grown; he must have his growing elsewhere." So it is with us all. Only fathers and mothers may contentedly be present at the growing. I hate to hear a singer who is learning, let her voice be never so sweet. I wish not to be asked in every note whether I will allow it. I wish every note to command me with sweet yet perfect empire.

Also I hate Early Poems.

A lovely Saturday afternoon, and I walked toward Fairhaven with Henry Thoreau, and admired autumnal red and yellow and, as of old, Nature's wonderful boxes in which she packs, so workmanlike, her pine seed and oak seed, and not less the keys of frost and rain and wind with which she unlocks them by and by.

Mankind have ever a deep common sense (using that word in the highest style) that guides their judgments, so that they are always right in their fames. How strange that Jesus should stand at the head of history, the first character of the world without doubt, but the unlikeliest of all men, one would say, to take such a rank in such a world. Well then, as if to indemnify themselves for this vast concession to truth, they must put up the militia — Alexander, Cæsar, Napoleon, etc. — into the next place of proclamation. Yet it is a pit to Olympus, this fame by that, or even by the place of Homer, Pindar and Plato.

I can be wise very well for myself, but not

for another, nor among others. I smile and ignore wo, and if that which they call wo shall
come to me I hope and doubt not to smile still.
They smile never and think joy amiss. All
their facts are tinged with gloom, and all my
pains are edged with pleasure. But if I intermeddle, if I quit my divine island and seek to
right them in particulars, if I look upon them
as corrigible individuals and their fortunes cura-
ble, I grow giddy and skeptical presently in
their company. Old age is a sad riddle which
this stony Sphinx reads us. How base to live,
as the old, when now their period of outdoor
activity is over, in their sensations; to exist to
trifles; to have the palate and the eye and ear
and skin so ignominiously wise and knowing;
to be a taster, and an inexhaustible quiddle; to
sell the sweet and noble human soul to all the
imps of spite and gloom on the cause of an ill-
done omelet, heavy cakes, or a draught of air.
I can only solve this sad problem by esteeming
it a slide in my lamp. It is a shade which adds
splendor to the lights. But if I intermeddle, if
I esteem it an entity, — already my own hair
grizzles. Age is to be parried and annihilated
to thee, O Son of God, by wrapping thyself in
God's eternal youth. Cast thyself frankly as

these sweet children do into the beauty and joy of this moment; do not addle the egg with thought, but generously sleep in thy sentiment, in thine act, the arms of the Wise God being around thee, and thou shalt take thy being again from him presently, refreshed and exalted. But seest thou not that in nature every set sun rises, every loss has a gain, nor shall even this hated phantom with its evil insignia of baldness, of toothless gums, cracked voice, defaced face, and fumbling, peevish trifling, stand in the wide beauty of the universe hopeless. There is recovery from this lapse, and awaking from this haggard dream.

But what is old age? what is the Fall? what Sin? what Death? lying as we do in this eternal Soul originating benefit forevermore. The dullest scholar learns the secret of Space and Time; learns that Time is infinite; that the instruments of God are all commensurate. Is not that lesson enough for a life? The Power that deals with us, the Power which we study and which we are to inherit as fast as we learn to use it, is, in sum, dazzling, terrific, inaccessible. It now benignly shows us in parts and atoms some arc of its magnificent circle, elements which are radically ours.

September 29.

A fair child went by who made me think, as others have done, that a mixture of Lethe adds to beauty.

The military eye which I meet so often darkly sparkling, now under clerical, now under rustic brows, — e. g., Robert Bartlett, W. Channing, and our William Shepherd here, — the city of Lacedæmon; and the poem of Dante, which seems to me a city of Lacedæmon turned into verses.

A fine melody again at the Church. I always thank the gracious Urania when our chorister selects tunes with solos for my singer. My ear waits for those sweet modulations, so pure of all manner and personality, so universal, that they open on the ear like the rising of the world.

A walk in the woods is only an exalted dream.

Some faces turn on the pivot of the collar-bone, with eyes that are shallow beads — no more : and some on a pivot at least as deep as the orbit of the sphere, so slow and lazily and great they move.

A man is a Diamond Edition of the world. What comedy, or what tragedy, like a John Barrett or John Brown or Mr. Smith or Mr. Clark, as we facetiously denominate these incarnations, with all he is and has, denoted in his countenance. The foolish science of Phrenology is yet founded on this very admiration, and sheds lights. Then my babies are the true academy of Sculpture.

In every house there is a good deal of false hospitality. Relatives come thither of all the degrees of cousindom and family acquaintances, who, like cats, frequent the place and not the man. The hero meets with content all this claim on time and labor and takes care that his "hospitality run fine to the last," as Lamb finely said. But not so the saint. He is so much the servant of absolute goodness, that he feels the falsehood of merely feeding and amusing these butterflies and beetles, and austerely tells them so.

When I was thirteen years old, my Uncle Samuel Ripley one day asked me, "How is it, Ralph, that all the boys dislike you and quarrel with you, whilst the grown people are fond of you?" Now am I thirty-six and the fact is reversed, — the old people suspect and dislike me,[1] and the young love me.

Never exhort, only confess. All exhortation, O thou hoarse preacher! respects others and not thyself, respects appearance and not facts, and therefore is cant.

Shall I not once paint in these pages an experience so conspicuous to me, and so oft repeated in these late years, as the Debating Club, now under the name of Teachers' Meeting, now a conference, now an æsthetic club, and now a religious association, but always bearing for me the same fruit; a place where my memory works more than my wit, and so I come away with compunction?

In correcting old discourses to retain only what is alive, I discover a good deal of matter which a strong common-sense would exclude. I seem however to discover in the same passages which I condemn the commendation of the ideal and holy life, and hence am annoyed by a discrepancy betwixt the two states. I love facts, and so erase this preaching. But also I venerate the Good, the Better, and did therefore give

[1] The natural shyness at bold thought and experiment.

it place. Cannot Montaigne and Shakspear consist with Plato and Jesus?

The whole world is in conspiracy against itself in religious matters. The best experience is beggarly when compared with the immense possibilities of man. Divine as the life of Jesus is, what an outrage to represent it as tantamount to the universe! To seize one accidental good man that happened to exist somewhere, at some time, and say to the new-born soul, Behold thy pattern; aim no longer to possess entire nature, to fill the horizon, to fill the infinite amplitude of being with great life, to be in sympathy and relation with all creatures, to lose all privateness by sharing all natural action, shining with the Day, undulating with the sea, growing with the tree, instinctive with the animals, entranced in beatific vision with the human reason. Renounce a life so broad and deep as a pretty dream, and go in the harness of that past individual, assume his manners, speak his speech, — this is the madness of Christendom. The little bigots of each town and neighborhood seek thus to subdue the manly and free-born. But, for this poor, dependent fraction of a life, they bereave me of that magnificent destiny which the young soul has embraced with auguries of immeasureable hope. I turn my back on these insane usurpers. The soul always believes in itself. It affirms the Eternity and Omnipresence of God which these deny. It knows that all which hath ever been is now, that the total world is my inheritance, and the life of all beings I am to take up into mine. By lowly listening, omniscience is for me. By faithful receiving, omnipotence is for me. But the way of the soul into its heaven is not to man, but from man. It leaves every form of life and doctrine that ever existed. It touches no book, or rite, or crutch, or guide, or mediator; it gives itself alone, original, pure, to the Lonely Original and Pure, who, on that condition, inhabits, leads and speaks through it. Then is it glad, young and nimble. It is not wise, but it sees through all things. It is not called religious, but it is innocent. It calls the Light its own and shares the pleasures of all creatures.[1]

And yet I know the dangers of this sort of speculation. It is somewhat not wholesome to be said in a detached form. It is not good to say with too much precision and emphasis that we are encroached upon by the claims of Jesus in

[1] A part of this passage is found in "The Over-Soul" (p. 296).

the current theology. It brings us into a cold, denying, irreligious state of mind. It is of no use to say, Quit Jesus and the saints and heroes. But without the saying, which is proud, and so, suicidal, let us turn our eyes to the Vast, the Good, the Eternal. There fasten the eyes, there build the perpetual hearth and house and altar of the soul. And dare to try thy pinions by flights into the Transcendent and the unknown. Thou awful Cause! hardly with sincerity can I ask that my eye may learn to keep upward, so prone is it ever to things around and below.

I was about to say and omitted it in the middle of the last page,—that we have nothing to do with Jesus in our progress, nothing to do with any past soul. The only way in which the life of Jesus or other holy person helps us is this,—that as we advance without reference to persons on a new, unknown, sublime path, we at each new ascent verify the experiences of Jesus and such souls as have obeyed God before. We take up into our proper life at that moment his act and word, and do not copy Jesus, but really are Jesus, just as Jesus in that moment of his life was us. Say rather, it was neither him nor us, but a man at this and at that time saw the truth, and was transformed into its likeness.

I must not bait my hook to draw men to me.
I must angle with myself and use no lower means.
Be Dion to Dion.

As much may be gleaned as gathered in straw-
berry-beds, grape-vines and books.

October 2.

It is strange how long our noviciate lasts;
that the period of our mastership still loiters,
that as long as we remain growing, and do not
inveterate, we are always subject to circumstances and do not control them. All the chemical agents act with energy on us, and we come,
greenhorns, to every conversation. The young,
the knowing, the fashionable, the practical, the
political, the belle, the Pharisee and the Sad-
ducee, all overact on us, and make us dumb.

Sad the complaints of the young people, —
sad their despondency and skepticism which
seem to spread every day. The young girl asks,
What shall I do? How shall I live? And there
is none to answer. It is vain to point them to
the uncultivated and pious. Could they bear the
ordeal of cultivation and leisure? If not, as
E. H. says, "I do not wish to be whipped by

toil all day, and whipped to bed at night." They must learn this fact,—that their sorrows are the ebbs of a happiness so delicate and spiritual, and if they are proportionate to the preceding flux, so are they also the preparation of a new tide.

Organization. — A chaste woman is indeed a poetic institution, but when you organize that idea by a stone convent with grated windows, shorn hair, dreadful vows, and terrific penalties, it is not chastity, but unchastity. The heart of a soldier is an impregnable castle, but if it be not, you add no strength with moats and mortars, ramparts, and cannon.

Aristocracy and Idealism. — 1. Society in our bright hours seems not to claim equality, but ought to be treated like children to whom we administer camomile and magnesia on our own judgment, without consultation. What we can do is law enough for them. And we glance for sanction at the historical position of scholars in all ages, whom we commend in proportion to their self-reliance. But when our own light beams less steadily and flickers in the socket, the pupil seems suddenly riper and more froward, and even assumes the mien of a patron whom we must court.

2. Do you say that all the good retreat from men and do not work strongly and lovingly with them? Very well; it is fit and necessary that they should treat men as ghosts and phantoms here for our behoof, here to teach us dramatically, as long as they have not yet attained to a real existence, existence in their own right, that is to say, until the uprise of the soul in them. Then instantly we shall, without tedious degrees, treat them as ourselves. Now they are not ourselves: why should we say they are?

The best effect of fine persons is felt after we have left their presence, as the greatest chemical energy of the prismatic spectrum is a little out of the spectrum.

How we hate this solemn Ego that accompanies the learned, like a double, wherever he goes! Let us be ravished by the fact and the thought, as these beautiful children are by the acorn, the hobby-horse and the doll,—rush into the object, nor think of our existence; though by the laws of nature, forever and ever, only the *subject* is consulted, let the *objects* be as many and as grand as they will.

I discern degrees in the proficiency of the malcontents of the day. I see some who, though not arrived at the chamber called Peace, have yet such redundant health that no poverty or unfriendly circumstance could much affect them; and others who are still seeking in the saloons of the city what not even solitude can give them.

The Transcendent is Economy also.

The woes of the time, — is not that topic enough? He that can enumerate their symptoms, expose their cause and show how they contain their remedies, comes to men from heaven with a palm branch in his hand.

October 7.

Only this strip of paper remains to me to record my introduction to Anna Barker last Friday at Jamaica Plains.[1] A new person is to

1 This lady became soon after the wife of Mr. Emerson's valued friend Samuel Gray Ward of Boston. She was bred a Quaker, but was born to adorn society. Though an invalid during the greater part of her long life, she was a person of great charm and beauty of character, and a strong influence in

me ever a great event, and few days of my quiet
life are so illustrated and cheered as were these
two in which I enjoyed the frank and generous
confidence of a being so lovely, so fortunate,
and so remote from my own experiences. She
seemed to me a woman singularly healthful and
entire. She had no detached parts or powers.
She had not talents, or affections, or accomplishments, or single features, of conspicuous beauty,
but was a unit and whole, so that whatsoever
she did became her, whether she walked or sat
or spoke. She had an instinctive elegance. She
had too much warmth and sympathy and desire
to please than that you could say her manners
were marked with dignity, yet no princess could
surpass her clear and erect demeanour on each
occasion. She is not an intellectual beauty, but
is of that class who in society are designated as
having a great deal of Soul, that is, the predomi-
nating character of her nature is not thought, but
emotion or sympathy, and of course she is not
of my class, does not resemble the women whom
I have most admired and loved, but she is so
perfect in her own nature as to meet these by the

the lives of many persons, the young especially. In middle life
she joined the Church of Rome, and was the means of bringing many into that Communion.

fulness of her heart, and does not distance me, as I believe all others of that cast of character do. She does not sit at home in her mind, as my angels are wont to do, but instantly goes abroad into the minds of others, takes possession of society and warms it with noble sentiments. Her simple faith seemed to be, that by dealing nobly with all, all would show themselves noble, and so her conversation is the frankest I ever heard. She can afford to be sincere. The wind is not purer than she is.

(From a loose sheet)

Eloquence. Lyceum. — Here is all the true orator will ask, for here is a convertible audience, and here are no stiff conventions that prescribe a method, a style, a limited quotation of books and an exact respect to certain books, persons or opinions. No, here everything is admissible, philosophy, ethics, divinity, criticism, poetry, humor, fun, mimicry, anecdotes, jokes ventriloquism, all the breadth and versatility of the most liberal conversation; highest, lowest, personal, local topics, all are permitted, and all may be combined in one speech; — it is a panharmonicon, — every note on the longest gamut, from the explosion of cannon, to the tinkle of a guitar.

Let us try if Folly, Custom, Convention and Phlegm cannot hear our sharp artillery. Here is a pulpit that makes other pulpits tame and ineffectual — with their cold, mechanical preparation for a delivery the most decorous, — fine things, pretty things, wise things, but no arrows, no axes, no nectar, no growling, no transpiercing, no loving, no enchantment.

Here he may lay himself out utterly, large, enormous, prodigal, on the subject of the hour. Here he may dare to hope for ecstasy and eloquence.

(From Journal E)

Concord, *October* 11.

At Waltham, last Sunday, on the hill near the old meeting-house, I heard music so soft that I fancied it was a pianoforte in some neighbouring farmhouse, but on listening more attentively I found it was the church bells in Boston, nine miles distant, which were playing for me this soft tune.

Horace Walpole, whose letters I read so attentively in the past summer, is a type of the dominant Englishman at this day. He has taste, common sense, love of facts, impatience of humbug, love of history, love of splendor, love of justice, and the sentiment of honour among gentlemen, but no life whatever of the higher faculties, no faith, no hope, no aspiration, no question even touching the secret of nature.

" Matter, which is itself privation, often scatters and dissolves what a more excellent Being than herself had wrought," says Plutarch (vol. iv, p. 12, " On Oracles ").

Those books which are for all time are written indifferently at any time. How can the age be a bad one which conveys to me the joys of literature? I can read Plutarch, and Augustine, and Beaumont and Fletcher, and Landor's *Pericles*, and with no very dissimilar feeling the verses of my young contemporaries Thoreau and Channing. Let those, then, make much of the different genius of different periods who suffer by them. I who seek enjoyments which proceed not out of time, but out of thought, will celebrate on this lofty Sabbath morn the day without night, the beautiful Ocean which hath no tides.

And yet literature, too, this magical man-provoking talisman, is in some sort a creature of time. It is begotten by Time on the Soul. And one day we shall forget this primer. But how

obviously initial it is to the writer. It is only his
priming. The books of the nations, the universal
books, are long ago forgotten of him who spake
them. We must learn to judge books by abso-
lute-standards. Criticism, too, must be transcendental. Society wishes to assign subjects and
method to its writers. But neither it nor you may
intermeddle. You cannot reason at will in this
and that other vein, but only as you must. You
cannot make quaint combinations, and bring to
the crucible and alembic of truth things far-
fetched or fantastic or popular, but your method
and your subject are foreordained in your nature,
and in all nature, or ever the earth was — or it
has no worth. All that gives currency still to any
book published to-day by Little and Brown is
the remains of faith in the breast of men that
not adroit book-makers, but the inextinguishable
soul of the Universe, reports of itself in articulate
discourse through this and that other man, today, as of old. The ancients strongly expressed
their sense of the unmanageableness of these
words of the God, by saying that the God made
his priest insane, took him hither and thither as
leaves are whirled by the tempest. But we sing
as we are bid. Our inspirations are very man-
ageable and tame. Death and Sin have whispered

in the ear of our wild horses and they are become drays and hacks.

It is very easy to hint keen replies to these statements of the independency of writers. It is easy to make persons ridiculous. Let us all, or any who say so, be ridiculous. Grant that we have been vain, boastful, cunning, covering our wretched pride with this claim of inspiration. Still the fact holds for ever and ever, that the soul doth so speak, and that the law of literature, giving its exact worth to every ballad and spoken sentence, is thus transcendent and only self-contained.

It certainly is never vitiated by any affectation, cant, dulness, or crime of those who speak for it. Their lie or folly recoils on them. Point out what abuses you will that might flow from the reception of this doctrine in weak and wicked heads, — the wind will still blow where it listeth, and the Eternal Soul will overpower the men who are its organs, and enchant the ears of those who hear them by the same right and energy by which long ago and now it enchants the mountains, and the sea, the air and the globes in their musical dance. "Thou shalt not plant a palm tree," said Pythagoras, intimating that, as that tree comes up best out of the ground self-sown, so Virtue and Wisdom are the direct proceeding of God, and are not to be overlaid and distorted by indiscreet meddling and art.

Men have yet to learn the beauty and depth of the doctrine of Trusts. O believe as thou livest that every sound that is spoken over the round world which thou oughtest to hear will vibrate on thine ear.[1] . . .

In all particulars the doctrine of the Soul must be taught. Men must be accustomed to ask if the thing they say of God holds. For the Father is with them.

A question which well deserves examination now is the Dangers of Commerce. This invasion of Nature by Trade with its Money, its Credit, its Steam, its Railroad, threatens to upset the balance of man, and establish a new, universal Monarchy more tyrannical than Babylon or Rome. Very faint and few are the poets or men of God. Those who remain are so antagonistic to this tyranny that they appear mad or morbid, and are treated as such. Sensible of this

[1] Here follows the passage thus beginning in "The Over-Soul" (*Essays*, First Series, pp. 293, 294). It was originally a part of a sermon preached by Mr. Emerson at East Lexington.

extreme unfitness they suspect themselves. And all of us apologize when we ought not, and congratulate ourselves when we ought not.[1]

Plutarch fits me better than Southey or Scott, therefore I say, there is no age to good writing. Could I write as I would, I suppose the piece would be no nearer to Boston in 1839 than to Athens in the fiftieth Olympiad. Good thought, however expressed, saith to us, "Come out of time, come to me in the Eternal."

We wish the man should show himself for what he is, though he be Iscariot. If the humour is in the blood, bring it out to the skin by all means.

October 16.

Friendship. — What needs greater magnanimity than the waiting for a friend, a lover, for years? We see the noble afar off.[2] . . . How sadly true all over human life is the saying, "To him that hath shall be given; from him that hath not shall be taken." Attentions are showered on the powerful, who needs them not.

1 This passage is followed by the greater part of the opening paragraph of Art (*Essays*, Second Series).

2 What follows is printed in "Friendship" (*Essays*, First Series, p. 212).

Friends abound for the self-trusting, and he retreats to his cliff.

Weather. — "If it be true that souls are naturally endued with the faculty of prediction, and that the chief cause that excites this faculty and virtue is a certain temperature of air and winds," etc. — PLUTARCH, *De Oraculis.*

"Hermes played at dice with the moon and won of her the seventieth part of each of her revolutions with which he made five new days and added to the year that Osiris might be born." — PLUTARCH, *Isis and Osiris.*[1]

Said Lidian, "How we covet insensibility! my boy whines and wails if I wake him." We are Buddhists all.

Nature mixes facts and thought to evoke a poem from the poet, but our philosophy would be androgynous, and itself generate poems without aid of experience.

October 18.

Lectures. — In these golden days it behooves me once more to make my annual inventory of

1 This myth is alluded to in "Experience" (*Essays*, Second Series, p. 46).

the world. For the five last years I have read each winter a new course of lectures in Boston, and each was my creed and confession of faith. Each told all I thought of the past, the present and the future. Once more I must renew my work, and I think only once in the same form, though I see that he who thinks he does something for the last time ought not to do it at all. Yet my objection is not to the thing, but with the form: and the concatenation of errors called *society* to which I still consent, until my plumes be grown, makes even a duty of this concession also. So I submit to sell tickets again.

But the form is neither here nor there. What shall be the substance of my shrift? Adam in the garden, I am to new name all the beasts in the field and all the gods in the sky. I am to invite men drenched in Time to recover themselves and come out of time, and taste their native immortal air. I am to fire with what skill I can the artillery of sympathy and emotion. I am to indicate constantly, though all unworthy, the Ideal and Holy Life, the life within life, the Forgotten Good, the Unknown Cause in which we sprawl and sin. I am to try the magic of sincerity, that luxury permitted only to kings and poets. I am to celebrate the spiritual powers in their infinite contrast to the mechanical powers and the mechanical philosophy of this time. I am to console the brave sufferers under evils whose end they cannot see by appeals to the great optimism, self-affirmed in all bosoms.

Jones Very only repeated, in a form not agreeable, the thought which agitated me in earlier years, when he said, "The same spirit which brings me to your door prepares my welcome." Shall I not say this in its extent of sense to the men and institutions of today? Think, and you annihilate the times. Drink of the cup which God proffers to your lips and these storming, anxious, contradicting, threatening crowds which surround you, mad with debt and credit, with banks and politics, with books and churches and meats and drinks, shall all flee away like ghosts from the new-born soul. They are much to you while the same blood flows in your veins and theirs. But let the man put off the merchant in you, and all this shall be pictures merely.

October 19.

Another day; the old game; up again, this wonderful but unhandsome machine, with thy hopes and shames; poor boasting augur, who sufferest as many misgivings on the edge of success as on the brink of failure, and tremblest with as many hopes on the eve of misfortune as on thy best day. And hark, New Day! they batter the grey cheek of thy morning with booming of cannon, and now with lively clatter of bells and whooping of all the village boys. An unwonted holiday in our quiet meadows and sandy valleys, and Cornwallis must surrender today.[1] Without sympathy with the merry crowd, the pale student must yet listen and perchance even go abroad to beg a look at the sun.

Who can blame men for seeking excitement? They are polar, and would you have them sleep in a dull eternity of equilibrium? Religion, love, ambition, money, war, brandy, — some fierce antagonism must break the round of perfect circula-

1 A popular and attractive feature in the annual Musters of the State Militia as late as 1856 was a representation of the surrender of Lord Cornwallis at Yorktown. Some jovial country colonel in blue and buff took the part of Washington, and another powdered red-coated officer, as the British general, gave up his sword to him. Old costumes and weapons from garrets lent an antiquarian interest to the historic farce.

" Recollect what fun we had, you 'n' I and Ezry Hollis,
Up there to Waltham Plain, last fall, along o' the Cornwallis ? "
                                LOWELL, *Biglow Papers*, First Series.

tion or no spark, no joy, no event can be. As good not be. In the country, the lover of nature dreaming through the wood would never awake to thought if the scream of an eagle, the cries of a crow or a curlew near his head, did not break the continuity. Nay, if the truth must out, the finest lyrics of the poet come of this coarse parentage; the imps of matter beget such child on the Soul, fair daughter of God.

And so I went to the Sham-Fight and saw the whole show with pleasure. The officer instantly appears through all this masquerade and buffoonery. I thought when I first went to the field that it was the high tide of nonsense, and indeed the rag-tag and bobtail of the county were there in all the wigs, old hats, and aged finery of the last generations. Then the faces were like the dresses, so exaggerated, — noses, chins and mouths, — that one could not reconcile them with any other dress than that frippery they wore. Yet presently Nature broke out in her old beauty and strength through all this scurf. The man of skill makes his jacket invisible. Two or three natural soldiers among these merry captains played out their habitual energy so well that order and reason appeared as much at home in a farce as in a legislature. Meantime the buffoons of a sham fight are soon felt to be as impertinent there as elsewhere. This organization suffices to bring pioneers, soldiers, outlaws and homicides distinct to view, and I saw Washington, Napoleon and Marat come strongly out of the mottled crew.

October 21.

How can I not record, though now with sleepy eye and flagging spirits, so fair a fact as the visit of Alcott and Margaret Fuller, who came hither yesterday and departed this morning? Very friendly influences these, each and both. Cold as I am, they are almost dear. I shall not, however, fill my page with the gifts or merits of either. They brought nothing but good spirits and good tidings with them of new literary plans here, and good fellowship and recognition abroad. And then to my private ear a chronicle of sweet romance, of love and nobleness which have inspired the beautiful and brave. What is good to make me happy is not however good to make me write. Life too near paralyses art. Long these things refuse to be recorded except in the invisible colors of memory.

Trust thy time also. What a fatal prodigality to contemn *our* age. One would say we could well afford to slight all other ages if only we value this one. Not for nothing it dawns out of Everlasting Peace, this pretty Discord, this great Discontent, this self-accusing Reflection. What apology, what praise, can equal the fact that here it is; therefore certainly in the vast Optimism here it ought to be? The great will seize with eagerness this novel crisis when the old and the new stand face to face, and reflection is for a time possible, and faith in the eternal stands in close neighborhood to exhausting analysis of the economical.

The very time sees for us, thinks for us; it is a microscope such as philosophy never had. Insight is for us which was never for any. And doubt not the moment and the opportunity are divine. He who shall represent the genius of this day, he who shall, standing in this great cleft of Past and Future, understand the dignity and power of his position so well as to write the laws of Criticism, of Ethics, of History, will be found, an age hence, neither false nor unfortunate, but will rank immediately and equally with all the masters whom we now acknowledge.

I heard with joy that which thou toldest me, O eloquent lady, of thy friends and mine, yet with my joy mingled a shade of discontent. Things must not be too fine. Parian marble will not stand exposure to our New England weather, and, though I cannot doubt the sterling sincerity of the mood and moment you describe, and though I am cheered to the bottom of my heart by these dear magnanimities which made their way to the light in the neighbourhood of all that is common, yet I dare not believe that a mood so delicate can be relied on like a principle for the wear and tear of years. It will be succeeded by another and another, and the new will sport with the old. Yet as it is genuine today, it will never be nothing.

A part of the protest we are called to make is to the popular mode of virtuous endeavor. "Will you not come to this convention and nominate a Temperance ticket? Let me show you the immense importance of the step." Nay, my friend, I do not work with those tools. The principles on which your church and state are built are false, and a portion of this virus vitiates the smallest detail even of your charity and religion. Though I own I sympathize with your desire and abhor your adversaries, yet I shall persist in wearing this robe, all loose and unbecoming as it is, of inaction, this wise passiveness until my hour comes when I can see how to act with truth as well as to refuse.

It pleases the great soul, that the present perception should arise in the universal heart of man of the Soul's all-sufficiency and so that literature, art, persons, space, time should be undervalued. Do not doubt that this mood is one sign in Heaven's eternal zodiack, or mistake the spirit of piety in which this old noblesse is assailed. It is not, as old men fancy, in a bragging spirit, that philosophy now tends to disparage books, and affirm that the reader of Shakspear is also a Shakspear, or he could find no joy in the page. Nor does the young student persuade himself that he could bodily restore the Parthenon, whilst he affirms the ultimate identity of the artist and the spectator; but only in the spirit of a child who says, I am but a child, but I am the heir of all. Certainly we concede that nothing has yet been greatly done, but we will not therefore distrust this great faith. Its boundlessness is already a grandeur. The greatness of this age is in its Prayer. You say you see no Miltons or Dantes, and only are disgusted by the flippant pretenders who decry

them. But take the same view of your poets
[that] we do whom this vision of God makes
happy, use your literature more impersonally,
strip it of this accurate individuality. Take all
that you call Dante, the whole mass of images,
thoughts and emotions, and believe, what is
certainly true, that it is not poorly confined to
certain Florentine flesh and blood, but that it is
an eternal flower of the world, a state of thought
indigenous in all souls, because in the One Soul
a sign of your zodiack, and so shall you in your
progress learn at last that the deified Alighieri
was only a type of the great class of divine
shapes to which he led you, the book a brute
harp-string which, vibrating on your ear, causes
you to see God and his angels, and that you
have a right, not derived, but original, to all the
pomp of real nature to which the name of Dante
was frontispiece. Observe, then, that this humour which offended you as brag is not so,
but is only a different manner of considering
literature, and leaves in the pupil as much
veneration for Shakspear and Homer as before; only they are made still alive, their power
still accessible and not a sepulchre to him.

Books. — In the statements we make so freely

that books are for idle hours [1] and when we flout
all particular books as initial merely, we truly
express the privilege of spiritual nature, but alas
not the fact and fortune of this low Concord and
Boston, of these humble Octobers and Novem-
bers of mortal life. [2] . . .

The Christianity represents no absolute fact
in history, but only the present and recent state
of thought. The traditional or conventional language on the subject is very ignorant. We choose
to speak as if only in one book, or one life, was
the pure light; but the wise know better; the experience of each intelligent reader belies the tale.
Whenever we are wise, every book we read
streams with an universal light. Whenever we are
wise, the whole world is wise and emblematic. The
great books do in that hour give us in every
page the most authentic tokens that they also
recognize the holiest law, the Unutterable. They
do not preach; they recognize it in strains of pure
melody. The Greek mythology — what a won-

1 See "The American Scholar" (*Nature, Addresses and
Lectures*, p. 91).

2 The rest of this long passage is the opening paragraph of
"Thoughts on Modern Literature," printed in the *Dial*, and
included in *Natural History of Intellect*, pp. 309, 310.

derful example is that of profound sense over-mastering the finite speakers and writers of the fables! Always and never the world is wise.

October 23.

Fact is better than fiction if only we could get pure fact. Do you think any rhetoric or any romance would get your ear from one who could tell, straight on, the history of man, who could reconcile your moral character and your natural history, who could explain your misfortunes, your fevers, your debts, your temperament, your habits of thought, your tastes, and in every explanation not sever you from the Whole, but unite you to it? Is it not plain that, not in senates, or courts, or chambers of commerce, but in the conversation of a true philosopher, the eloquence must be found that can agitate, convict, inspire and possess us and guide us to a true peace?[1] I look upon the Lecture-room as the true church of today and as the home of a richer eloquence than Faneuil Hall or the Capitol ever knew.

1 All of this entry, thus far, is printed in "Domestic Life." (See *Society and Solitude*, pp. 107, 108.) It is reproduced here because of the curious change in the text in the printed volume, seeming to show the mellowing of the author's character. There "the dwelling house" takes the place of "the conversation of a true philosopher."

Michel Angelo is as well entitled to the sur-
name Colossal as Charles to his *Magne*, or Alfred
to his *Great*.

The genius of Michel aims at Strength in all
figures, not in gods and prophets alone, but in
women and in children; a divine Strength, ti-
tanic, aboriginal before the world was; a strength
anterior to all disease. The colossal in him is not
in the outline or particular drawing, but is intrinsic; and so appears in all; to this, Beauty
is made incidental.

Michel esteemed the human form the best
ornament, and so uses no other in each cornice
or compartment, only a new and wondrous attitude of sleep or energy.

See a knot of country people working out
their road-tax or laying a new bridge. How close
are they to their work. How they sympathize
with every log, and foreknow its every nod and
stir with chain and crowbar, and seem to see
through the ground all the accidents of preser-
vation and decay.

Truth of Character. Temperance. — Truth will
cure all our ails. I hate the giving of the hand
unless the whole man accompanies it. I hate
giving seven pounds of rice or sugar to a poor

person whose whole character is disagreeable to me.[1] . . .

But now men are multiplex. The good offices they do are not their genuine aim, the mere flower and perfume of their nature, but are a compliance and a compliment, and contradicted by other actions on the same day. Their temperance is a plume, a feather in the cap, this ostentatious glass of cold water and dry, raw, vegetable diet that makes your blood run cold to see, is not the joyful sign that they have ceased to care for food in nobler cares, but no, they peak and pine and know all they renounce. Temperance when it is only the sign of intrinsic virtue is graceful as the bloom on the cheek that betokens health, but temperance that is nothing else but temperance is phlegm or conceit. Is it not better they should do bad offices and be intemperate so long as that is their ruling love? So at least they should not be hypocrites. Also I lament that people without character, seeing the homage that is paid to character, demand the homage, and feel seriously injured and bewail themselves if it is withholden; and then the silly friends affect to yield that homage,

1 The rest is in "Domestic Life" (*Society and Solitude*, p. 109).

and so lie and steal and transform themselves into the similitude of apes and serpents.

October 26.

There is that in us which mutters and that which groans and that which chants and that which aspires.

The piano educates, and the evening game, as well as the sciences and afflictions. Abolition is poetic, has produced good verses, Whittier's, for example; phrenology never one, but prose only. There are facts which turn curled heads round at church and send wonderful eyebeams across assemblies, from one to one, never missing in the thickest crowd, which it behooves the philosopher also to remember. One must not in scrutiny of causes forget, any more, that a large part of the content of men in institutions which poets esteem odious arises from the rude health of men, a health which makes a hard board pew as soft a seat as an ottoman in a palace, and the drowsiest sermon as agreeable a circumstance as music and dancing to another man.

Rest and Love. — There are two elements of which our nature is mixed, most unequally in different individuals. The first is Rest, predominant in manifold facts, from the vision of reason, the contemplation of the infinite, to the simple satisfaction in permanence, the love of what is old, Old Age itself, Sleep and Death. The second is Love.

The Past. — The Centuries are conspirators against the sanity and majesty of the soul. The greatness of Greece consists in this, that no Greece preceded it.

October 27.

Garrison. — Don't seek to vamp and abut principles. They were before you were born, and will be when you are rotten. You might as well paint the sky blue with a bluebag.

The old thought which I loved in my youth when the roar of politics fell harshest on my ear, that presently government would cease to be sought by gentlemen and would be despatched by a few clerks, is now embodied, and, as far as I heard last night, very ably and truly preached by the Non-Resistants with Garrison at their head, a man of great ability in conversation, of a certain longsightedness in debate which is a great excellence, a tenacity of his proposition which no accidents or ramblings in the conversation can divert, a calmness and method in unfolding the details of his argument, and an eloquence of illustration, which contents the ear and the mind, — thus armed with all the weapons of a great apostle — no, not yet, until I have remembered his religion, which is manifest, his religious trust in his principles, and his clearness from any taint of private end. And yet the man teases me by his continual wearisome trick of quoting texts of Scripture and his Judaical Christianity, and then by the continual eye to numbers, to societies. Himself is not enough for him.

But to the principle of non-resistance again, Trust it. Give up the government without too solicitously inquiring whether roads can be still built, letters carried, and title-deeds secured when the government of force is at an end.[1] . . .

Again it seems clear that we should never cumber ourselves with maintaining either popular religion or popular Sabbaths or popular Laws, if we do not want them ourselves. Are they now maintained by [us] because the world needs them? Let the world maintain them. And you shall find, if the deacons and the

[1] The continuation of this passage is found in "Politics" (*Essays*, Second Series, p. 220).

priests all fail, the bank presidents and the chambers of commerce, yea, the very inn-holders and democrats of the county would muster with fury to their support.

Prophecy is not more sacred than the knowledge of the present. It is only the fixing the eye on the hill-top before you, instead of the fields around. Believe thy faintest presentiment, and thou art a prophet. And how all my experience admonishes me not to throw up an abstraction because I cannot solve to flesh and blood the objections they make to it. I am always sure to see those objections highly solved, self-solved, by cleaving to the law. A law has eagle-wings, and its own path to heaven and to earth.

In our modern reforms there's a little too much commentary on the movement by the mover.

It is not to be contested that a selfish commerce and government have got possession of the masses. Whilst we plead for the Ideal we do not pretend that we have the majority.[1]

I wrote to S. G. Ward, "There are fewer

1 The passage thus beginning occurs in "Thoughts on Modern Literature," first printed in the *Dial* (*National History of Intellect*, p. 317).

painters than poets." [1] Ten men can awaken
me by words to new hope and fruitful musing
for one that can achieve the miracle by forms.
Besides, I think the pleasure of the poem lasts
longer. And yet the expressive arts ought to go
abreast and as much genius find its way to light
in design as in song, and probably does, so far
as the artist is concerned, but the eye is a
speedier student than the ear. By a grand or a
lovely form it is astonished or delighted once
for all, and quickly appeased, whilst the sense of
a verse steals slowly on the mind and suggests a
hundred fine fancies before its precise import is
settled. Or is this wholly unjust to the noble
art of design and only showing that I have a hun-
gry ear but a dull eye? Will you let me say that
I have conceived more highly of the possibilities of the art sometimes in looking at weather-
stains on a wall, or fantastic shapes which the
eye makes out of shadows by lamplight, than
from really majestic and finished pictures? [2]

1 See *Letters from Ralph Waldo Emerson to a Friend,*
1838–1853 (edited by Charles Eliot Norton ; Houghton,
Mifflin & Co., 1899). Mr. Ward had lent his friend a
portfolio containing the large engravings of Michel Angelo's
frescoes in the Sistine Chapel.

2 This coincides with the advice of Leonardo da Vinci
to artists in his *Treatise on Painting*.

October 28.

The world can never be learned by learning all its details.

Variety of topic and of illustration may be a sign of poverty and not of wealth, as the double and treble plots of Spanish plays, and the overcrowding of action, indicate a lack of genius to expand one action to just and majestic issues.

The Age. — One would say that the present Reflective Period had not reached its meridian and will endure for some time yet, who considered that no great analyst except Kant has yet appeared, and Kant is rather a technical analyst than an universal one such as the times tend to form.

The Age, what is it? It is what the being is who uses it, — a dead routine to me, and the vista of Eternity to thee. One man's view of the age is confined to his shop and the market, and another's sees the roots of Today in all the Past and beneath the Past in the Necessary and Eternal. Let us not dwell so fondly on the characteristics of a single Epoch as to bereave ourselves of the permanent privileges of man.

We ought never to lose our youth. In all natural and necessary labors, as in the work of a farm, in digging, in splitting, rowing, drawing water, a man always appears young — is still a boy. So in doing anything which is still above him, — which asks all his strength and more; somewhat commensurate with his ability, so that he works up to it, not down upon it, — he is still a youth. But if his work is unseasonable, as botany and shells or the Greek verbs at eighty years of age, or playing Blindman's Buff, we say, Go up, thou baldhead!

Best Gift. — The dreams of youth, the passion of love are the constant reproduction of the vision of the Ideal, which God will not suffer a moment to remit its presence or to relax its energy as a coagent in history.

October 31.

No article so rare in New England as Tone.

November 3.

In Boston I visited the gallery of Sculpture and saw the Day and Night of Michel Angelo. I find in Michel more *abandon* than in Milton. . . . Wonderful figure and head of Day. The head suggests not only, as when I first saw it in Florence, the sun new risen resting over the brow of a hill, but, when better seen, a whole rough landscape of woods and mountains. I see reason for this figure being called Day: and I called the Night, Night.

The Jove of Phidias pleases me well. In the afternoon I visited Alcott and in the evening Ward came to see me, and the next morning again brought me Raphael's designs to show me that Raphael was greater than Angelo, great as Shakspear. But in making this scale we must be very passive. The gods and demigods must seat themselves without seneschal in our Olympus, and as they can instal themselves by seniority divine, so will I worship them, and not otherwise. I had told Alcott that my First Class stood, for today, perhaps thus: Phidias, Jesus, Angelo, Shakspear; or if I must sift more sternly still,—Jesus and Shakspear were two men of genius.

The common reply to the physician is,—"See how many healthy men use the foods and liquors and practices which you reprehend." And men see in this fact a treachery in Nature herself, instead of esteeming it the bending goodness of the god, the resistance of the Soul, the moral purchase, the intercession of the spirit, the elasticity straining still against the noxious wrong and giving the poor victim still another and yet another chance of self-recovery and escape.

Health. — Is it becoming or agreeable to your imagination that the bursts of divine poetry, that the new delineations of God and his world should be the inspirations of opium or tea?

It is the condition of inspiration — Marry Nature, and not use her for pleasure.

He who has not yet departed from his innocence stands in the highway which all souls must travel, and, solitary as he may at moments seem to himself, he is lovely, and that which we seek in society : so that he appears to all beholders to stand betwixt them and the sun, a transparent object, and whoso journeys towards that person, journeys towards the sun. But he who departs from his innocency must be loved for himself and not for virtue: the time given to courting his affection is lost to any other object, and the affection itself is a false and fugitive affection.

It is only known to Plato that we can do without Plato.

Older! Older! We wish sign, in praising or describing aught, that the eye has seen other things. Deep eyes that have drank more of this wine than others.

Nose and Teeth. — I saw at the Athenæum with great pleasure that old head of Jove attributed to Phidias. It is sublime in general and in all the details except the nose, which did not beseem the father of the gods. Indeed, it is not easy to imagine the shaping of that feature (long ago excluded from epic poetry) worthily for such a form. And this is strange. Yet the nose of Cæsar and of Pitt suggest " the terrors of the beak." I have mentioned elsewhere that the teeth in the physiognomy express limitation. For that reason it is very plain that no painter could dare to show the teeth in the head of Jupiter.

The City delights the Understanding. It is made up of finites: short, sharp, mathematical lines, all calculable. It is full of varieties, of successions, of contrivances. The Country, on the contrary, offers an unbroken horizon, the monotony of an endless road, of vast uniform plains, of distant mountains, the melancholy of uniform and infinite vegetation; the objects on the road are few and worthless, the eye is invited ever to the horizon and the clouds. It is the school of Reason.

The problem which belongs to us to solve is new and untried. Born in the age of calculation and criticism, we are to carry it, with all its triumphs, and yield it captive to the universal Reason. Educated in the very shop and the mill, taught that nature exists for use and the raw material of art, conveyed, clothed, fed by steam, educated in traditions, and working in state, in church, in education, and in charities by mechanical methods, we are yet made to hear the auguries and prophecies of the Soul, which makes light of all these proud mechanisms, breathes on them and they become ashes and shadows, and calls us to the Holy and the Eternal, not by the Past, but by the Present, not by men, but alone, not by Bibles, but through thought and lowliest submission of heart. I see already this effort in eminent individuals. They are renouncing that which had been their pride: they encounter scorn and live with scorned men. They acquire a serener, heavenlier eye and brow. They avow and defend what yesterday they contradicted; and gain daily a reliance on principles and the habit of reposing child-like on the lap of the incessant Soul.

The greatness of all our heroes is to be revised. All reputations each age revises. Very few immutable men has History to show. We are to issue a *Quo warranto* and revoke the charters of fame. There are all degrees of greatness, and this foolish praising, so vague and superlative, must be retrenched. . . .

November 6.

People hold to you as long as you please yourself with the Ideal life only as a pretty dream and concede a resistless force to the limitations of the same, to structure, or organization, and to society. But as quickly as you profess your unlimited allegiance to the first, so far as to be no longer contented with doing the best you can in the circumstances, but demand that these mountain circumstances should skip like rams and the little hills like lambs before the presence of the Soul, then they distrust your wisdom and defy your resolutions. And yet Nature is in earnest. That aspiration in every heart which they like that you should paint, or carve, or chaunt,—anything but enact,—is not a castle in the air. They moreover admit it in the moral world; they concede that a perfect justice should be sought and done; but an intellectual equality, an intellectual society, a mode of domestic life, in which trifles should at last descend to their place, confectionery should come down, and character, art, and joy ascend, this is an incredible proposition. But what they concede destroys the force of their denial. Nature is unique throughout. The prayer of the soul predicts its own answer in facts. The moral nature is not a patch of light here, whilst the social world is a lump of darkness there, but tends incessantly to rectify and ennoble the whole circumference of facts.

Never was anything gained by admitting the omnipotence of limitations, but all immortal action is an overstepping of these busy rules. In Rome, a consul was thanked by the Senate because he had not despaired of the Republic.

Today a letter came to me from John Sterling. So have I two friends in England to make the heart and mind glad.[1]

A great man stands on God. A small man stands on a great man.

1 See *Correspondence of John Sterling and Emerson*; Houghton, Mifflin & Co., 1897.

A man's subject always lies in his recent thought and habits, and is to be found by just observations, not in odd moments, but in sane moments.

Honor him whose life is a perpetual victory.[1] . . . Virtue was never yet a good Whig.

Ward showed me a volume of Raphael's designs by way of evincing Raphael's title to stand in the first class of men of genius. The book did certainly surprise me with the opulence of his genius, and if this were a question in which details of power had any place, this would be unexceptionable evidence. But it is a question not of talents but of *tone*, and not particular merits, but the mood of mind into which one and another can bring us is the only relevant testimony.

Prudence governs the world, and not Religion or Science or Art. Mr. Cunard sends the steam-packet from Boston to England, and not I. In order that principles should rig and man and sail the ship, it needs to begin far back, and bring about a new state of society. At present,

1 What follows is printed in "Worship" (*Conduct of Life*, p. 237).

a right-minded individual can only live so as to point at these ends, to imply Love and Art and Knowledge in every moment of his life.

An admirable account of the Battle of Lützen is contained in the fourth volume of the Harleian Miscellany, translated from the French, though, if it were not so stated, I should not suspect a translation. The piece was printed 1633, 4to, 45 pages, — far superior to anything I remember in Schiller's War.

The story of the Battle of Lützen is worthy of Plutarch. " Gustavus was never weary though ever busied, as if action had been his nourishment." " He would often say ' That he was willing to bear with others' infirmities, as the phlegm of some and the wine of others, and that therefore reciprocally his choler deserved some support.' And, to say truth, this passion may challenge and win connivance from him who shall duly consider his working spirit never weakened though ever bended," etc., etc.

In the same volume is Cavendish's " Negotiations of Cardinal Wolsey," printed in London 1641.

Cavendish, who was Wolsey's Gentleman Usher, being sent before him when in France to secure Lodgings at Champaigne, relates that on his arriving at Champaigne, being sat at dinner in his inn over against the market place, he "heard a great noise and clattering of bills and looking out I saw the officers of the town bringing a prisoner to execution, and with a sword cut off his head. I demanded what was the offence. They answered me, 'For killing of red deer in the forest near adjoining.' And incontinently they held the poor man's head upon a pole in the market place between the stag's horns, and his four quarters set up in four places of the forest."

Certainly this anecdote is not a specimen of Law as we know it in America. Government is here less ferocious, but it has not yet become amiable. Does the Custom House, does the Statute Book associate itself with any idea of Gladness, of Genius, of Holiness, of the progress of man? When we look at a plant, at a gem, at a landscape, we behold somewhat accordant with, though inferior to, our own nature. But I ask if a man should go to walk in the woods and should there find suspended on the oaks or bulrushes electioneering placards setting forth the pretensions of Mr. Van Buren or Mr. Harrison, whether the new train of thoughts thus awakened would harmonize with the place, or would exalt his meditation?

Is not the breast of man the home of the Vast and the Awful, as well as the gay and convenient? The (Holy) Ideal still soars above us, let us mount as we will, and is as far from the heights of thought as from the chaffering of the market.

Our moods do not believe in each other.[1] . . .

Books. — Linnæus's *Tour in Lapland,* and two French novels. I read the first as White's *Selborne,* or Plutarch, or Elgin marbles, or the cold, moist morn itself. The latter is lamp-smoke and indigestion.

November 9.

We are helped along by good and bad; ambition, want, vanity, and such *canaille* spur us to industry. I have no love for Lord Brougham, yet the recital of his immense and unweariable activity inspires good resolutions in me.

So comes ever the question whether our profane mode of educating children even up to manhood by emulation is purely noxious.[2] . . .

1 The rest of the passage is printed in "Circles" (*Essays,* First Series, p. 306).

2 The long passage in "Education," including the dis-

And yet the familiar observation of the universal compensations might suggest the fear that so summary a step of a bad humour was more jeopardous than its continuance; it is driven into the constitution and has infected the brain and the heart.

The same difference is between the Revival of Religion or the partaking of the Lord's Supper, and the life of spiritual obedience.

The book that alarms one man, threatening the disorganization of society, is heard of by one of higher principle with no more emotion than the cheeping of a mouse in the wall.

The question between men is, Are they still advancing? or, are the seals set to their character and they now making a merchandise simply of that which they can do? In general, men of genius who know no period are incapable of any perfect exhibition, because, however agreeable it may be to them to act on the public, it is always a secondary matter. They are humble, self-accusing, moody men, whose worship is toward the Ideal Beauty which chooses to be

cussion of corporal punishment, follows (*Letters aud Biographical Sketches,* p. 154).

courted in sylvan solitudes, in retired libraries,
in nocturnal conversations with a few; with one
companion, or in silent meditation. Their face
is forward and their heart is in this heaven. By
so much are they disqualified for a perfect success in any of the arenas of ambition to which
they can give only a divided affection. But the
man of talents, who has attained and has ceased
to advance, has every advantage in the controversy. He can give that cool and commanding
attention to the thing to be done, as shall secure
its just performance.

Fashionists. — Do not be afraid of cold water,
nor cold weather, nor cold countenances. Frost
is wholesome and hardens the constitution.
There will always be in society certain persons
who are very mercuries of its approbation and
so whose glance will at any time determine for
the curious their standing in the world. These
are the mercuries of the lesser gods. Accept
their coldness as a good omen of grace with
the loftier deities. And be not so weak as to
quarrel with these functionaries. They are
clear in their office, nor could they be there
and thus formidable to you without their own
merits.

Our exaggeration of all fine characters arises from the fact that we identify each in turn with the soul. Presently the individual warps and shrinks away and we accuse him. It is very hard to find an ideal in history. By courtesy we call saints and heroes such, but they are very defective characters.[1] I cannot easily find a man I would be.

It is only low merits that can be enumerated. Fear when your friends say to you what you have done well, and say it through. But when they cannot say it, when they stand beside you with uncertain, timid looks of respect and yet half dislike, inclined to suspend their judgment of you for years to come, then you may begin to hope and to trust.

November 13.

Do something; it matters little or not at all whether it be in the way of what you call your profession or not, so it be in the plane or coincident with the axis of your character. The reaction is always proportioned to the action, and it is the reaction that we want. Strike the hardest blow you can, and you can always do this by work

[1] Compare what is said to this effect in the third page of " Nominalist and Realist " (*Essays*, Second Series).

which is agreeable to your nature. This is economy.

Self-culture. — In hard times, cultivate yourself, and you cannot lose your labor. A just man, a wise man, is always good property; the world cannot do without him, be the fashions or the laws or the harvest what they may. But if he seek to suit the times he miserably fails. Even Plato and Kant can hardly be trusted to write of God. As soon as one sets out to write in the course of his book of the Divine mind, the love of System vitiates his perception. He grows a little limitary. The truest account of that Idea would be got by an observation and record of the incidental expressions of the most intelligent men when they speak of God quite simply and without any second thought.

Hospitality. — Who is timid and uneasy and fleeting but the master of the house, when his house is full of company? He should be glad that such brave and wise men are happy around his hearth, and he is tormented instead with fantastic supposition. He hates every civil thing that is said to him, as if it implied that their freedom was less than he had wished it. He scorns to treat any one with particular kindness, as if it were some encroachment on that rude freedom he desires should prevail. It would give him some contentment if they would put his real generosity to the proof by hard knocks and abusive personalities levelled at himself. What a fine sentiment lay under the bold usage of the Romans when they set buffoons and satirists about the triumphing consul to warn and insult him! So they took off this slight delirium and vacillation of success, and gave to the day a solid content.

Alcott seems to need a pure success. If the men and women whose opinion is fame could see him as he is and could express heartily as these English correspondents their joy in his genius, I think his genius would be exalted and relieved of some spots, with which a sense of injustice and loneliness has shaded it.[1]

1 Alcott's *Records of a School* awakened the lively interest of several earnest Englishmen, who wrote letters welcoming his high ideas on Education. First of these was John Pierpont Greaves, a merchant, who, when his trade was ruined by Napoleon's wars, went to Switzerland and became the friend of Pestalozzi, and in England worked for Infant Schools and Emancipation. Other correspondents were W. Oldham, John Heraud, who conducted the *Monthly Magazine*, which took notice of the American Transcendentalists, and Charles

But no great man will ever drill. None will ever solve the problem of his character according to our preconceived notions or wishes, but only in his own high, unprecedented way.

A good sentence, a noble verse which I meet in my reading, are an epoch in my life. From month to month, from year to year, they remain fresh and memorable. Yet when we once in our writing come out into the free air of thought, we seem to be assured that nothing is easier than to continue this communication at pleasure indefinitely. Up, down, around, the kingdom of thought has no enclosures, but the Muse makes us free of her city. Well, the world has a million writers. One would think then that thought would be as familiar as the air and water, and the gifts of each new hour exclude the repetition of those of the last. Yet I remember a beautiful verse for twenty years.

November 14.

We cannot overvalue our Age. All religious considerations lead us to prefer it. Then it is our all. It is the world. As the wandering sea-

Lane and Henry G. Wright, masters of the school founded in Alcott's honor in Surrey, England, and named for him.

bird which, crossing the ocean, alights on some rock or islet to rest for a moment its wings and to look back on the wilderness of waves behind and forward to the wilderness of waters before, so stand we perched on this rock or shoal of Time arrived out of the Immensity of the Past and bound and road-ready to plunge into immensity again.

Generosity does not consist in giving money or money's worth.[1]

The poor therefore are only they who *feel poor*, and poverty consists in feeling poor.[2] . . .

S. M. F. writes me that she waits for the Lectures, seeing well, after much intercourse, that the best of me is there. She says very truly; and I thought it a good remark which somebody repeated here from S. S.,[3] that I "always seemed to be on stilts." It is even so. Most of the persons whom I see in my own house I see across a gulf. I cannot go to them

1 The rest of the passage is found in "Domestic Life" (*Society and Solitude*, pp. 114, 115).

2 The rest of this passage is in "Domestic Life" (p. 118).

3 Perhaps Sarah Shaw, later the wife of Mr. George R. Russell of Boston.

nor they come to me. Nothing can exceed the frigidity and labor of my speech with such. You might turn a yoke of oxen between every pair of words; and the behavior is as awkward and proud. I see the ludicrousness of the plight as well as they. But, having never found any remedy, I am very patient with this folly or shame, patient of my churl's mask, in the belief that this privation has certain rich compensations, inasmuch as it makes my solitude dearer, and the impersonal God is shed abroad in my heart more richly, and more lowly welcome for this porcupine impossibility of contact with men. And yet in one who sets his mark so high, who presumes so vast an elevation as the birthright of man, is it not a little sad to be a mere mill or pump yielding one wholesome product at the mouth in one particular mode, but as impertinent and worthless in any other place or purpose as a pump or a coffee-mill would be in a parlor or a chapel? I make rockets: must I therefore be a good senator?

Mimicry. — We cannot hear anyone mimic the notes and sounds of the lower animals, as frogs, birds, insects, without instantly conceiving a new and immense extension possible to the descriptiveness and energy of language.

One Mind. — All languages are inter-translateable.

Systems. — I need hardly say to anyone acquainted with my thoughts that I have no System. When I was quite young, I fancied that by keeping a manuscript Journal by me, over whose pages I wrote a list of the great topics of human study, as, *Religion, Poetry, Politics, Love,* etc., in the course of a few years I should be able to complete a sort of encyclopædia containing the net value of all the definitions at which the world had yet arrived. But at the end of a couple of years, my Cabinet Cyclopædia, though much enlarged, was no nearer to a completeness than on its first day. Nay, somehow the whole plan of it needed alteration, nor did the following months promise any speedier term to it than the foregoing. At last I discovered that my curve was a parabola whose arcs would never meet, and came to acquiesce in the perception that, although no diligence can rebuild the universe in a model by the best accumulation of disposition of details, yet does the world reproduce itself in miniature in every event that transpires, so that all the laws of nature may be read in the smallest fact. So that the truth-speaker may dismiss all solicitude as to the proportion and congruency of the aggregate of his thoughts, so long as he is a faithful reporter of particular impressions.

Literature is now critical. Well, analysis may be poetic. People find out they have faces, and write Physiognomy; sculls, and write Phrenology; mysteries of volition and supervolition, and explore Somnambulism. Chemistry is criticism on an apple, and a drop of water, and the glassy air, which to our fathers were wholes, but which we have resolved. Is not the sublime felt in an analysis as well as in a creation?

Nature loves analogies, not repetitions. And those eclectics are doomed to an agreeable surprise who have fancied the Creator so poor in invention that he can produce but three or four Ages or Schools of thought, and having run through so short a gamut, must needs repeat the old tune to infinity.

Once more, it is not the analyst who is unhappy or who desponds. It is the idler who does not the work of the time, who is not in its spirit, the frivolous and sensual who have the vices of their class, modified, of course, by the character of the era, and so we have frivolity and sensuality with cant, because the time is decorous, and with a smattering of letters and philosophy, because the time is social and analytic.

It is not when I analyse that I am unhappy. That is common to all men, and independent of circumstances; in so much that the peculiar disadvantages of any time or mode sink into nothing beside it. The real danger of American scholars is not analysis, but sleep, or that they be not scholars. There is a town in which it is said all the inhabitants are on their backs at 2 P. M.

November 15.

We are accustomed to speak of our National Union and our Constitution as of somewhat sacred. Individual character and culture are sacred, but these bands are trivial in the comparison. The language of the newspapers will undergo a great change in fifty years. The precious metals are not quite so precious as they have been esteemed. The spirit of political economy is low and degrading. Man exists for his own sake and not to add a laborer to the State. There-

fore, I never can forgive a great man who suc-
cumbs so far to the mere forms of his day as
to peril his integrity for the sake of adding to
the weight of his personal character the authority of office, or making a real government titular.
Adams, Clay and Webster electioneer. And Nature does not forgive them, for thus they compromise their proper majesty, and are farther than
ever from obtaining the adventitious.

Our life is infested by unjust persons, by fools,
by paltry fellows who win a political importance
— by all these tormentors who exercise a power
of annoyance sadly disproportioned to the short-
ness of the term in which we converse with the
Ideas of Religion, Wisdom and Society. Yet the
power to annoy which is given to these agents
for a season, we give. It is merely an outward
or reflex exhibition of our defects. With the uprise of the soul these recede and decay.

In the beginning of thought we discriminate
between all those means and labors which contribute to a well-being of the senses, and those
in which the means and the end are one, or which
seek an absolute good, as, Justice. Whatever
proposes this end without end is sacred in our

eyes. All the mechanic arts contribute nothing to this end. The commerce of the world forwards this end no more than the Indian and his wampum belt. The forms of government — an Eastern despotism and a Western Democracy — are indifferent to it. But Love, Friendship, Poetry, Solitude are friendly to the Conscience.

You would have me at advantage, O friend; you would come to face me by having first wronged me. You would cheat me of the majesty which belongs to every human being.

November 16.

Politics. — It is plain that the statesman occupies himself only with the measure, not with the opinion of the people. By directing all his understanding and affection on the fact, and not allowing the people or their enemies to arrest it, he is able to make his hands meet to come at his end. If the people must meddle with what they don't understand, he reprimands them if they would check, he encourages them if they would distrust his movement. Is it not plain then that when the eye of the political agent veers too frequently from the measure to the opinion of the people, and in course of time fastens on the opinion mainly, he must lose just so much steadiness of conduct and therewith so much success?

In this country there is *no measure* attempted for itself by legislatures, but the opinion of the people is courted in the first place, and the measures are perfunctorily carried through as secondary.

Extra fortunam est quicquid donatur amicis.

J. C. SCALIGER.

November 17.

The Sabbath, . . . that frankincense out of a sacred antiquity!

Why should they call me good-natured? I too, like puss, have a retractile claw.

What just theology is in the popular proverb, " Every man for himself and the Lord for us all."

Death. — And where is he now? O, he is dead, poor fellow! That is the sentiment of mankind upon death, that the dead, be he never so wise, able, or contented, is a poor fellow.

Men kill themselves. And run the risk of great absurdity; for our faculties fail us here to say what is the amount of this freedom, this only door left open in all the padlocked secrets of nature, . . . this main entry and royal staircase admitting apparently to the Presence-Chamber, yet so designedly it seems left wide. It may be that he who sheathes his knife in his own heart does an act of grand issues, and it may be a preposterous one. I think I would not try it until I had first satisfied myself that I did not baulk and fool myself. The question is whether it is the way *out*, or the way *in*.

Board. — L. C. B. went to board in the country, and complained that she got bad air, bad light, bad water, bad fire, bad sound, bad food, and bad company. The house shook with rats and mice, smelt of onions, the oil in the lamp would not burn, the water was foul, the wood on the fire was soggy and made no flame, the children stunned her, the table was poverty itself, and the people vulgar and knavish, and when she would walk abroad she could not draw the bolt. I advised her to publish her adventures under the name of Bad Board, or the Baroness Trenck.

Homerides. — It is strange how hard we find it to conceive of the organization of any other

Ideas than those under which we live. We do not see that what we call Church, State, School, are only ideas embodied which have succeeded to other ideas and must give place hereafter to new. A new thought will orb itself in a moment. Our savants cannot believe that the Greek bards should be able to carry in the memory several thousand lines, as the Iliad and the Odyssey; for we have no need of such memories. As little could one of these minstrels conceive of the faculty of one of Whitwell and Bond's clerks, who, I have heard, can add up five columns of figures by one numeration instead of five. Mr. Chase, a clerk of Waterston, Pray and Co., will with a ruler add up any number of columns, — three, four, or five figures at one ascent of the column.

Temperance. — Who argues so sourly for beef and mutton against the man of herbs and grains? The fat and ruddy eater who hath just wiped his lips from feeding on a sirloin, whose blood is spouting in his veins, and whose strength kindles that evil fire in his eye. It is not then the voice of man that I hear, but it is the beef and brandy that roar and rail for beef and brandy. But shall these play the judge in their own cause?

The Bible. — The transcendent, I have said, is economy also. Literary accomplishments, skill in grammar, logic and rhetoric can never countervail the want of things that demand voice. Literature is but a poor trick when it busies itself to make words pass for things. The most original book in the world is the Bible. This old collection of the ejaculations of love and dread, of the supreme desires and contritions of men, proceeding out of the region of the grand and eternal, by whatsoever different mouths spoken, and through a wide extent of times and countries, seems the alphabet of the nations, and all posterior literature either the chronicle of facts under very inferior Ideas, or, when it rises to sentiment, the combinations, analogies or degradations of this.

It is in the nature of things that the highest originality must be moral. The only person who can be entirely independent of this fountain of literature and equal to it, must be a prophet in his own proper person. Shakspear, the first literary genius of the world, leans on the Bible : his poetry supposes it. If we examine this brilliant influence, Shakspear, as it lies in our minds, we shall find it reverent, deeply indebted to the traditional morality, — in short, compared with the tone of the prophets, *Secondary*. On the other hand, the Prophets do not imply the existence of Shakspear or Homer, — advert to no books or arts, — only to dread Ideas and emotions. People imagine that the place which the Bible holds in the world, it owes to miracles. It owes it simply to the fact that it came out of a profounder depth of thought than any other book, and the effect must be precisely proportionate. Gibbon fancied combinations of circumstances that gave Christianity its place in history. But in nature it takes an ounce to balance an ounce.

I have used in the above remarks the *Bible* for the Ethical Revelation considered generally, including, that is, the Vedas, the Sacred writings of every nation, and not of the Hebrews alone; although these last, for the very reason I have given, precede all similar writings so far as to be commonly called *The Book*, or Bible, alone.

Eyes. — Women see better than men. Men see lazily, if they do not expect to act. Women see quite without any wish to act. Men of genius are said to partake of the masculine and feminine traits. They have this feminine eye, a function so rich that it contents itself without asking any aid of the hand. Trifles may well be studied by him, for he sees nothing insulated; the plaid of a cloak, the plaits of a ruffle, the wrinkles of a face, absorb his attention and lead it to the root of these matters in universal Laws.

NOBLESSE

Quoique je ferme un corps, je ne suis qu'une idée :
Plus ma beauté vieillit, plus elle est decidée :
Il faut, pour me trouver, ignorer d'où je viens :
Je tiens tout de lui qui reduit tout à rien.

MME. DU DEFFAND,
Letters of H. Walpole.

November 18.

We are constrained to compare continually the inspiration of Shakspear with that of Isaiah, and each new fact with an old standard. Comparisons are odious, we say, and we feel a certain poverty of mind in a too sudden reference of some new merit to one or a few measures. Yet who does not see in this inevitable instinct which forces the rudest to compare, the confession of one Substance, of one Cause, of one mind ?

Scholar and Soldier. — Unius ætatis sunt qui fortiter fiunt ; quæ, vero, pro utilitate reipublicæ scribuntur, æterna

VEGETIUS.

Animal Magnetism. — "Extasi omnia prædi-
cere." — See Burton's *Anatomy of Melancholy*,
vol. i, p. 12.

November 19.

Society quarrels with the Clerisy, or learned
class, if they shall sell their wisdom for money.
But Society compels them to this course. Once,
before Malthus was in vogue, the world thought
its health and grace consisted in its clerisy. The
state magnificently maintained them. No one
could spend money so well, of course, as the
most cultivated. The state took care that the
best qualified should be the richest benefactors.
But times are changed. The church is not now
the resort of all or almost all this class. They
are gone out hence, and the ecclesiastics are not
drawn to the church by their nature, but by
convenience. Of course the church has lost the
veneration of the people ; and they do not like
to pay for its support. Meantime the scholars
out of the church have the same needs as before : the same fitness to be the almoners of the
state : for all the expenditure of a truly cultivated man is like the expenditure of a temple,
religious and public. They have a right, — have
they not ? — in proportion to their enlarged sight
to exert a large power, to direct the means of

the community, to select and aid and enrich the youth of genius and virtue. Shall they then, since the state is no state, gives them no place, desert also their function in the commonwealth, untimely deny themselves and those whom they ought to serve the first means of education? Shall they kill, through a fatal economy, every generous proposition of culture to the community, forbear assembling themselves together, grudge the miles of travel that will bring them face to face with poets and sages, deny themselves the sight of a picture, a statue, and a concert of music, a correspondence with distant philosophers and the interchange of books and apparatus?

Or shall they forsake their duties, since they are so straitened by your penury, and go dig in the fields and buy and sell in the markets, to the detriment of all learning and civility in the commonwealth, in order that they may have that share of external power which their insight has made a higher need to them? If not, then leave open to them the resource of selling the works which are the only vendible product of so many laborious days and watching nights, and whose price ought to be esteemed sacred, and not vile.

Death. — " When people are going to die their faults come out," was one of Aunt Mary's old sayings.

November 20.

Ah, Nature! the very look of the woods is heroical and stimulating. This afternoon in a very thick grove where Henry Thoreau showed me the bush of mountain laurel, the first I have seen in Concord, the stems of pine and hemlock and oak almost gleamed like steel upon the excited eye. How old, how aboriginal these trees appear, though not many years older than I. They seem parts of the eternal chain of destiny whereof this sundered will of man is the victim. Is he proud, high-thoughted and reserved sometimes? Let him match if he can the incommunicableness of these lofty natures, beautiful in growth, in strength, in age, in decay. The invitation which these fine savages give, as you stand in the hollows of the forest, works strangely on the imagination. Little say they in recommendation of towns or a civil, Christian life. Live with us, they say, and forsake these wearinesses of yesterday. Here no history or church or state is interpolated on the divine sky and the immortal year.

O Lord! unhappy is the man whom man can make unhappy.

This country is not an aristocracy, but a cacocracy rather. This town is governed in Wesson's bar-room; and the Country in bar-rooms.

November 21.

The best of Literature is in the feeling of Immortality it awakens. The names of Scaliger, Cardan, Galen, Sallust, Livy, suggest ideas of immortal leisure, of elegance and Olympian thoughts. And the reading these books, or the exercise of the same faculties in compositions of our own, makes, for the time, death somewhat incredible and out of nature.

You teach your boy to walk, but he learns to run himself.

I am charmed with the pensive beauty of the younger Sibyl of Raphael's Four Sibyls, as I see the single head in this fine chalk drawing in Ward's portfolio. What delights me especially is to observe that in a drawing so wonderfully bold and yet precise, the face has a liquid softness. Genius must have copied what genius drew.

In Guido's Aurora I enjoy the distinct expression of morning health and earnestness. It breathes the dawn. What profound health these Hours have and how firmly they tread the clouds. With the most masculine force in every part of the picture, there is no convulsion, no straining, no foam, no ado, but the most flowing grace and ease. What fine propriety in all the details, in the arrangement of the horses, in the disposition of the group, in the variation of the attitude and drapery of the figures on the foreground. Then the horse is nothing but a morning cloud. The little sea-landscape in the corner is matutinal also.

November 26.

Ward has given me the Endymion with friendliest letter.¹ It shall hang by Carlyle's Guido.

1 Of this beautiful copy, in a warm reddish sepia, of the bas-relief in the Capitoline Museum of the sleeping Endymion and his dog, Mr. Emerson wrote, — " I confess I have difficulty in accepting the superb drawing which you ask me to keep. In taking it from the portfolio, I take it from its godlike companions to put it where it must shine alone. Besides, I have identified your collection with the collector ; I have been glad to learn to know you through your friends. They tell me very eloquently what you love, and a portfolio seems to me a more expressive vehicle of taste and character than a bunch

Temperance. — The caterpillar and cow and robin mix the sun and blue sky with their diet. We hide our bread in cellars and basements. It matters not how plain is the fare which is spiced by the sun and sky, as mountaineers and Indians know.

November 27.

Unconsciousness. — Happy is he who in looking at the compositions of an earlier date knows that the moment wrote them, and feels no more call or right to alter them than to alter his recollections of a day or a fact. We pretend sometimes to find somewhat of this sacredness in our scrolls; but I speak of one who should know it.

When once and again the regard and friendship of the noble-minded is offered me, I am made sensible of my disunion with myself. The head is of gold, the feet are of clay. In my *worthiness* I have such confidence, that I can court solitude. I know that if my aspirations should demonstrate themselves, angels would not disdain me. Of my *unworthiness*, the first person I meet shall apprize me. I shall have so little

of flowers. This beautiful Endymion deserves to be looked on by instructed eyes." — See *Letters from Ralph Waldo Emerson to a Friend,* p. 15.

presence, such pitiful, gingerbread considerations, so many calculations, and such unconcealable weariness of my company, — that in my heart I beseech them begone, and I flee to the secretest hemlock shade in Walden woods to recover my self-respect. *Patimur quisque suos manes!* But when I have shriven myself to the partridges, I am gay again and content to be alone. Then I am let into the secret, daily history of others to whom that grace and conversation I covet is given, and find such savage melancholy, such passion, discontent and despair, that suddenly I count myself the happiest of men, and will know the sweetness of bread and water, and live with the jays and sparrows still.

November 28.

It seems a matter of indifference what, and how, and how much, you write, if you write poetry. Poetry makes its own pertinence, and a single stanza outweighs a book of prose. One stanza is complete. But one sentence of prose is not. But it must be poetry.

I do not wish to read the verses of a poetic mind, but only of a poet. I do not wish to be shown early poems, or any steps of progress. I wish my poet to be born adult. I do not find youth or age in Shakespear, Milton, Herbert, and I dread minors.

Shelley is never a poet. His mind is uniformly imitative; all his poems composite. A fine English scholar he is, with taste, ear, and memory; but imagination, the original authentic fire of the bard, he has not. He is clearly modern, and shares with Wordsworth and Coleridge, Byron, and Hemans the feeling of the Infinite, which so labors for expression in their different genius. But all his lines are arbitrary, not necessary,[1] and therefore, though evidently a devout and brave man, I can never read his verses.

The same secondariness pervades Wilson's poetry. Scott and Crabbe are objective and have not the feeling of the Infinite. But from Crabbe's poems may the Muses preserve me! . . .

Genius and Reform. — And where were the men of genius whilst these coarse missionaries were

1 This judgment of Shelley was printed in the *Dial* in 1840 (see " Thoughts on Modern Literature," in *Natural History of Intellect*, p. 319), but in that paper Richter, Chateaubriand, and Manzoni are associated with Wordsworth, instead of Coleridge, Byron, and Hemans, as here.

making odious the high doctrines of temperance, love, and the life of nature, which they had first broached in solemn hymns? Alas, master, the Devil put them in their own keeping; their own mouths. For their fine organization the pleasures of sense were doubly attractive. Palaces, sofas and delicious tables amused them like other men, and more than other men, and in their holiday they forgot to resume their task. I saw them each taking himself in charge, to keep himself silent, nor plague the world longer with the harsh counsel of reform, drugging and quieting, how he best could, the nerves that were once harpstrings on which every sunbeam played music.

Why is our diet and table not agreeable to the imagination, whilst all other creatures eat without shame? We paint the bird pecking at fruit, the browsing ox, the lion leaping on his prey, but no painter ever ventured to draw a man eating. The difference seems to consist in the presence or absence of the world at the feast. The diet is base, be it what it may, that is hidden in caves or cellars or houses. . . . Did you ever eat your bread on the top of a mountain, or drink water there? Did you ever camp out

with lumbermen or travellers in the prairie?
Did you ever eat the poorest rye or oatcake with
a beautiful maiden in the wilderness? and did
you not find that the mixture of sun and sky
with your bread gave it a certain mundane sa-
vour and comeliness?

November 30.

Keats. —

" And scarce three steps ere Music's golden tongue
    Flattered to tears this aged man and poor." [1]

" So Saturn as he walked into the midst
    Felt faint, and would have sunk among the rest,
    But that he met Enceladus's eye
    Whose mightiness and awe of him at once
    Came like an inspiration." [2] —

1 Mr. Emerson loved to repeat these lines, as also the Saturn
passage given in the text. In the Journal he also copied the
passages beginning —

" As when upon a trancèd summer night " —

and

" As Heaven and earth are fairer, — fairer far, —
    Than Chaos and blank Darkness " —

and

" One avenue was shaded from thine eyes."

2 Here follow the greater part of two long paragraphs first
printed in the *Dial* "Thoughts on Modern Literature," and
included in the volume *Natural History of Intellect,* pp.
314–316.

December 1.

We are misled by an ambiguity in the use of the term Subjective. It is made to cover two things, a good and a bad. The great always introduce us to facts; small men introduce us always to themselves. . . .

Would you know the genius of the Writer, do not enumerate his talents or his feats, but ask thyself what spirit he is of? Has he led thee to Nature because his own soul was too happy in beholding her power and love? or has he only shown you stars and mountains, woods and lovely forms as *his house*, bribing you by the splendor of his palace to come and see *him?* What has Lord Byron at the bottom of his poetry, but, *I am Byron, the noble poet, who am very clever, but not popular in London?* The little can see nothing in nature but their own stake, and their most discursive regards are still economical. And as Scaliger says, in reference to Montaigne's gossiping account of himself, that he likes red wine, but never drinks white, — "Who the devil wants to know what wine you drink?"

The water we wash with never speaks of itself, nor does fire, or wind, or tree. Neither does the noble natural man; he yields himself to your occasion and use, but his act expresses a reference to universal good.

Rob was tender and timid as a fawn in his affections, yet he passed for a man of calculation and cold heart. He assumed coldness only to hide his *woman's heart*. There is a play in which the sister is enamoured of her brother, and when they embrace, she exclaims, " J'ai froid."

In taking, this afternoon, farewell looks at the sibyls and prophets of Michel Angelo, I fancied that they all looked not free, but necessitated; ridden by a superior will, by an Idea which they could not shake off. It sits in their life. The heads of Raphael look freer certainly, but this obedience of Michel's figures contrasts strangely with the living forms of this age. These old giants are still under the grasp of that terrific Jewish Idea before which ages were driven like sifted snow, which all the literatures of the world — Latin, Spanish, Italian, French, English — tingle with; but we sleek, dapper men have quite got free of that old reverence, have heard new facts on metaphysics, and they are quite ready to join any new church. We are travellers, and not responsible.

Let the painter unroll his canvas. Millions of eyes look through his.

We are not at home in nature. We confess our unworthiness inadvertently in all we say of it. The unusual beauty of the sunset attracts us and the soul dares not say, "Behold my peace passed into nature also!" but we mendicantly say, "What a scene for a painter or for a poet!" or more superficially still, "What an Italian sky!"

"*Society*," like wealth, is good for those who understand it. It is a foolish waste of time for any who do not. It seems impossible for anyone to expand in the crowd to his natural dimensions. It seems vain to expect any sentiment, any truth and human encouragement. All character seems to fade away from all the accomplices. Every woman seems to be suffering for a chair, and you accuse yourself and commiserate those you talk to. . . . He must be rich, and of a commanding constitution, who can stand this malaria. It spoils the best persons for me.

I will never quarrel with a man because he makes little of the forms, laws, and usages of the world. He cannot do so, if he be thoughtful and earnest, but by the force of his perception. He sees that the soul is a creator, and instantly makes light of all your present works, since he knows it can very easily make more when these are gone; a secret which others do not know, and so contradict him with petulance.

It is very pleasant to me to hear of any fine person that he or she is a reader of Swedenborg. It is an uncomputed force, — his influence on this age, his genius still unmeasured. He is the fabulist, the Cebes, the better Æsop of the last ages. How bland, how warm, how renovating it works on the cold crudities of Calvinism or Unitarianism!

Gather yourself into a ball to be thrown at a mark.

Lectures. — In Boston, December 4, I read the first lecture of my course on the Present Age; with the old experience that when it was done, and the time had come to read it, I was then first ready to begin to write.[1]

1 The lectures of this course, lasting into February of the following year, were as follows: I, Introductory; II and III,

There is no hope so bright but it is the beginning of its own fulfilment. The dearer it is to us, the more it engages the hands to work for it, and approaching by nature to its object in proportion to its justice, it enlists heaven and earth to work in its behalf.

O Age! he who embraces thee heartily finds all ages in thee. The magazine of the gods, which every age dispenses in its own way, is now thine, and thou hast thine own expenditure.

And lo! how fast the great Critic, who now instructs, — discerns, separates the dead from the living, the flesh from the spirit! See the living veins and strata run, detaching as bark and burr what we thought was stock and pith. See laws to be no laws, and religions to become impieties, and great sciences mistakes, and great men perverters.

It is in the order of nature one of the curbs and ligaments, that great good is first contended against before it is heartily appropriated, as the

Literature; IV, Politics; V, Private Life; VI, Reforms; VII, Religion; VIII, Ethics; IX, Education; X, Tendencies.

heroes first made war against the Amazons whom they afterwards married.

Sunday, *December* 8.

My Friends. — I read with joy Sterling's noble critique on Carlyle in the *Westminster Review*. All intellectual ability seems to have somewhat impersonal and destructive of personality ; and yet I read with warm pride because a man who has offered me friendship gives this unequivocal certificate of his equality to that office. O friend ! you have given me that sign which high friendship demands, namely, ability to do without it. Pass on, we shall meet again. . . . I woke this morn with devout thanksgiving for my friends, the old and the new. I think no man in the planet has a circle more noble. They have come to me unsought : the great God gave them to me. Will they separate themselves from me again, or some of them ? I know not, but I fear it not, for my relation to them is so pure that we hold by simple affinity ; and the Genius of my life being thus social, the same affinity will exert its energy on whosoever is as noble as these men and women, wherever I may be.[1]

1 Although the last three sentences are printed ("Friendship," *Essays*, First Series, p. 194), they are given here

JOHN STERLING

A man with his thoughts about him distinguishes at first sight those fancies which are momentary, and the revelations of the soul: knows among his reveries which is a circumstance and which is a thought, a flower, as well as a man walking knows which is the wall and which is the road. Well, thus among my fancies it occurs that the mind of this Age will endure no miracle, and this, not because of unbelief, but because of belief. It begins to be that the sun and the moon and the man who walks under them are miracles that puzzle all analysis; and that to quit these and go gazing for I know not what parish circumstances or Jewish prodigies is to quit the eternal signs scrawled by God along the dizzy spaces of the Zodiack, for a show of puppets and wax lights.

I say how the world looks to me without reference to Blair's Rhetoric or Johnson's Lives. And I call my thoughts The Present Age, be-

because of their connection with Emerson's high friendship with Sterling, continued until his death, four years later. Emerson and he never met in the flesh, but their lives had run strangely parallel up to this time, and their religious experiences, their desire to become poets, and their noble humanity showed that they might have been more to each other at closer range than Carlyle and Emerson could ever have been.

cause I use no will in the matter, but honestly record such impressions as things make. So transform I myself into a dial, and my shadow will tell where the sun is.

It is dangerous to "crush the sweet poison of misusèd wine" of the affections.[1] . . .

[December 11, after the general lecture, Mr. Alcott mentions in his journal that Mr. and Mrs. Emerson came to his house with several of the persons who had attended the lecture, Margaret Fuller, Miss White (probably later the wife of Lowell), Mr. Bartlett (Sidney?), Mr. Wilson and Mr. Palmer.]

December 21.

All things that speak of heaven speak of peace :
Peace hath more might than war : high brows are calm :
Great thoughts are still as stars : and truths, like suns,
Stir not, but many systems tend around them.

BAILEY, *Festus.*

December 22.

I do not care what you write, but only that you should show yourself a man by writing.

1 For the rest of the passage, see " Friendship" (*Essays,* First Series, p. 195).

Why should we go to our grandfathers for all our rules and tests for measuring the Age and our state of Society, and not rather take those that are near and dear to us? Do not I know what I want? Must I ask thee, Reverend Doctor of Divinity, or thee, O learned Chief Justice of the Bench? . . .

It is the necessity of my nature to shed all influences. Who can come near to Kehama? Neither the rain, neither the warm ray of love, nor the touch of human hand. It seemed, as I mused in the street in Boston on the unpropitious effect of the town on my humor, that there needs a certain deliberation and tenacity in the entertainment of a thought, — a certain longanimity to make that confidence and stability which can meet the demand others make on us. I am too quick-eyed and unstable. My thoughts are too short, as they say my sentences are. I step along from stone to stone over the Lethe which gurgles around my path, but the odds are that my companion encounters me just as I leave one stone and before my foot has well reached the other, and down I tumble into Lethe water. But the man of long wind, the man who receives his thought with a certain phlegmatic entertainment and unites himself to it for the time, as a sailor to his boat, has a better principle of poise and is not easily moved from the perpendicular.

The material is nothing, — bitumen, wood, or stone; the *proportion* is all. Proportion makes permanence, beauty, grandeur. So is it with this daily life; here lie the same materials for all men, the common day, the common men, the common woes, necessities, and, deep under all, the uplifting sentiment of the Good. Out of these selfsame elements the sot builds his sty, and the hero his prevailing character, — Pantheon, shall I say.

In my dream I saw a man reading in the Library at Cambridge, and one who stood by said, " He readeth advertisements," meaning that he read for the market only, and not for truth. Then I said, Do I read advertisements?

Unbecoming is this shamefacedness of ours, this fear of poverty, — for presently the wonderful spectacle of the universe will withdraw from us; we shall be old, blind, deaf, and die. Yet though we be brave, let us not be ungraceful.

Let us stand too much in regard of the beauty of nature to be pert or foolish. Hide, from a great motive, or not at all. We are brothers, and the worst of us is a miracle beyond analysis.

Let us only not be frivolous or vulgar. Let not the sun shine and the infinitude of moral nature exist in vain for us. If we have seen that under our wooden or brick houses the living magical Earth lay, yet lay not still a moment, but whirled forever on in its orbit, true to the orbs of its system, and its system just to its vast sympathy with nature; if we have seen that under our ridiculous routine of selfish trade and government bloomed unhurt the life of God, and found ever and anon vent in our consciousness and in our action, that we have not set ourselves systematically and invariably to stifle it, and so kill ourselves, but in sane moments have opened it a passage into the laws and institutions, have let our private bark follow the course of the river, and be blown in the path of the monsoon, have not selected for honour the mean and the dead in whom no virtue lived, and such therefore as honour could not cleanse or great aims enliven, but have let our votes follow Ideas, and our elections express our character and aspiration, so that the highest sentiment cheered us in the assembly of the people, and the ballot was a voice of truth and veneration, — then the State will stand, then the Laws will be memorable and beautiful for long thousands of years, — will shine by intrinsic light as easily through many as through a few ages. Should not a man be ennobled by his vote? Is it not a prayer? Now he and his candidate are both degraded.

Treat Things Poetically. — Everything should be treated poetically, — law, politics, housekeeping, money. A judge and a banker must drive their craft poetically as well as a dancer or a scribe. That is, they must exert that higher vision which causes the object to become fluid and plastic. Then they are inventive, they detect its capabilities. If they do not this, they have nothing that can be called success, but the work and the workman become blockish and near the point of everlasting congelation. All human affairs need the perpetual intervention of this elastic principle to preserve them supple and alive, as the earth needs the presence of caloric through its pores to resist the tendency to absolute solidity. If you would write a code, or logarithms, or a cookbook, you cannot spare the poetic impulse. We must not only have hydrogen in balloons, and steel springs under coaches, but we must have fire under the Andes at the core of the world. No one will doubt that battles must be fought poetically who reads Plutarch or Las Casas. Economy must be poetical, inventive, alive: that is its essence, and therein is it distinguished from mere parsimony, which is a poor, dead, base thing: but economy inspires respect,—is clean and accomplishes much.

Love is only the reflection of a man's own worthiness from other men.

Some books leave us free and some books make us free.

December 24.

We are to write on this topic not by black art of any kind, not by trick, or journey work, or direction; not stimulated by strong waters, or by fashion, or by praise, or money, but feeling the power of the Past Ages laid on our hand. We are to stand all-related, all accomplished, having covenanted with truth that we will bear witness for it, though by our silence.

Let us not rashly judge an age shallow,—so

we accuse only ourselves. For not by might or disease of man came in this posture of affairs and thoughts we call Today, but it is the fruit towards which a whole past eternity has flowered and ripened, and it is not weak, but the sprouting seed of all that shall ever be.

December 25.

All life is a compromise. We are haunted by an ambition of a celestial greatness, and baulked of it by all manner of paltry impediments. But each of us can do somewhat marked, either lucrative or graceful or kind or wise or formidable.[1] . . .

December 26.

The whole world travails to ripen and bear the sufficiency of one man. The wise man is the State. Louis XIV was right. The wise man needs no army, fort, or navy: he loves men too well. Even if they turn on him, he is invulnerable.[2] He needs no bribe or feast or palace to

1 This sentence and a long passage which follows it are printed in " Politics " (*Essays*, Second Series, pp. 217–219).

2 Although much of the following paragraph has been printed (see " Politics," *Essays*, Second Series, p. 216), it is fuller here, and is given therefore, and also because of its beauty. One of Mr. Emerson's friends suggested that much of the passage would be most appropriate for his epitaph.

draw friends to him. He is supremely fair. He
angles with himself and with no other bait. He
asks no vantage ground, no favorable circumstance. The obedient universe bends around
him, and all stars lend their ray to the hour and
the man. Nature speaks *ex tempore* to him and
lights up a sudden festival whithersoever he
bends his steps. He needs no library, for he
has not done thinking; no church, for he is
himself a prophet; no statute book, for he hath
the Lawgiver; no money, for he is value itself;
no road, for he is at home where he is; no
experience, for the life of the Creator shoots
through him, and from him animates brute
things and turns them immediately to their desired ends. He has no personal friends, for he
does not need to husband and educate a few to
share with him a select and poetic life, who has
the spell to draw the select prayer and piety of
all men unto him. His relation to all men is
angelic. His memory is myrrh to them, his
presence frankincense and flowers.

I have heard that it is not usually beauty
which inspires the strongest passion. I can even
believe that Aspasia was not beautiful, seen *tête-
à-tête*, but almost plain and homely, yet in a

circle of dames in a gallery or across the apartment, hers was the only face on which the eye would fix, and when all were gone, the only one whose form and behaviour the heart would remember.

Treat your friend as a spectacle.[1] . . . Be not so much his friend that you can never know your man, like fond mammas who shut up their boy in the house until he is almost grown a girl. Reverence is a great part of friendship. There must be very two before there can be very one.[2] . . .

Whoso sees Law does not despond.[3] . . .

Pleasant these jets of affection that relume a young world for me again. Delicious is a just and firm encounter of two in a thought, in a feeling. But we must be tormented presently by baffled blows, by sudden unseasonable apathies, by epilepsies of wit and of animal spirits in the heyday of friendship and thought. Our faculties do not play us true.

1 The rest of the passage is in "Friendship" (*Essays*, First Series, p. 209).

2 See "Friendship," pp. 208, 209.

3 See "Considerations by the Way" (*Conduct of Life*, p. 264). This passage is followed by others from "Friendship."

AUTHORS OR BOOKS QUOTED OR REFERRED TO
IN JOURNAL FOR 1839

Vedas; Pythagoras; Cebes; Aristotle; Galen;
Livy; Sallust; Vegetius *apud* Burton; Saint
Augustine, *Confessions;*

The Welsh Bards; Dante, *Purgatorio, Paradiso*; Petrarch; Michel Angelo; Melancthon,
Cardan and Scaliger, *apud* Burton;

William Cartwright and Edward Powell, *On
John Fletcher;*

Donne; Burton, *Anatomy of Melancholy;*
Bentley; William Penn; Linnæus, *Tours in Lapland*; Blair, *Rhetoric;*

Gilbert White, *Natural History of Selborne;*
Harleian Miscellany, French Account of Battle
of Lützen, Cavendish on Negotiations of Cardinal Wolsey;

Walpole, *Letters of Madame du Deffand;*
Bentley; Crabbe;

Burns; Samuel Rogers; Campbell;

Humboldt; Chateaubriand; Hazlitt, *Remains;* Wilson;

Hallam, *Literature of Europe;* Las Casas;
Manzoni; Maroncelli;

Keats, *Hyperion;* Shelley; Mrs. Hemans;

Southey; Cooper; Irving; Everett; Stone, *Life of Brant*;

Lieber; Dr. Follen; Graeter;

Dickens, *Oliver Twist*; Forster, *Cromwell*; Bailey, *Festus*;

John Sterling; Bryant; Horace Mann; Hawthorne; Jones Very; W. Ellery Channing, Frederic H. Hedge;

Fraser's Magazine.

JOURNAL

PREPARATION OF ESSAYS

SYMPOSIA

FRIENDS

THE DIAL APPEARS

BROOK FARM PROJECT

JOURNAL XXXI

1840

(From Journals E and F)

Se maì continga che 'l poema sacro
Al quale ha posto mano e cielo e terra
Si che m' ha fatto per piu anni macro,

. . . .

DANTE, *Il Paradiso*, xxv.

(From F)

January, 1840.

GUY wished all his friends dead on very slight
occasion. Whoever was privy to one of his
gaucheries had the honour of this Stygian op-
tation. Had Jove heard all his prayers, the planet
would soon have been unpeopled. At last it
occurred to Guy that, instead of wringing this
hecatomb of friends' necks every morning, he
would dine better if he gave as much life as he
now took. He found to his astonishment the em-
bryos of a thousand friends hid under his own
heart, and that for every offence he forgave, and
for every great choice he made, suddenly from
afar a noble stranger knocked at his street gate.

What is the State?
The Hero is the State:
The Soul should legislate,
Postponing still the measure to the man;
One sage outweighs all China and Japan.

No man may have any measure which is to be preferred a moment to the man itself. The State may avail as long as it can be treated as wise man. After that, stop. Coax it not. Lie not unto it nor for it.

The influence of character, that is the Theocracy. It is never nothing. It is never omnipotent, but in the inspired moments of each people prevails. In each of our towns and cities, there are periods when the influence of genius predominates for a season over a circle of minds. (The power of Swedenborg at this moment is an impure theocracy.) The influence of a preacher, of a book, of a character of singular worth, exerts this magnetism: the recipients feel that they do not so much borrow the light as find the same light in their breast which flames so high from this inspired brother. The effect of Jesus on men, after an immense deduction is made for false reception of all kinds, is an impure theocracy.

But character is scarcely allowed any rule at

all. Everything governs but that. It is a force not yet known. Rarely a young man, a young woman, reckoned fastidious and whimsical, goes alone, doth somewhat, or forbears somewhat, in contradiction to all custom, out of private motions, — hath insuperable reluctances which are not to be expressed, or invincible urgencies to particular action. But this is a spirit which does not love much the old, hard people, but rather haunts childhood and tender youth. There is a great deal of theocracy in a blush. Nothing is incredible of this power. Its feeblest motion is a counterbalance for mightiest monarchies.

I have read Plato's Dialogue, "The Politician," in Cousin. He seems to me, as before, to owe his fame to the fact that he is a great Average Man.[1] . . .

It is pedantry to estimate nations by the census, or the geographical extent, by coin, or antiquity. We compromise ourselves when we depart from necessary standards, — that is, from their importance to the mind of the period. If

[1] For the rest of this passage, see "Plato" (*Representative Men*, p. 61).

Russia is a scarecrow, that fact at least tells somewhat of them whom it scares. If England, France and Italy draw the steps of all travellers, that fact characterizes at least the traveller. But to measure miles and count hands is brute, — indicates hopeless formalism.

We want one miracle by way of evidence; this, namely, that a mind not profound should become profound. The teaching which has that miracle to show will go round the world.

Man of genius belongs to Monarchy, Aristocracy and Democracy equally.

The scholar verifies the Duke of Ormond's experience, who went to court because there only he could see his equals, and stayed away because there he could see a superior.

Genius avails always itself of a fact as language for its abstractions.

The capital crime with which the church stands charged is its Poverty. Truth is always rich, all-related, all explaining. But our church is a little byeway, an eddy, a nook, wherein you hear

some words and notions you will hear of no-
where else, and which will not explain to the
handcart-man, his cart, nor to me my pen and
ink, my sex, my form and face.

" Les événements ont des causes dans lesquelles
ils sont préconçus, comme nos actions sont ac-
complies dans notre pensée, avant de se repro-
duire, au dehors ; et les pressentiments, les
prophéties sont *l'aperçu* de ces causes." Louis
Lambert's psychological maxim at fifteen years
of age in Balzac's *Le Livre Mystique*.

February 3.

Every man passes his life in the search after
friendship, and here is the letter which he writes
to each candidate for his love.[1] . . .

1 Here follows the letter printed in "Friendship" (*Essays*,
First Series, p. 198). In December, Mr. Emerson had sent
to his friend Samuel G. Ward, in Boston, at his request, a
paper on Burke, but, in his letter, said, "I think I might
qualify this anodyne by sending you one of last winter's composition, a piece which I wrote in good heart, and trust you
may find some sparks still alive in the cinders. The argument were fitter for rhyme ; but that comes only by special
favor of the skies." This was probably "Friendship," as
would appear from Mr. Emerson's next letter. (See *Emerson's Letters to a Friend*. Letters VI and VII.)

Character plus Sensibility.—They were self-centred: Willow was not. He went to them more than was due. He would be poised, and they should pass and repass. Yet was this mobility of his only superficial, and in manners. The flintiest brow in the hall did not surmount a purpose as fast as his to its natural objects, or one as impatient of a false position. He was a rocking stone, always tilting, but never overthrown.

[Here follows the dialogue between Xenos and Iole, which occurs in "Character" (*Essays*, Second Series, p. 90).]

February 19.

I closed last Wednesday, 12th instant, my course of lectures in Boston, on "The Present Age," which were read on ten consecutive Wednesday evenings (except Christmas evening).

　　　I. Introductory. (4 December.)
　　　II. Literature.
　　III. Literature.
　　　IV. Politics.
　　　V. Private Life.
　　　VI. Reforms.
　　VII. Religion.

VIII. Ethics.

IX. Education.

X. Tendencies.

I judge from the account rendered me by the sellers of tickets, added to an account of my own distribution of tickets to my friends, that the average audience at a lecture consisted of about 400 persons. 256 course tickets were sold and 305 evening tickets or passes. I distributed about 110 to 120 course tickets.

These lectures give me little pleasure. I have not done what I hoped when I said, I will try it once more. I have not once transcended the coldest self-possession. I said I will agitate others, being agitated myself, I dared to hope for extasy and eloquence. A new theatre, a new art, I said, is mine. Let us see if philosophy, if ethics, if chiromancy, if the discovery of the divine in the house and the barn, in all works and all plays, cannot make the cheek blush, the lip quiver, and the tear start. I will not waste myself. On the strength of Things I will be borne, and try if Folly, Custom, Convention, and Phlegm cannot be made to hear our sharp artillery. Alas! alas! I have not the recollection of one strong moment. A cold mechanical preparation for a delivery as decorous, — fine things, pretty things, wise things, — but no arrows, no axes, no nectar, no growling, no transpiercing, no loving, no enchantment.

And why?

I seem to lack constitutional vigor to attempt each topic as I ought. I ought to seek to lay myself out utterly, — large, enormous, prodigal, upon the subject of the week. But a hateful experience has taught me that I can only expend, say, twenty-one hours on each lecture, if I would also be ready and able for the next. Of course, I spend myself prudently; I economize; I cheapen; whereof nothing grand ever grew. Could I spend sixty hours on each, or, what is better, had I such energy that I could rally the lights and mights of sixty hours into twenty, I should hate myself less, I should help my friend.

I ought to be equal to every relation.[1] . . .

I saw a maiden, the other day, dressed so prettily and fancifully that she gave the eye the same sort of pleasure that a gem does, — a fine opal, or the coloured stones. When I remem-

1 Here follows the paragraph thus beginning in "Friendship" (*Essays*, First Series, p. 200).

ber what fairy pleasure I found in some cornelians or agates which I saw for an hour when a very little boy, I think none but children and savages enjoy gems.

I wrote S. G. Ward : —

I see persons whom I think the world would be richer for losing: and I see persons whose existence makes the world rich. But blessed be the Eternal Power for those whom my lawless fancy, even, cannot strip of beauty, and who never for a moment seem to me profane.

(From F)

How much we augur in seeing an unusual natural phenomenon, as, for instance, an electric spark. Already we are groping for its ethics.

What absence of all sadness in the drops of the snow-bank.

What nimble, gigantic creatures our thoughts are. What Saurians, what palæotheria these? Ὁ ποίκιλος, rich, leopard-skinned man! who art a palace of sweet sounds and sights, and carriest in thy brain the City of God; in thy cunning senses the morning and the night; the unfathomable galaxy and the realms of Right and Wrong.

Rich past! One word of the old book is so penetrating to my imagination. What shall I say of thy world of old words and virtues and crucifixions and gifts to men? And yet, poor and thoughtless though today is, I count this instinct sacred which bids me slight thy admirable wealth, even in my starving poverty, as a testimony to my faith in my more admirable possibilities.

February 21.

Self-respect is demanded of us by the most general considerations. We stand here for nature and humanity. They bid us make them comely and honorable.

The aim of art is always at somewhat better than nature, but the work of art is always inferior to nature.

The book only characterizes the reader. Is Shakspear the delight of the Nineteenth Century? That fact shows whereabouts we are in the ecliptic of the Soul.

Ah! that I could reach with my words the force of that rhetoric of things in which the Divine mind is conveyed to me, day by day, in what I call my life; a loaf of bread, an errand to the town, a temperate man, an industrious man.

PROVIDENCE, *March* 28.[1]

Send Very's Poems to Carlyle and Wordsworth.

PROVIDENCE, *March* 30.

When the materialist represents mind as the result of body and, at the perishing of body, deceasing — he tells us that this is true, though not so satisfactory to our pride. This last remark is a fatal concession. Nature is always true, there is no lie, no betrayal in it, and yet, it seems in all the individuals there arises this feeling, on hearing his statement, that it is less satisfactory to our pride than something else. In other words, all the individuals feel, Here is some wrong, some crack; something else is desirable than that you say is done, something else is best. Then surely something else must be true.

Nature is in continual flux. Everybody is an hourly mercury of the state of its Soul. So much for phrenology and physiognomy.

---

1 Mr. Emerson seems to have been giving several lectures there at about this time.

Some men write better than they speak. Of such I had rather see the manuscript than see the man. For what he speaks he says to me, but what he writes he says to God.

I said to C. S., The difference between persons is not in Wisdom, but in knack.' . . .

(From E)

April.

By confession we help each other; by clean shrift, and not by dictation.

I like manners and their aristocracy better than the *morgue* of wealth. It is a gay chivalry, a merit, and indicates certainly the presence of a sense of beauty. I am always a fool to these mannered men at the first encounter. The Southerner holds me at arm's length; he will not let me measure him, and after twenty-four hours my opinion shall still not be worth the telling, — such a cloak is his *politesse*. And yet, O stately friend, do not presume on this gay privilege of thine. Yonder simple countryman, on whom you have yet bestowed no smile, strikes down all your glittering and serried points with

1 The paragraph thus beginning (with "art" substituted for "knack") occurs in "Intellect" (*Essays*, First Series, p. 333).

a wave of his hand, and overawes you, as does some
grey friar a circle of armed barons. He oversteps
with a free stride all your spaces marked with
ribbons and etiquette, for he does not respect
them; he is dignified by a higher thought, viz.,
by a humanity which slights all this, and over-
stands it, as a sane man an insane.

Death in a novel, or a poem, is but the mechanical sublime, manage it how you will. Lay
any emphasis on it, and it only betrays the poverty of the writer; the feeblest action, the faintest thought must always be superior to the most
imposing death in fable.

Ah, my poor countrymen! Yankees and Dollars have such inextricable association that the
words ought to rhyme. In New York, in Boston, in Providence, you cannot pass two men in
the street without the word escaping them in the
very moment of encounter, "dollars," "two
and a half per cent," "three per cent."

April 7.

What does that fact signify, that nobody in
this country can draw a hand except Allston?
asserted by Mr. Cole, I think.

At Providence I was made very sensible of the desire of all open minds for religious teaching. The young men and several good women freely expressed to me their wish for more light, their sympathy in whatever promised a better life. They inquired about the new Journal of next July. I was compelled to tell them that the aims of that paper were rather literary than psychological or religious. But the inquiry and the tone of these inquirers showed plainly what one may easily see in Boston and Cambridge and the villages also — that what men want is a Religion.

The railroad makes a man a chattel, transports him by the box and the ton; he waits on it. He feels that he pays a high price for his speed in this compromise of all his will. I think the man who walks looks down on us who ride.

I see with great pleasure this growing inclination in all persons who aim to speak the truth, for manual labor and the farm.[1]

In all my lectures, I have taught one doctrine, namely, the infinitude of the private man. This the people accept readily enough, and even with

1 Here follow passages printed in " Man the Reformer " (Nature, Addresses, and Lectures, pp. 233, 238).

loud commendation, as long as I call the lecture
Art, or Politics, or Literature, or the Household; but the moment I call it Religion, they
are shocked, though it be only the application
of the same truth which they receive everywhere
else, to a new class of facts.

The case of the menaced and insulted mon-
arch is not quite aloof from our own experience. We have tasted that cup too. For see this
wide society, in which we walk, of laboring men.
We allow ourselves to be served by them. We
pay them money and then turn our backs on
them.[1] . . .

(From F)

April 9.

We walked this afternoon to Edmund Hosmer's and Walden Pond. The South wind blew
and filled with bland and warm light the dry
sunny woods. The last year's leaves flew like
birds through the air. As I sat on the bank of the
Drop, or God's Pond, and saw the amplitude of
the little water, what space, what verge, the little
scudding fleets of ripples found to scatter and
spread from side to side and take so much time to

1 For the rest of this long passage on Service, see " Man the
Reformer " (*Nature, Addresses, and Lectures,* pp. 252, 253).

cross the pond, and saw how the water seemed made for the wind, and the wind for the water, dear playfellows for each other, — I said to my companion, I declare this world is so beautiful that I can hardly believe it exists. At Walden Pond the waves were larger and the whole lake in pretty uproar. Jones Very said, " See how each wave rises from the midst with an original force, at the same time that it partakes the general movement!"

He said that he went to Cambridge, and found his brother reading Livy. "I asked him if the Romans were masters of the world? My brother said they had been : I told him they were still. Then I went into the room of a senior who lived opposite, and found him writing a theme. I asked him what was his subject? And he said, Cicero's Vanity. I asked him if the Romans were masters of the world? He replied they had been : I told him they were still. This was in the garret of Mr. Ware's house. Then I went down into Mr. Ware's study, and found him reading Bishop Butler, and I asked him if the Romans were masters of the world? He said they had been : I told him they were still." [1]

1 An interesting memoir of Very was written by Mr. W. P. Andrews, and several of his poems were printed at the

Very obvious is the one advantage which this singular man has attained unto, that of bringing every man to true relations with him. No man would think of speaking falsely to him. But every man will face him, and what love of nature or what symbol of truth he has, he will certainly show him. But to most of us the society shows not its face and eye, but its side and its back. To stand in true relations with men in a false age is worth a fit of insanity, is it not?[1]

(From E) *April* 27.

My little boy says, "I want something to play with which I never saw before," and thus lives over already in his experience the proclamation of Xerxes advertising a reward for a new pleasure. I tell him that the sun and moon are good playthings still, though they are very old; they are as good as new. So are eating and drinking, though rather dangerous toys, very good amusements, though old ones; so is water which we wash and play with; but he is not persuaded by my eloquence.

end. Mr. Emerson used to praise "The Strangers" and "The Barberry," and included them in his *Parnassus.*

1 The last paragraph is printed in "Friendship" (p. 203), but it seemed better to let it stand here in its connection.

There seems a strange propensity to egotism in the mind of several eminent spiritualists whom I have known, disproportion, a sad exaggeration which disables them from putting their act and word aloof from them, detaching it, and seeing it as a pitiful, shrivelled apple, at its best a disgrace to the tree and to nature; and this in souls of unquestionable power and greater nearness to the secret of God than others. It is sadly punished too, and that speedily, inasmuch as this habit always leads men to humour it, to treat the patient tenderly, not roundly, and so shut him up gradually in a narrower selfism, and exclude him from the great world of God's cheerful, though fallible, men and women. I had rather be insulted whilst I am insultable.

James Naylor, George Fox, Luther, are eminent examples of it long ago; and now we have poets, critics, abolitionists, prophets, and philosophers infected with the same elephantiasis.

There is an important *équivoque* in our use of the word unconscious, a word which is much played upon in the psychology of the present day. We say that our virtue and genius are unconscious, that they are the influx of God, and the like. The objector replies that to represent

the Divine Being as an unconscious somewhat
is abhorrent, etc. But the unconsciousness we
spake of was merely relative to us; we speak,
we act, from we know not what higher principle, and we describe its circumambient quality
by confessing the subjection of our perception
to it, we cannot overtop, oversee it, — not see
at all its channel into us. But in saying this, we
predicate nothing of its consciousness or unconsciousness in relation to itself. We see at once
that we have no language subtle enough for dis-
tinctions in that inaccessible region. That air is
too rare for the wings of words. We cannot say,
God is self-conscious, or not self-conscious; for
the moment we cast our eye on that dread nature, we see that it is the wisdom of wisdom,
the love of love, the power of power, and soars
infinitely out of all definition and dazzles all
inquest.

True Criticism is inexhaustible. Every new
thought supersedes all foregone thought and
makes a new light on the whole world.

All spontaneous thought is irrespective of all
else. It is for those who come after to find its
relation to other thoughts.

If there be need of a new Journal, that need is its introduction : it wants no preface. It proceeds at once to its own ends, which it well knows, and answers now for the first time. That consummated fitness is a triumphant apology. It will ignore all the old, long constituted public or publics which newspapers and magazines address. It ignores all newspapers and magazines. It is so real, so full of its own authentic aim which it exists to attain, that it knows them not; not seeing them to fill any place which this mind esteems real, it has no thought to waste on them. It speaks to a public of its own, a newborn class long already waiting. They, least of all, need from it any letters of recommendation.

It is of course too confident in its tone to comprehend an objection, and so builds no outworks for possible defence against contingent enemies. It has the step of Fate, and goes on existing, like an oak or a river, because it must. If the projected Journal be what we anticipate, — and, if not, we should not care for it, — it does not now know itself in the way of accustomed criticism ; it cannot foretell in orderly proportions what it shall do ; its criticism is to be poetic, not the peeping, but the broad glance of the American man on the books and things of this hour.

Its brow is not wrinkled with circumspection, but serene, cheerful, adoring. It has all things to say, and no less than all the world for its final audience.

There are, no doubt, many dogs barking at the moon, and many owls hooting in this Saturday night of the world, but the fair moon knows nothing of either.

April 30.

Waldo looks out today from my study window and says, "These are not the woods I like to look at."—"And what woods do you like to look at?"—"Those that I see from the window of the nursery."

May 4.

Waldo says, "God is very glorious, he always says his prayers, and never 'haves (behaves) naughty."

May 6.

Yesterday with the Club[1] at Medford.

Superlative. — It is somewhat sad that a word of such sacred meaning as *Glory* should now be the emptiest of all words, and scarcely in a lifetime shall we hear it used without disgust.

1 "Symposium."

In conversation, Alcott will meet no man who will take a superior tone. Let the other party say what he will, Alcott unerringly takes the highest moral ground and commands the other's position, and cannot be outgeneralled. And this because, whilst he lives in his moral perception, his sympathies with the present company are not troublesome to him, never embarrass for a moment his perception. He is cool, bland, urbane, yet with his eye fixed on the highest fact. With me it is not so. In all companies I sympathize too much. If they are ordinary and mean, I am. If the company were great, I should soar: in all mere mortal parties, I take the contagion of their views and lose my own. I cannot outsee them, or correct, or raise them. As soon as they are gone, the Muse returns; I see the facts as all cultivated men always have seen them, and am a great man alone.

Every man supposes himself not to be fully understood or appreciated.[1] . . .

Strange how hard it is for cultivated men to free themselves from the optical illusion by

1 The rest of the passage is printed in " Circles " (*Essays*, First Series, p. 306).

A. BRONSON ALCOTT

which a great man appears an institution. They know and have observed in particular instances that the demonstration of a strong will, of a vast thought, at once arrested the eyes and magnetized the wills of men, so that society and events became secondaries and satellites of a man; and the genesis of that man's thought is not now explored after the laws of thought, but externally in his parentage, in his country, climate, college, election by his fellow - citizens, and the like, — as we know is the tenor of vulgar biography. And yet, though familiar with this fact, the moment Jesus is mentioned, they forget their knowledge, and accept the apparatus of prophecy, miracle, positive supernatural indication by name and place, and claim on his part to extraordinary outward relations;—all these, which are the prismatic hues and lights which play around any wonderful genius, they regard as of an adamantine reality, and in the selectest society where Beauty, Goodness and the Soul are named, these men talk of " preaching Christ," and of "Christ's being the ideal of man," etc., etc.

We are halves: we see the past in Memory, but do not see the future. They say, that, at times, this hemisphere completes itself, and Foresight becomes as perfect as Aftersight.

May 9.

Is it not pedantry to insist that every man should be a farmer as much as that he should be a lexicographer? Suppose the doctrine of the right estate of man finds him at sea, shall he therefore scrape together what dust and refuse he can find on deck, and dibble in a flowerpot, or shall he learn to use the ropes, to stand at the wheel, to reef a sail and draw a fish out of the sea and be a farmer of the sea? In like manner, if the doctrine of universal labor find him in the midst of books, whose use he understands, and whose use other men wish to learn of him, shall he cast away this his skill and usefulness to go bungle with hoe and harrow, with cows and swine which he understands not? Should he not rather farm his books well and lose no hour of beneficent activity in that place where he now is? — The Doctrine of the Farm is merely this;¹ . . .

Where is the fertile earth? Where the farmer

¹ The rest of the passage is printed in "Man the Reformer" (*Essays*, First Series, pp. 240, 241).

is. Where do books become great engines but where the scholar is?

May 10.

Self-trust. — If you have no talent for scolding, do not scold ; if none for explaining, do not explain ; if none for giving parties, do not give parties, however graceful or needful these acts may appear in others.

I said once, that every one should read proudly, not too anxious to find himself in Æschylus or in Spinoza, but quite ready to dismiss the book as an inadequate interpreter of his consciousness. I said again, that the scholar must not fear the excess of influence of any author, but follow with heart and strength the master whom he loved, leaving father and mother, house and land behind him, and by and by the over-influence would abate and the light of this would blend with the general day. Do these two statements clash ? I think not. He is to give himself to that which draws him, because that is his own ; and he is to refuse that which draws him not, because it draws him not.

The Age. — The age is marked by " an increasing tenderness for human life."

If a man knows the law, he may settle himself in a shanty in the pine forest, and men will and must find their way to him as readily as if he lived in the City Hall.

(From F)

I begin to dislike animal food. I had whimsies yesterday after dinner which disgusted me somewhat. The man will not be much better than the beast he eats.

Conformity is the ape of harmony.

I have supped with Gods to-night,
Shall I come under wooden roofs?
As I walked on the hills
The great stars did not shine aloof,
But they hurried down from their deep abodes
And hemmed me in their glittering troop.[1]

All spontaneous thought is irrespective of all

1 From 1838 for many years Mr. Emerson's longings to express himself in verse resulted in fragments (scattered through some journals, and in his special Verse-books) which he never published, but which were collected after his death, forming a fairly connected whole called " The Poet," and printed in the Appendix to the *Poems*. The lines given here occur in better form in " The Poet " (*Poems*, p. 314).

else. It is for those who come after to find its relation to other thoughts.

The Soul.—I think whenever we are addressed greatly we greet the brave speaker, and are by him instantly admonished how we ought to speak.

It is the highest power of divine moments that they abolish even our contritions.[1] . . .

Can we never extract this maggot of Europe out of the brains of our countrymen?[2] Plato and Pythagoras may travel, for they carry the world with them and are always at home, but our travellers are moths and danglers.[3]

Wordsworth has done as much as any living man to restore sanity to cultivated society.

Beware when the great God lets loose a new thinker on this planet.[4] . . .

1 Here follows the passage thus beginning in " Circles " (*Essays*, First Series, p. 317).

2 These lines are in " Culture " (*Conduct of Life*).

3 This passage is followed by that in " Friendship " on European travel (*Essays*, First Series, p. 214). This is followed by the sentences about the brook in " Nature " (*Essays*, Second Series, p. 178).

4 The rest of the passage is printed in " Circles" (*Essays*, First Series, pp. 308, 309).

But ah, we impute the virtues to our friends, and afterwards worship the face and feature to which we ascribe these divine tenants.

Labor with the hands that you may have animal spirits. Be not an opium-eater. Cold water has no repentance. But do not let debt and the bondage of housekeeping fret you out of the knowledge of the value of house, husbandry, property. Suppose you have reformed, and live on grains and black-birch bark and muddy water, that you may have leisure. Well, what then? What will you do with the long day? Think? What! All day? Do you not see that instantly taste and arithmetic and power will plan plantations and build summer-houses and carve gods? We must have a basis for our delicate entertainments of poetry and philosophy in our handicraft. We must have an antagonism in the tough world for all the variety of our spiritual faculties or they will not be born.

In regard to this Goethe I have to add that a man as gifted as he should not leave the world as he found it.[1] . . .

1 Much of what follows may be found in "Thoughts on Modern Literature," originally printed in the *Dial* (*Lectures and Biographical Sketches*, p. 333).

Yet how is the world better for Goethe? What load has he lifted from men or from women? There is Austria, and England, the old and the new, full of old effete institutions and usages, full of men born old, and the question still incessantly asked by the young, "What shall I do?" with forlorn aspect. But let some strong Zeno, some nervous Epaminondas, Moses or Isaiah come into our society, and see how he defies it, and enables us to brave it, to come out of it, and re-make it from the corner-stone. There is hardly a life in Plutarch that does not infuse a new courage and prowess into the youth and make him gladder and bolder for his own work.

(From E)

May 17.

In architecture, height and mass have a wonderful effect because they suggest immediately a relation to the sphere on which the structure stands, and so to the gravitating system. The tower which with such painful solidity soars like an arrow to heaven apprizes me in an unusual manner of that law of gravitation, by its truth to which it can rear aloft into the atmosphere those dangerous masses of granite, and keep them there for ages as easily as if it were a feather or a scrap of down. Then, great mass, especially in height, has some appreciable proportion to the size of the globe, and so appears to us as a splinter of the orb itself.

The earth is gay in these days with the blossoming of all fruit-trees. An apple-tree near at hand is a great awkward flower, but seen at some distance it gives a wonderful softness to the landscape.

There are many things which teach that high lesson that success depends on the Aim, not on the means. Look at the mark, not on your arrow. And herein is my hope for all reform in our vicious modes of living. Let a man direct his inquiry on details in attempting an amelioration, and he will be met at every step by unanswerable objections, insoluble difficulties. But let him propose to himself a grand Aim, to live a Prophet, a Helper, a member of the Morning and of Nature, one whom the flowering tree and the summer wind and the sovereign stars shall recal to the remembrance of men, and be the newborn child of absolute Love, — a pure Power, a calm and happy Genius through whom, as through a lens, the rays of the universe converge to the joy of the eye that seeth, — and I think he shall be floated into his place of activity and happiness by might and mind sublime over all these rocks and shoals that now look insuperable. Fix his heart on magnificent life, and he need not know the economical methods: he shall be himself astonished at the great solution of the problem of means.[1]

Living has got to be too ponderous than that the poor spirit can drag any longer this unnecessary baggage-train. Let us cut the traces. The bird and the fox can get their food and house without lies, and why not we? A great Aim shall bring it, as if ravens brought it, the bread of love, apples, pomegranates, berries and corn, not stolen from nature, not polluted nor polluting.

There is this plea always considerable when it is said, Let the bard, the priesthood, receive no contributions, but be rather tent-makers and ploughmen as others are; namely, that in the experience of all sedentary men that degree of

---

[1] Compare "The Poet" (Poems, Appendix): —

> Means, dear Brother? Ask them not;
> Soul's desire is means enow;
> Pure content is angels' lot,
> Thine own Theatre art thou.

manual labor which is necessary for the main-
tenance of a family indisposes and disqualifies
for intellectual exertion.[1] . . .

Latent heat performs a great office in nature.
Not less does *latent joy* in life. You may have
your stock of well-being condensed into extasies,
trances of good fortune and delight, preceded
and followed by blank or painful weeks and
months; or, you may have your joy spread over
all the days in a bland, vague, uniform sense of
power and hope.

Yet is this figure of a stock of well-being only
rhetorical, or rather relative to certain limitations.
For the latent heat of an ounce of wood or stone
is inexhaustible, and the power of happiness of
any soul is not to be computed or drained.

May 18.

Criticism must be transcendental, that is, must
consider literature ephemeral, and easily entertain the supposition of its entire disappearance.
In our ordinary states of mind, we deem not
only letters in general, but most famous books

1 The rest of the paragraph is found in "Man the Reformer " (p. 241), and is followed by much of the matter on
the next two pages of that lecture.

parts of a preëstablished harmony, fatal, unalterable, and do not go behind Dante and Shakspear, much less behind Moses, Ezekiel, and St. John. But man is critic of all these also, and should treat the entire extant product of the human intellect as only one age, revisable, corrigible, reversible by him.

We have more traditions than the most resolute skeptic has yet interrogated or even guessed. How few cosmogonies have we. A few have got a kind of classical character, and we let them stand, for a world-builder is a rare man. And yet what ghosts and hollow, formless, dream-gear these theories are; how crass and inapplicable; how little they explain; what a poor handful of facts in this plentiful universe they touch. Let me see. — Moses, Hesiod, Egyptian lore of Isis and Osiris, Zoroaster, Menu — with these few rude poems, or extracts from rude poems, the nations have been content when any clever boy, black or white, has anywhere interrupted the stupid uproar by a sharp question, "Would any one please to tell me whence I came hither?" To be sure that question is contrary to the rules of good society in all countries. For society is always secondary, not primary, and delights in secondaries. It is gregarious and parasitic and loves to lay its egg like the cow-troopial in a nest which other birds have built, and to build no nest itself. Absolute truths, previous questions, primary natures, Society loathes the sound of and the name of. " Can you not as well say Christ as say truth?" it asks. "Who are you, child, that you must needs ask so many questions? See what a vast procession of your uncles and aunts who never asked any. Can't you eat your dinner and read in the books? besides, I hate conversation, it makes my head ache." But if the urchin has wild eyes, and can neither be coaxed nor chidden into silence, and cares not a pin for the Greeks and Romans, for art or antiquity, for Bible or Government, for politics or money, and keeps knocking soundly all night at the gate, then at last the good world condescends to unroll for him these solemn scrolls as the reports of the Commissioners from the East, from the South, from the North and the West, to whom his question had been formerly referred. If the poor lad got no answer before, he has got none now. — What birth do these famous books of Genesis reveal? Do they explain so much as the nest of a bluebird or the hum of a fly? Can they tell him the pedigree of the smallest effect?

Can they detect the virtue of the feeblest Cause? Can they give him the least hint of the history of the eyes he has worshipped, or disclose his relations to the summer brook and the waving corn? And yet every man is master of the whole Fact, and shall one day find himself so.

May 25.[1]

In the golden age men did not lay up property for their children, for the marriages were equal and the children abler than their parents.

In the golden age men did not study the song of the bird by writing down, with Nuttall, the notes in awkward syllables, *che*, *che*, *che*, etc., but the chaste and simple hermit found himself intelligent of the song by the love in his own heart. Neither did they know too much of bird or beast, and peep after them; but treating them brotherly and greatly, they without pains saw through their being.

In the golden age a brave pleasure was not purchased too dearly, like a poet's day, by many leaden days; but every joy was embosomed in joys like a lupine in the woods.

People wish to be settled. It is only as far

1 Mr. Emerson's birthday.

as they are unsettled that there is any hope for them. You admire this tower of eternal granite defying the assault of ages. Yet a little waving hand built this huge wall.[1] . . .

Criticism is timid. . . . When shall we dare to say, only that is poetry which cleanses and mans me?

Hate this childish haste to print and publish; for the hours of light come like Days of Judgment at last, and cast their glory backward, forward, above, below. Then, poor child, all the folly stands confessed in thy scrolls and detaches itself from the true words.

By help of tea, tea was renounced.

I went to the circus. . . . One horse brought a basket in his teeth, picked up a cap, and selected a card out of four. All wonder comes of showing an effect at two or three removes from the cause. Show us the two or three steps by which the horse was brought to fetch the basket,

[1] The rest of the passage occurs in " Circles " (*Essays*, First Series, pp. 302, 303), and is followed by the passage beginning, " In the thought of tomorrow," etc. (p. 305).

and the wonder would cease. But I and Waldo
were of one mind when he said, "It makes me
want to go home." [1]

A pleasant walk and sail this fine afternoon
with George Bradford. I threatened by way of
earnest-penny in this absorbing Reform to renounce beef and the Daily Advertiser. There is
ever a slight suspicion of the burlesque about
earnest, good men. It is very strange, but we
flee to the speculative reformer to escape that
same slight ridicule.

I think it ought to be remembered in every
essay after the Absolute Criticism that one circumstance goes to modify every work of literature, this, namely, that books are written generally by the unmagnetic class of mankind, by
those who have not the active faculties, and who
describe what they have never done. This circumstance must certainly color what they say
of character and action.

May 28.

At Bartol's, our club was enriched by Ed-

[1] The story is not all told here. It was when the painted
clown began his fooleries that the little boy said, "Papa, the
funny man makes me want to go home," and Mr. Emerson
always cherished this evidence of his refinement.

ward Taylor's presence. I felt in a higher degree the same happiness I have formerly owed to that man's public discourses, the exhilaration and cheer of so much love poured out through so much imagination. For the time, his exceeding life throws all other gifts into deep shade, "philosophy speculating on its own breath," taste, learning and all,—and yet how willingly every man is willing to be nothing in his presence, to share this surprising emanation, and be steeped and ennobled by the new wine of this eloquence. He gives sign every moment of a certain prodigious nature. No man instructs like him in the power of man over men. Instantly you behold that a man is a Mover,—to the extent of his being, a Power, and in contrast with the efficiency thus suggested, our actual life and society appears a dormitory. We are taught that earnest, impassioned action is most our own, and invited to try the deeps of love and wisdom, —we who have been players and paraders so long. And yet I think I am most struck with the *beauty* of his nature. This hard-featured, scarred and wrinkled Methodist, whose face is a system of cordage, becomes whilst he talks a gentle, a lovely creature—the Amore Greco is not more beautiful.

In conversation we pluck up the eternal Ter-
mini which bound the common of Silence.[1]

Old Age. — Sad spectacle that a man should
live and be fed that he may fill a paragraph
every year in the newspapers for his wonderful
age, as we record the weight and girth of the
Big Ox or Mammoth Girl. We do not count
a man's years until he has nothing else to count.

What can we do in dark hours? We can abstain. In the bright hours we can impart.

Reform. — The world accuses the Scholar of
a tendency to idealism. And why tends he
thither? he loves the warm sun and the magnetic person as well as they, but finding that
your facts and persons are grown unreal and
phantastic by reason of the vice in them, he nears
that most real world of Ideas within him, and
aims to recruit and replenish nature from that
source. Let ideas obtain and establish their
sway again in society, let life again be fair and
poetic, and we shall gladly be objective, lovers,
citizens and philanthropists.

1 The rest of this long passage on this subject is printed in
" Circles " (*Essays,* First Series, pp. 310, 311).

The books of men of genius are divers or dippers. When they alight on the water, they soon disappear, but after some space they emerge again.[1] Other books are land-birds which, falling in the water, know well that their own safety is in keeping at the top, they flutter and chirp and scream, but if they once get their heads under they are drowned forever.

May 30.

Wrote letters yesterday by "British Queen" to John Sterling and Richard Monckton Milnes.[2]

Was it Æsop or Epictetus who, being sold for a slave at the market, cried out to all comers, "Who'll buy a master?" I should like to buy or hire that article. My household suffers from too many servants. My cow milks me. A rope of sand for Asmodeus to spin I cannot find.[3] Now if so many dollars as I could amass would fetch the good husband or gardener who would tell

1 This thought appears in verse in "The Poet" (see *Poems*, Appendix, pp. 309, 310).

2 Who was reviewing Mr. Emerson's writings in England.

3 Asmodeus is mentioned in the book of Tobit in the Apocrypha, and in the Talmud. This image, the keeping a troublesome demon occupied with sand-ropes, occurs in "Behavior" (*Conduct of Life*), and in "Resources" (*Letters and Social Aims*).

me what I ought to do in garden and barnyard, would summon me out to do it, even with a little compulsion, when I resisted, — that would put me well.

May 31.

We can never see Christianity from Christendom; but from the pastures, from a boat in the pond, from the song of a starling, we possibly may. Cleansed by the elemental light and wind, steeped in the sea of beautiful forms which the field offers us, we may chance to cast a right glance back upon biography. We must be great to see anything truly. Our weak eyes make goblins and monsters. But man thyself, and all things unfix, dispart, and flee. Nothing will stand the eye of a man, — neither lion, nor person, nor planet, nor time, nor condition. Each bullies us for a season; but gaze, and it opens that most solid seeming wall, yields its secret, receives us into its depth and advances our front so much farther on into the recesses of being, to some new frontier as yet unvisited by the elder voyagers. And yet alas for this infirm faith, this will, not strenuous, this vast ebb of a vast flow! I am God in nature, I am a weed by the wall.

Has the naturalist and the chemist learned his craft who has explored the gravity of atoms and the elective affinities?[1] . . .

The use of literature is to afford us a platform whence we may command a view of our present life.[2] . . .

June 1.

The Buddhist expresses the true law of hospitality when he says, "Do not flatter your benefactors." The bread that you give me is not thine to give, but mine when the great order of nature has seated me today at your table. Do not let me deceive you by my thanks into the notion that you are aught but the moderator of the company for the hour, though you call yourself rich man and great benefactor, perhaps.

The capital or stock of man our estimates always overlook; it is not set down in any invoice. Ruined! are you? Have you not earth and water? Have you not gravity, chemistry, love, cause and effect, time, fate, men? Do not all these

1 Here follows the analogy that all that belongs to men comes to them. See "Circles" (*Essays*, First Series, p. 314; also end of second motto to "Compensation").

2 The rest of the paragraph is found in "Circles" (p. 312).

circulate through you, and you through them?
What in God do you whimper for? What else
wouldst thou have, O child?

A personal influence is an *ignis fatuus.*[1] . . .

Our American letters are, we confess, in the
optative mood.[2] . . .

The swallow over my window ought to weave
that straw in his bill through all my web also of
speculations.

Standing. — All men have learned one use of
their feet, — to go; but another use, — to stand,
— few have learned. We lean upon a wall, on a
book, on a man. Is it not strange, too, that, in
French, there should be no word for *stand?* Is it
that the Frenchman knows only a leaning and
referred existence, and cannot stand?

1 This paragraph is found in " Nominalist and Realist "
(*Essays*, Second Series, p. 229), except that there the names
of Washington and Franklin are substituted for Dr. Channing
and Garrison in the Journal.

The next entry is that on the Greek sculpture having all
melted away (" Circles," p. 302).

2 The rest of the passage occurs in " The Transcendentalist "
(*Nature, Addresses, and Lectures,* p. 342).

All great men have written proudly, nor cared to explain. They knew that the intelligent reader would come at last, and would thank them. So did Dante, so did Machiavel. What else has Goethe done in this hated *Meister?* [1] . . .

Bat and Ball.—Toys, no doubt, have their philosophy, and who knows how deep is the origin of a boy's delight in a spinning top? In playing with bat-balls, perhaps he is charmed with some recognition of the movement of the heavenly bodies, and a game of base or cricket is a course of experimental astronomy, and my young master tingles with a faint sense of being a tyrannical Jupiter driving spheres madly from their orbit.

June 4.

Self-reliance sanctifies the character, for whoso is of that habit does not gossip or gad; is not betrayed by excess of sympathy into trifles, but ignores what he should ignore.

In looking at pictures, you must stop soon. You may see one or two, but, after turning over

1 The long criticism of Goethe follows, first printed in the *Dial*, which may be found in "Thoughts on Modern Literature" (*Natural History of Intellect*, pp. 329–333).

seven or eight, you see no more. And when you do chance to see one, bid it good-bye, you will never see it again.

Waldo says, "The flowers talk when the wind blows over them." My little boy grows thin in the hot summer, and runs all to eyes and eye-lashes.

June 11.

Who has more self-repose than I masters me by eye and manner, though he should not move a finger; who has less is mastered by me with the like facility.

I finish this morning transcribing my old essay on Love, but I see well its inadequateness. I, cold because I am hot, — cold at the surface only as a sort of guard and compensation for the fluid tenderness of the core, — have much more experience than I have written there, more than I will, more than I can write. In silence we must wrap much of our life, because it is too fine for speech, because also we cannot explain it to others, and because somewhat we cannot yet understand. We do not live as angels, eager to introduce each other to new perfections in our brothers and sisters, and frankly avowing our delight in each new trait of character, in the magic of each new eyebeam, but that which passes for love in the world gets official, and instead of embracing, hates all the divine traits that dare to appear in other persons. A better and holier society will mend this selfish cowardice, and we shall have brave ties of affection, not petrified by law, not dated or ordained by law to last for one year, for five years, or for life; but drawing their date, like all friendship, from itself only; brave as I said, because innocent, and religiously abstinent from the connubial endearments, being a higher league on a purely spiritual basis. This nobody believes possible who is not good. The good know it is possible. Cows and bulls and peacocks think it nonsense.

Sunday, *June* 14.

Tranquil and great sailed or slept the clouds today in the northeastern horizon as I walked and mused on my friends. I thought, why should I play with the young people this game of idolatry?[1] . . .

The great man will not be prudent in the popular sense.[2] . . .

1 The rest of the passage is found in "Circles" (*Essays*, First Series, p. 307).

2 The rest is found in "Circles" (pp. 314, 315).

Our countrymen love intoxication of some sort. One is drunk with whiskey, and one with party, and one with music, and one with temper. Many of them fling themselves into the excitement of business until their heads whirl and they become insane. But ambition is for strong heads, not for weak ones. It is droll that the Laurel in our woods is called Lamb-kill, and even the larger laurel Spoon-hunt.

Dr. Abernethy's rule for diet to the invalid was, "Live on sixpence a day and earn it."

It is a superstition to insist on vegetable, or animal, or any special diet. All is made up at last of the same chemical atoms. The Indian rule shames the Graham rule. A man can eat anything, — cats, dogs, snakes, frogs, fishes, roots and moss. All the religion, all the reason in the new diet is, that animal food costs too much. We must spend too much time and thought in procuring so varied and stimulating diet and then we become dependent on it.

Admiral Keppel said of the Scots, "They are excellent soles, but terrible bad upper-leathers."

June 18.

Edmund Hosmer taught me by his generous care of my interest, in the matter of the cow, that the part which each man should look at in driving a bargain with his neighbor is his neighbor's interest, and not his own.

What right have I, because there is money in my pocket, to furnish me with toys and comforts on an idle or wicked day? If I have not in my conscience earned a right to what I desire, let me not buy; the money is not mine, though it lie in my drawer.

A gay and pleasant sound is that of the whetting of the scythe. A summer sound. Yet, as my mowing Dr. Bugbee replied to me, what is there more lonesome and sad than the sound of a whetstone or rifle when it is too late in the season to make hay?

Diet. — I like Henry Thoreau's statement on Diet: " If a man does not believe that he can thrive on board nails, I will not talk with him."

Ye rogues, my company eat turf and talk not;
Timber they can digest and fight upon 't;
Old mats, and mud with spoons, rare meats, — your
        shoes, slaves,

Dare ye cry out of hunger and those extant?
Suck your sword hilts, ye slaves, if ye be valiant,
Honor will make them marchpane.

BEAUMONT AND FLETCHER, *Bonduca.*

June 19.

On the 17th June the mercury stood at 96°
in the shade at 1 o'clock P. M.

(From E)

June 21.

Can we not be so great as to offer tenderness
to our friend, — tenderness with self-trust? Why
should we desecrate noble and beautiful souls by
intruding on them? [1]

[In his letter to Mr. S. G. Ward, of June 22,
Mr. Emerson wrote: "I am just now finish-
ing a Chapter on Friendship (of which one of
my lectures last winter contained a first sketch)
on which I would gladly provoke a commentary.
I have written nothing with more pleasure, and
the piece is already indebted to you, and I wish
to swell my obligations. If I like it when I read
it over, I shall send it to you." [2]]

[1] Here follows the long passage, thus beginning, found in
"Friendship" (pp. 210, 211).
[2] *Emerson's Letters to a Friend.*

Of a man we should ask, Has he invented a Day? an action? every act, every moment, every mode of being he showed us? Alas! often he invented nothing: he was a speaking ape; he did not rise to an original force, — not for an instant, — and we are hardly able in thought to detach him from his body, and we talk well pleased of having put him in the ground.

A lover does not willingly name his mistress; he speaks of all persons and things beside; for she is sacred. So will the friend respect the name of his friend. Name him for pride and he is already ceasing to be yours. The base lover is piqued by the natural dignity of the virgin which overawes and disconcerts him, do what he can. He desires to possess her, that so, at least, he may recover his tongue and his behaviour in her presence. Thus he steals the victory, which he ought greatly to earn by raising his own character to the royal level of hers. The same ethics hold of thy friendship. Worship the superiorities of thy friend. Wish them not less by a thought, but hoard and tell them all: they are the uplifting force by which you are to rise to new degrees of rank.

Self-reliance applied to another person is reverence, that is, only the self-respecting will be reverent.

June 24.

The least sense of power, as the newly attained skill to make corn grow, or to row a boat, raises the spirits, and from it a new wisdom immediately flows.

We love to paint those qualities which we do not possess.[1] . . . I, who suffer from excess of sympathy, proclaim always the merits of self-reliance.

Channing's poetry and ———'s have a certain merit which unfits them for print. They are proper manuscript inspirations, honest, great, but crude. They have never been filed or defiled for the eye that studies surface: the writer was not afraid to write ill; had a great meaning too much at heart to stand for trifles, and wrote lordly for his peers alone. This is the right poetry of hope, no French correctness, but Hans Sachs and Chaucer rather.[2]

We are never so fit for friendship as when we cease to seek for it, and take ourselves to friend.

[1] See "Prudence," opening paragraph (*Essays*, First Series).

[2] Yet Channing's refusal to mend his verses was a trial to his friend.

Once I was in love, and whenever I thought of what should happen to me and the maiden, we were always travelling; I could not think of her otherwise. Again I was in love, and I always painted this maiden at home.

Why should I wish to do or write many things, since any one well done contains my history? Why should I see with regret the felling of the woods, and fear lest my son should lack the lessons his father drew from nature, when I have known myself entertained by a single dewdrop or an icicle, by a liatris, or a fungus, and seen God revealed in the shadow of a leaf? Nature is microscopically rich, as well as cumulatively. Why should I covet a knowledge of new facts and skills, when I know that they are only other illustration of laws daily playing before my eyes?[1] . . .

Each new fact I look upon, as this steaming of hot air from the wide fields upward, is a new word that I learn and hive, well assured the use for it will come presently, as the boy learns with good hope his Latin vocabulary. What is it

[1] Several sentences, thus introduced are in "The Poet" (*Essays*, Second Series, p. 32).

to be a poet? What are his garland and singing robes?[1]

(From a loose sheet)

Originality. — Talent without character is friskiness. The charm of Montaigne's egotism, and of his anecdotes, is, that there is a stout cavalier, a seigneur of France, at home in his château, responsible for all this chatting. Now suppose it should be shown and proved that the famous "Essays" were a *jeu d'esprit* of Scaliger, or other scribacious person, written for the booksellers, and not resting on a real status, picturesque in the eyes of all men, would not the book instantly lose almost all its value?

(From E)

Montaigne. — The language of the street is always strong. What can describe the folly and emptiness of scolding like the word *jawing?* I feel too the force of the double negative, though clean contrary to our grammar rules. And I confess to some pleasure from the stinging rhetoric of a rattling oath in the mouth of truckmen and teamsters. How laconic and brisk it is by the side of a page of the *North American Review.*

---

1 The rest of the passage is in "Poetry and Imagination" (*Letters and Social Aims*, p. 36).

Cut these words and they would bleed; they are vascular and alive; they walk and run. Moreover they who speak them have this elegancy, that they do not trip in their speech. It is a shower of bullets, whilst Cambridge men and Yale men correct themselves and begin again at every half sentence.[1]

I know nobody among my contemporaries except Carlyle who writes with any sinew and vivacity comparable to Plutarch and Montaigne. Yet always this profane swearing and bar-room wit has salt and fire in it. I cannot now read Webster's speeches. Fuller and Browne and Milton are quick, but the list is soon ended. Goethe seems to be well alive, no pedant. Luther too.

Nature. — I think I must do these eyes of mine the justice to write a new chapter on Nature. This delight we all take in every show of night or day, of field or forest or sea or city, down to the lowest particulars, is not without sequel, though we be as yet only wishers and

---

1 Sentences from the above paragraph occur in the chapter "Art and Criticism," printed only in the Centenary Edition (*Natural History of Intellect*, p. 288), and in "Montaigne" (*Representative Men*, p. 168).

gazers, not at all knowing what we want. We are predominated herein, as elsewhere, by an upper wisdom, and resemble those great discoverers who are haunted for years, sometimes from infancy, with a passion for the fact or class of facts in which the secret lies which they are destined to unlock, and they let it not go until the blessing is won. So these sunsets and starlights, these swamps and rocks, these birdnotes and animal forms off which we cannot get our eyes and ears, but hover still, as moths, round a lamp, are no doubt a Sanscrit cipher covering the whole religious history of the universe, and presently we shall read it off into action and character. The pastures are full of ghosts for me, the morning woods full of angels. Now and then they give me a broad hint. Every natural fact is trivial until it becomes symbolical or moral.

How I am touched and gladly surprised by hearing the chemist propounding the theory of heat, viz., that every particle of matter is in constant revolution round its own axis, slower or faster, alike in a column of smoke, or a stone jug. Increase the heat, and you accelerate the revolution by separating the atoms; increase the heat again, and the particles acquire such freedom that the form is changed to liquid; increase the heat again, and they gyrate in larger circles and become gas and (as we call it) die, or enter into the universe again. Shall we not apply the moral for our consolation to these men of fire and these men of stone that sit around us? The dullest lump is yet amenable to this law of fire. Warm him with love, and he too must begin to feel new freedom, and presently to become luminous with thought and glowing with affection.

No inventory is complete. The farmer does not count the sparrows and bobolinks that breed in his meadow in his account of his poultry, and the selectmen assess on me no tax for my use of the woods, where I find first sight, second sight, and insight. The asters and eupatoriums are maturing their leaves and buds, the gerardia is getting ready its profuse flowers, warning me that my book should be ended before their capsules are filled with seed.

Now for near five years I have been indulged by the gracious Heaven in my long holiday in this goodly house of mine, entertaining and entertained by so many worthy and gifted friends, and all this time poor Nancy Barron, the mad-woman, has been screaming herself hoarse at the Poor-house across the brook and I still hear her whenever I open my window.

The Best are never demoniacal or magnetic, but all brutes are. The Democratic Party in this country is more magnetic than the Whig. Andrew Jackson is an eminent example of it. Van Buren is not, — but his masters are, who placed him in his house. Amos Kendall and Woodbury. Mr. Hoar is entirely destitute of this element. It is the prince of the power of the air. The lowest angel is better. It is the height of the animal; below the region of the divine.

June 29.

Today at the Cliff we held our *Villegiatura.* I saw nothing better than the passage of the river by the dark clump of trees that line the bank in one spot for a short distance. There Nature charmed the eye with her distinct and perfect painting. As the flowing silver reached that point, it darkened, and yet every wave cel-ebrated its passage through the shade by one sparkle. But ever the direction of the sparkles was onward, onward. Not one receded. At one invariable pace, like marchers in a procession to solemn music, in perfect time, in perfect order, they moved onward, onward, and I saw the warning of their eternal flow.[1] Then the rock seemed good to me. I think we can never afford to part with Matter. How dear and beautiful it is to us![2] . . . The flowers lately, especially when I see for the first time this season an old acquaintance, a gerardia, a lespedeza, have much to say on Life and Death. "You have much discussion," they seem to say, "on Immortality. Here it is: Here are we who have spoken nothing on the matter." And as I have looked from this lofty rock lately, our human life seemed very short beside this ever renewing race of trees. Your life, they say, is but a few spinnings of this top. Forever the forest germinates: forever our solemn strength renews

[1] This was the view southwestward from Fairhaven Hill, and the same sight may be seen now (1911) on a sunny afternoon, when ripples gleam out of the dark reflection of the pines on the opposite bank.

> Far seen, the river gleams below,
> Tossing one sparkle to the eyes.
> I catch thy meaning, wizard wave
> The river of my Life replies.

[2] From "Peter's Field" (*Poems*, p. 364). Continued in "Nature" (*Essays*, Second Series, p. 171).

its knots and nodes and leaf-buds and radicles. Grass and trees have no individuals, as man counts individuality. The continuance of their race is immortality; the continuance of ours is not. So they triumph over us; and when we seek to answer, or to say something, the good tree holds out a bunch of green leaves in your face, or the woodbine five graceful fingers, and looks so stupid-beautiful, so innocent of all argument, that our mouths are stopped and Nature has the last word.

A notice of modern literature ought to include (ought it not?) a notice of Carlyle, of Tennyson, of Landor, of Bettina, of Sampson Reed.

We chide the citizen because, with all his honest merits, he does not conceive the delicacies and nobility of friendship, but we cannot forgive the poet if he does not substantiate his fine romance by the municipal virtues of justice, fidelity and pity.

The simplest things are always better than curiosities. The most imposing part of this Harrison celebration of the Fourth of July in

Concord, as in Baltimore, was this ball, twelve or thirteen feet in diameter, which, as it mounts the little heights and descends the little slopes of the road, draws all eyes with a certain sublime movement, especially as the imagination is incessantly addressed with its political significancy. So the Log Cabin is a lively watchword.[1]

I think we must give up this superstition of company to spend weeks and fortnights. Let my friend come and say that he has to say, and go his way. Otherwise we live for show. That happens continually in my house, that I am expected to play tame lion by readings and talkings to the friends. The rich live for show: I will not.

(From F)

July 6.

It is very easy to represent a farm, — which in most hours stands for the organization of the

---

[1] The political campaign for Harrison and Tyler was at its height, with its watchword, —

> " Tippecanoe
> And Tyler too," —

its Log Cabin, and "Hard Cider"; and it is said that even venerable citizens helped to "keep the ball a-rollin'!" up gravest needs of man, — as a poor trifle of a few pea-vines, turnips and a henroost.

> The name of death was never terrible
> To him that knew to live.
>
> *Double Marriage.*

The rankest materialist must build his house, — no matter how deep and square on blocks of granite he lays his foundations, — must set it last, not on a cube, but on a mass which rounds off to an almost perfect sphericity and lies floating in soft air and goes spinning away thousands of miles the hour, — he knows not whither.

Heroism made easy is that for which people are always seeking to find some recipe. But God saith, It shall not be. Heroism means difficulty, postponement of praise, postponement of ease, introduction of the world into the private apartment, introduction of eternity into the hours measured by the sitting-room clock.

We see the river glide below us, but we see not the river that glides over us and envelopes city streets or along country roads. Mr. Emerson was pleased with the symbolism, and alludes to it in "The Poet" (*Essays*, Second Series, p. 16).

us in its floods.[1] A month ago, I met myself, as I was speeding away from some trifle to chase a new one, and knew that I had eaten lotus and been a stranger from my home all this time. And now I see that, with that word and thought in my mind, another wave took me and washed my remembrance away, and only now I regain myself a little and turn in my sleep.

Increase our Faith.— Practical faith we have not. Let us believe in unity until our actions are united. Let us not believe, as we do now, in means and medicines, but in our action recognize that the world flows ever from the soul, and, instead of attacking the toothache or the dyspepsia, or any other symptom, raise the aim of the man, — and toothache and indigestion, cramp and croup, pain and poverty, will disappear in troops, as now in troops these calamities come.

It makes no difference what a saintly soul eats or drinks; let him eat venison or roots, let him drink champagne or water, nothing will harm him or intoxicate or impoverish him; — he eats as though he eat not, and drinks as though he drank not. But we are skeptics over our dinner-table, and therefore our food is noxious and our

1 Compare, in the *Poems*, the " Two Rivers."

bodies fat or lean. Looking as we do at means, and not at grand ends, being in our action disunited, our bodies have come to be detached also from our souls, and we speak of our health.

Our expense is almost all for conformity. It is for cake that we all run in debt, — not the intellect, not the heart, not beauty, not worship, that costs us so much.[1] . . .

The ends of Society will appear; now, we live solitary; men of genius, being apart, half snore and spend their time in girding at society for not thinking as they do, but do nothing to convert it. But these hermits, when brought near and acting directly on each other, shall sleep no more, but be put on their mettle.

I have better servants than taste and attention to polish and adjust my relations to my friend, namely, Time and Fate, or the prevailing harmony of nature. These harden, these attemper and polish my relation to the smoothness and finish that will weather all accidents and stand for eternity.

1 The rest of this long passage in "Man the Reformer" (*Nature, Addresses, and Lectures*, pp. 244, 245).

Our quarrel with every man we meet is not with his kind, but with his degree. There is not enough of him; that is the only fault.

We pretend to our friends that we do not need direct communication — neither actions, nor gifts, nor conversation — to keep their influence whole. But it is a pretence.

It makes a great difference as to the force of any sentence whether there be a man behind it or no.[1] . . .

Filled with her love, may I be rather grown
Mad with much heart than idiot with none.
                                        DONNE.

No Spring nor Summer's beauty hath such grace
As I have seen in one Autumnal face.
                                        DONNE.

There is always this impassable gulf between the men of the world and the men of principle. The practical man hears the theory or the advice of the prophet and laughs or is angry at such raving. For he says, Look at the tools with which this world of yours is to be built.[2] . . .

1 The rest of the paragraph is found in "Goethe" (*Representative Men*, p. 282).

2 For the rest of this paragraph, see "Man the Reformer" (*Nature, Addresses, and Lectures*, p. 252).

A man of principles is nature. But the worlds-man cannot once withdraw his eye from his actual neighbors, or cease to believe that you are dreaming of making them do the deeds of angels, their wills remaining as they are.

Someone said to me, "But if we were simpler should we not talk more of ourselves?" I reply, Not of this named and mortal me. When I have talked of myself, I am presently punished by a sense of emptiness, and, as it were, flatulency, that I have lost all the solemnity and majesty of being.

Love and intellect, each in their perfection become the other. Love is beautiful in action, but can never be spoken without some cloying or fulsomeness until it becomes quite pure, like Fénelon's, or St. John's. Less than a Saint, it is but a goody.

Osman. — Osman was a poor and simple man and was neglected in his youth, being esteemed a person of narrow intellect, whilst his brothers were able and ambitious men. His features were mean and irregular, his form was unproportioned, his movement was awkward and he had a bass, unmu-

sical voice. He was, therefore, never instructed
in any trade or art, but was put to household
chares, and later, to aid a small farmer in his
husbandry. Not until he reached the middle age
was he at all remarked, but left in obscurity,
served last, and no notice taken of what he said.
Osman thought no more of himself than others
thought of him, but acquiesced in this low and
menial place which was assigned to him, and
with great respect to others who, he doubted
not, had superior parts, and with great good
humor, did all that was required of him. Much
serving made him very meek and very useful.
He could turn his hand to any ordinary work,
and do it well. As there was no one to serve
him, he learned to serve himself, and, as happens where a man waits on his own wants, he made
them very few. He was social and affectionate in
his nature as a dog, and readily talked with all
who availed themselves of his hands to end some
odd piece of work. Nobody dreamed of being
either civil or of assuming any airs before poor
Osman, so that he knew everybody for just what
they were, as they all knew him. Although
affable enough, he really spoke little during the
day, and was of a grave, quiet deportment. In
his youth he had been sickly, but these long

habits of light daily work established his constitution, and when he had counted thirty-five years
he began to be much considered for his probity
and his wisdom. Everybody who knew him liked
him, as if he had been their brother. The farmers
said he worked like the rain or the wind, which
need nobody's aid, but do their charity themselves. He had a strong memory, and having
neither selfishness nor learning to cloud it, it
might be depended on like a thermometer or a
sun-dial. He was temperate in his diet, and, on
account of his ill-health in childhood, had been
bred to prefer a vegetable nutriment.[1]

You must steadily prefer your own native
choices against all argument and all example.
(If you stand by them, they will certainly bring
you out safe into reality and excellence, at last,

[1] Mr. Emerson, through many years, occasionally diverted
himself by writing the traits and adventures of the imagi-
nary Osman, many of which — by no means all — were auto-
biography. In this instance Osman's experiences are humbler
and more practical and he has a social gift, the absence of
which in himself Mr. Emerson used sometimes to deplore,
and yet often said, "Solitude is my doom, and my strength."
But in many other cases Osman appears a sublimed self, a sort
of ideal man.

unworthy and contemptible as they may now seem.) Defend them against the multitude, and defend them against the wise. He who told you of them is wiser than the colleges, wiser than the holy men.

Cannot you, instead of contributing to Bunker Hill Monument, or the Charity Lecture, learn to serve yourself? Society is full of infirm, lazy people who are incessantly calling on others to serve them.[1] . . .

Whenever I read Plutarch or look at a Greek vase I am inclined to accept the common opinion of the learned that the Greeks had cleaner wits than any other people in the Universe. But there is anything but Time in my idea of the antique. A clear and natural expression by word or deed is that which we mean when we love and praise the antique. In society I do not find it; in modern books seldom; but the moment I get into the pastures I find antiquity again. Once in the fields with the lowing cattle, the birds, the trees, the waters and satisfying outlines of the landscape, and I cannot tell whether this is Tempe, Thessaly and Enna, or Concord and Acton.

[1] The long paragraph thus beginning is printed in "Man the Reformer" (pp. 246, 247).

What is so bewitching as the experiments of young children on grammar and language? The purity of their grammar corrects all the anomalies of our irregular verbs and anomalous nouns. They carry the analogy thorough. *Bite* makes *bited*, and *eat*, *eated* in their preterite. Waldo says there is no "telling" on my microscope, meaning no name of the maker, as he has seen on knife-blades, etc. "Where is the wafer that *lives* in this box?" etc. They use the strong double negative which we English have lost from our books, though we keep it in the street. " I wish you would not dig your leg," [1] said Waldo to me. Ellen calls the grapes "green berries," and when I asked, "Does it rain this morning?" she said, "There 's tears on the window."

But what is so weak and thin as our written style today in what is called literature? We use ten words for one of the child's. His strong speech is made up of nouns and verbs, and names the facts. Our writers attempt by many words to suggest, since they cannot describe.

There is a difference between one and another

---

[1] The suggestion of a possible unhandiness with the spade implied was long thrown up against Mr. Emerson in the domestic circle.

moment of life in their authority and subsequent effect.[1] . . .

Waldo asks if the strings of the harp open when he touches them !

As for walking with Heraclitus, said Theanor, I know nothing less interesting; I had as lief talk with my own conscience.[2]

You fancy the stout woodchopper is thinking always of his poverty, compared with the power and money of the capitalist who makes the laws. I will not deny that such things have passed through his mind, for he has been at a Caucus with open mouth and ears. But now he is thinking of a very different matter, for his horse has started in the team and pulled with such a spring that he has cleared himself of the harness — hames and all — and he, as he mends the broken tackle, is meditating revenge on the horse. " Well, you may draw as fast as you like up the mile hill; You shall have enough of it, if you like to draw, Damn you !" — the horse, that is, and not the capitalist.

1 Here follows the opening passage of " The Over-Soul."
2 Possibly a reflection on a recent walk with the sad and austere Jones Very.

Let every man shovel out his own snow, and the whole city will be passable.

Read a translation of the *Prometheus Chained*. . . . It seems to be the first chapter of History of the Caucasian Race.

It is, besides, a grand effort of Imagination. Imagination is not good for anything unless there be enough. That a man can make a verse or have a poetic thought avails not, unless he has such a flow of these that he can construct a poem, a play, a discourse. Symmetry, proportion we demand, and what are these but the faculty in such intensity or amount as to avail to create some whole? . . .

There is no irregular, auroral shooting in Æschylus, but calm, equal strength; in Plato most of all men. But Æschylus treated of Greek subjects. What should we treat? The Poet in 1840 and in New England, what does that signify?

Who shall quarrel with literature as unnatural and pedantic? What is a man but Nature's final success in self-explication?[1] . . .

1 The rest of the passage is printed in "Art" (*Essays*, First Series, p. 352).

Prometheus is noble. He is the Jesus of the old mythology, and plays with much exactness the part assigned to the Nazarene in the Genevan theology. He is the friend of man. Stands between the *unjust justice* of the Eternal Father and the frail race of man; then readily suffers all things on their account.[1] It is a pity he should be so angry. Anger continued and indulged becomes spleen. A single burst of indignation is heroic enough, but a persisting expression of it degenerates fast into scolding. Prometheus scolds, and Eteocles in "The Seven"; and Electra in Sophocles.

[Here is the first thought of the quatrain "Memory":—]

> The dreams of the night
> Are shadows of the thoughts of the day
> And thy fortunes as they befall thee
> Are the ghosts of thy will,
> The children of thy spiritual body.

[Here it begins to take form:—]

> Let the dreams of night recall
> Shadows of the thoughts of day

1 The last two sentences occur in "History" (*Essays*, First Series).

And see thy fortunes as they fall
Each secret of thy will betray.

[The finished poem is in quatrain, "Memory," *Poems*, p. 295.]

(From E)

July 10.

Nature invites to repose, to the dreams of the Oriental sages; there is no petulance, no fret; there is eternal resource and a long to-morrow, rich and strong as yesterday. We should be believers in Necessity and Compensation, and a man would have the air of pyramids and mountains, if we forsook our petulant mates and kept company with leaves and waters.

[Here follows the opening passage of "History" in the first volume of *Essays*, about the uniform recognition of gentility in the elder dramatists.]

All diseases run into one, Old Age. We grizzle every day.[1] . . .

1 Here follows the passage thus beginning in "Circles" (*Essays*, First Series, p. 319).

" Faith and Hope "; these words are used in the church as if they were as unmeaning as Selah and Amen.[1] . . .

July 13.

The Graces of sleep not three, but three thousand; no man is ever awkward, ever sly, canting, or otherwise false whilst asleep. Only one thing they do amiss, the sleepers,— sn—e.

Carlyle shall make a statement of a fact, shall draw a portrait, shall inlay nice shades of meaning, shall play, shall insinuate, shall banter, shall paralyze with sarcasm, shall translate, shall sing a Tyrtæan song, and speak out like the Liturgy, or the old English Pentateuch, all the secrets of manhood. This he shall do and much more, being an upright, plain-dealing, hearty, loving soul of the clearest eye and of infinite wit, and using the language like a protean engine which can cut, thrust, saw, rasp, tickle or pulverize as occasion may require. But he is not a philosopher: his strength does not lie in the statement of abstract truth. His contemplation has no wings.

He exhausts his topic. There is no more to be said when he has ended. He is not suggestive.

1 The rest of the passage is in " Man the Reformer " (*Nature, Addresses, and Lectures,* pp. 249, 250).

Every new history that shall be written will be indebted to him. It will not be stately, but will go now into the street and sitting-room and the ale-house and kitchen.

What he has said shall be proverb; nobody shall be able to say it otherwise.

It does not need that a poem should be long. Life, I have written above, is unnecessarily long, and poems are, as we learn when we meet with a line

"In the large utterance of the early gods,"

or Milton's "beyond the manhood of a Roman recovery," moments of personal relation, smiles and glances how ample. Borrowers of eternity, they are. Some mellow, satisfying sessions we have in the woods in cool summer days.

Education aims to make the man prevail over the circumstance. The vulgar man is the victim of the circumstance. In the stagecoach, he is no man, but a tedious echo of each new accident of the journey, absorbed in the heat, in the cold, in the bad horses, in the fret of a crowded carriage. In the rain, he can think of nothing but that he wishes it would stop; in the drought, he waits till the rain fall; in debt, he postpones his being until his note is paid; in dull company, until the company is gone; and never rallies himself to sink the circumstance and these encroaching trifles into their proper nothingness before the energies, the sweetness, the riches, the aspirations of a human mind.

The common man has no time. One circumstance delivers him over to another. Now he cannot be, for he is travelling. Then he cannot be, for he has arrived in a new place; now, because he labors, then because he rests.

July 15.

Behaviour. — I like to see a man or a woman who does not palter or dodge, whose eyes look straight forward, and who throws the wisdom he or she has attained into the address and demeanor. What blandishment in the pronouncing of your name. Your name is commended to your ear ever after it has been spoken by a man like Otis or a woman like A—— W——.

July 17.

"Sunshine was he
On the cold day
And when the dogstar raged
Shade was he and coolness,"

says the Arabic poet translated by Goethe
(vol. vi).

The hottest weather, so long continued, that
I have noticed; — redhot noons, — the mercury
reaches 93° in the shade — the crops are drying
up. Let me be coolness and shade. The gardener floods his vines with water out of the well,
sure that the good Rain will in the year fill his well,
though it delays to feed his garden. So is he
"coolness and shade." In the winter he covers
his asparagus with straw, and in the cold spring
his young tomatoes with glass. So is he to them
"Sunshine," but I weep with the weepers and
fear with the fearers and am not a tower of defence, but a foolish sympathy.

July 18.

96° Fahrenheit. What right has the man of
genius to retreat from work and indulge himself?
The popular literary creed is: "I am a man of
genius; I ought not therefore to labor." But
genius is the power to labor better and more
availably than others. Deserve thy genius. Exalt
it. The good, the illuminated sit apart from the
rest, censuring their dulness and vices, as if they
thought that by sitting very grand in their chairs
the very brokers and congressmen would see the
error of their ways and flock to them. But the

good, the wise must learn to act and carry this very salvation to the brokers and the demagogues which they need.

July 26.

Beside the self-repose which manners express the Alleghanies seem to me the drifting sand.

Tantalus is but a name for you and me. *Transmigration* of Souls: that too is no fable.[1] . . .

Go to the forest, if God has made thee a poet, and make thy life clean and fragrant as thy office.

> True Bramin in the morning meadows wet
> Expound the Vedas in the Violet.

Thy love must be thy art. Thy words must spring from love, and every thought be touched with love. Only such words fly and endure. There are two ways of speaking: one, when a man makes his discourse plausible and round by considering how it sounds to him who hears it, and the other mode when his own heart loves and so infuses grace into all that drops from him. Only this is living beauty. Nature also must

1 See the passages thus beginning in " History " (*Essays*, First Series, p. 32); and these, in the Journal, are followed by the image of Proteus, in " History," p. 31.

teach thee rhetoric. She can teach thee, not only to speak truth, but to speak it truly. Only poets advance with every word. In most compositions there is one thought which was spontaneous, and many which were added and abutted: but, in the true, God writes every word.

Shall the scholar write every word in his mind, — how bad as well as how good he is,— like Rabelais and Goethe? or shall he be an eclectic in his experience? Is there not then cant when he writes more chastely than he speaks if you should hear his whispers? Let him then mend his manners and bring them within the mark which he trusts his pen to draw.

I cannot . . . travel with parties of pleasure or with parties of business. The frivolous make me lonely. Neither can I well go to see those whom I esteem, unless they also esteem me, for I can bestow my time well at home. I have thus found that I cannot visit any one with advantage for a longer time than one or two hours.

Love should always make glad, never gloomy. We talked of *Deerbrook* in these days, Miss Martineau's novel. It is a good book to read: there is much observation and much heroism in

it, and people will be the better for reading. Yet
the author is of that class who mistake a private
for an universal experience and venture to record it. A perfectly sound nature may accept all
his own experience for the uniform experience
of mankind, and so record it. But a man par-
tially sick may not. If he record his morbid passages they will be accepted only by the sick for
general truths. To the well they will be offensive.

It is a delicate matter—this offering to stand
deputy for the human race, and writing all one's
secret history colossally out as philosophy. Very
agreeable is it in those who succeed: odious in
all others.

It is good when one of these heroines remarks
that all martyrdoms looked mean when they happened. It is ill when she suggests to a third person
what her lover must have suffered on her account,
for of that a woman can never say little enough.

Character makes an overpowering present, a
cheerful, determined hour which fortifies all the
company by making them see that much is possible and excellent that was not thought of.[1] . . .

1 The rest of the paragraph is in " Circles " (*Essays*, First
Series, p. 321).

July 31.

Talked with Elizabeth Hoar last night on Landor whom I read for a few minutes yesterday. We agreed that here was a book of Sentiment (*Pericles and Aspasia*), sentiment in the high and strict sense that one could hardly read it without learning to write with more elegance. The inimitable neatness of the sentences and then the wonderful elegance of suppression and omission which runs through it might polish a dunce.

A newspaper in Providence contains some notice of Transcendentalism, and deplores Mr. Emerson's doctrine that the argument for immortality betrays weakness. The piece seems to be written by a woman. It begins with round sentences, but ends in Ohs and Ahs. Yet cannot society come to apprehend the doctrine of One Mind? Can we not satisfy ourselves with the fact of living for the Universe, of lodging our beatitude therein? Patriotism has been thought great in Sparta, in Rome, in New England even, only sixty years ago. How long before *Universalism* or Humanity shall be creditable and beautiful?

[The first number of the *Dial* was issued in July, Miss Fuller being the literary editor, and Mr. George Ripley the business manager. Mr. Cabot, in his Memoir of Emerson, volume ii, pp. 403-409, gives an interesting account of the *Dial* and Mr. Emerson's relation to it.]

And now I think that our *Dial* ought not to be a mere literary journal, but that the times demand of us all a more earnest aim. It ought to contain the best advice on the topics of Government, Temperance, Abolition, Trade, and Domestic Life. It might well add to such compositions such poetry and sentiment as now will constitute its best merit. Yet it ought to go straight into life with the devoted wisdom of the best men and women in the land. It should — should it not? — be a degree nearer to the hodiurnal facts than my writings are. I wish to write pure mathematics, and not a culinary almanac, or application of science to the arts.

Every history in the world is my history. I can as readily find myself in the tragedy of the Atrides as in the Saxon Chronicle, in the Vedas as in the New Testament, in Æsop as in the

Cambridge platform, or the Declaration of Independence. The good eye, the good ear, can translate fast enough the slight varieties of dialect in these cognate tongues. The wildest fable, the bloodiest tragedy is all too true.[1]

Let fiery hope nourish you in the angelic region. — ZOROASTER.

August 9.

A man of genius or a work of love or beauty cannot be compounded like a loaf of bread by the best rules, but is always a new and incalculable result like health. Do not therefore rattle your rules in our ears, we must behave and do as we can. The *ancients*, the *antique;* I see in all that is excellent under that name somewhat near to me. It is the genius of the European family. The discovery and the planting of America and the American Revolution and mechanic arts are Greek, Attic, Antique, in this sense, as much as the Parthenon or the *Prometheus Chained*. I can easily see in our periodical literature, for example, a diffused and weakened Athens.

---

1 The third page in " History " (*Essays*, First Series) is much to this effect.

The poet cannot spare any grief or pain or terror in his experience: he wants every rude stroke that has been dealt on his irritable texture. I need my fear and my superstition as much as my purity and courage to construct the glossary which opens the Sanscrit of the world.[1]

C. delights in the beauty of clouds, the shining people of the sky; and I felt that they, with their hard and fawn-coloured surface and broad edges of glory, were the flowers of the upper element, and the fittest symbols in nature of an illustrious life. The clock by which we measured our stay in this field of outsight and upsight was one of these splendid clouds which lost its large dimension and nearly faded in the air whilst we stood.

[Here follow some verses from a poem by Mrs. Wells:—

"My own delighted, laughing boy," etc.]

---

1 Compare "The Poet":—

> Thanked Nature for each stroke she dealt;
> On his tense chords all strokes were felt;
> The good, the bad, with equal zeal
> He asked, he only asked, to feel.

Poems, Appendix, p. 316.

Love makes us little children. We never attain a perfect sincerity in our speech except we
feel a degree of tenderness. And lovers use the
monosyllables and the short and pretty speech
of children. Love takes off the edges and the
ceremonies of speech and says Thee to one,
and you to many.

Do not *say* things. What you *are* stands over
you the while and thunders so that I cannot
hear what you say to the contrary.

(From F)

August 16.

After seeing Anna Barker I rode with Margaret [Fuller] to the plains. She taxed me, as
often before, so now more explicitly, with in-
hospitality of Soul. She and C. would gladly be
my friends, yet our intercourse is not friendship, but literary gossip. I count and weigh, but
do not love. They make no progress with me,
but however often we have met, we still meet
as strangers. They feel wronged in such relation and do not wish to be catechised and criti-
cised. I thought of my experience with several
persons which resembled this : and confessed
that I would not converse with the divinest per-

son more than one week. M. insisted that it was no friendship which was thus so soon exhausted, and that I ought to know how to be silent and companionable at the same moment. She would surprise me, — she would have me say and do what surprised myself. I confess to all this charge with humility unfeigned. I can better converse with George Bradford than with any other. Elizabeth Hoar and I have a beautiful relation, not however quite free from the same hardness and fences. Yet would nothing be so grateful to me as to melt once for all these icy barriers, and unite with these lovers. But great is the law. . . . But this survey of my experience taught me anew that no friend I have surprises, none exalts me. This then is to be set down, is it not? to the requirements we make of the friend, that he shall constrain us to sincerity, and put under contribution all our faculties.

I read in Rabelais that Thomas Walleys, an English Dominican friar, published a book in which he spiritualized Ovid's Metamorphoses.

August 18.

Gaston de Foy was a pleasant man, but he was no saint. He said he had little faith in prayer, and never used it but for one class of persons, namely, his benefactors. Their chance, he thought, of any return for their kindness was so small, that, if there was a possibility that a prayer should be effective, these ought to have the benefit of it.

September 1.

One fact the fine conversations of the last week — now already fast fading into oblivion — revealed to me, not without a certain shudder of joy, that I must thank what I am, and not what I do, for the love my friends bear me. I, conscious all the time of the shortcoming of my hands, haunted ever with a sense of beauty which makes all I do and say pitiful to me, and the occasion of perpetual apologies, assure myself to disgust those whom I admire, — and now suddenly it comes out that they have been loving me all this time, not at all thinking of my hands or my words, but only of that love of something more beautiful than the world, which, it seems, being in my heart, overflowed through my eyes or the tones of my speech. Gladly I learn that we have these subterranean, — say rather, these supersensuous channels of communication, and that spirits can meet in their pure upper sky without the help of organs.[1]

Granted that my theory of the world born out of the side of man is a false one, and that it is pedantry in us helpless and ignorant people to make this vast pretension, when we do not want a dollar the less, not a yard of cloth, not a loaf of bread less than other people who do not talk of their relations to the universe. Well, you do not talk of such things, but only of stocks and streets, the Cunard boats, and the politics of the new administration. Well, it is just as much pedantry in you not to talk of that which really is there, and makes the dignity of politics and trade, viz., your relation to the world. Each was a half view; granted. But one half view was nobler, and therefore truer, than the other.

September 5.

The objection to the popular Christianity is a philosophical one. It is in the nature of things that persons can never usurp in our minds the

[1] The poem which serves as the motto of "Manners" (*Essays*, Second Series), beginning, —

> Grace, Beauty and Caprice
> Build this golden portal,

was written in these days.

authority of Ideas. Every man is at last, in his purest thought, an Idealist, and puts all persons at an infinite distance from him, as every moralist is at last in his purest thought an Optimist. Now Christianity goes to invest persons with the rights of Ideas, which is absurd.

Mr. W. remarked that in the courts of justice it seemed to him that the judge, the jurors, and the witnesses, mutually tried each other.

September 8.

We should be very rich if we could speak the truth, for, since that is the law of our progress, in proportion to our truth we should coin the world into our words. If we, dear friends, shall arrive at speaking the truth to each other we shall not come away as we went. We shall be able to bring near and give away to each other the love and power of all the friends who encircle each of us, and that society which is the dream of each shall stablish itself in our midst, and the fable of Heaven be the fact of God.

(From E)

I went into the woods.[1] I found myself not

1 The substance of what follows occurs in "Nature" (*Essays*, Second Series, pp. 192, 193 and 198), but it seemed so attractive in its personal form that it is given here.

wholly present there. If I looked at a pine-tree or an aster, *that* did not seem to be Nature. Nature was still elsewhere: this, or this was but outskirt and far-off reflection and echo of the triumph that had passed by and was now at its glancing splendor and heyday, — perchance in the neighboring fields, or, if I stood in the field, then in the adjacent woods. Always the present object gave me this sense of the stillness that follows a pageant that has just gone by.

It was the same among men and women as among the silent trees. Always it was a referred existence; always an absence; never a presence and satisfaction. Thus I was looking *up to Nature*.

Afterwards, I was for a season active, devout and happy, and, passing through the woods, the trees and asters looked *up at me*. There was I, and there were these placid creatures around, and the virtue that was in them seemed to pass from me into them.

Nature is thus a differential thermometer detecting the presence or absence of the divine spirit in man.

September 10.

It was the oblique and covert way in which the good world was training to the discovery that a man must have the saintly and the poetic character; that by taste he must worship beauty, and by love of the invisible, if it were only of Opinion, must carry his life in his hand to be risked at any instant.

September 11.

Would it not be a good cipher for the seal of the Lonely Society which forms so fast in these days, Two porcupines meeting with all their spines erect, and the motto, " We converse at the *quill's* end " ?

I would labour cheerfully in my garden every day, if when I go there it did not seem trifling. It is so easy to waste hours and hours there in weeding and hoeing, and as pleasant as any other play, that I can impute to you no merit that you labour. Nothing is easier or more epicurean.

Character establishes itself and blows a grand music through whatever instrument, though it were an oat pipe or a cornstalk viol. If love be there, I shall find it out, though I only see you eat bread or make some trifling but necessary request. The reform that is ripening in your mind for the amelioration of the human race I shall find already in miniature in every direction to the domestics, in every conversation with the assessor, with your creditor, and with your debtor.

The monastery, the convent, did not quite fail, many and many a stricken soul found peace and home and scope in those regimens, in those chapels and cells. The Society of Shakers did not quite fail, but has proved an agreeable asylum to many a lonesome farmer and matron. The College has been dear to many an old bachelor of learning. What hinders, then, that this Age, better advised, should endeavor to sift out of these experiments the false, and adopt and embody in a new form the advantage?

September 12.

Sarah Clarke,[1] who left us yesterday, is a true and high-minded person, but has her full proportion of our native frost. She remarked of the *Dial*, that the spirit of many of the pieces was lonely.

(From F)

September 16.

The questions which have slept uneasily a long time are coming up to decision at last.

1 Miss Clarke, the sister of Rev. James Freeman Clarke, was a friend of Mr. Emerson's from the days when she was one of the scholars in the school in Boston kept by his brother William and himself. She devoted her life to art.

Men will not be long occupied with the Christian question, for all the babes are born infidels; they will not care for your abstinences of diet, or your objections to domestic hired service; they will find something convenient and amiable in these. But the question of property will divide us into odious parties. And all of us must face it and take our part. A good man now finds himself excluded from all lucrative employments.[1] . . . There is so much to be done that we ought to begin quickly to bestir ourselves. Lidian says well that it is better to work on institutions by the sun than by the wind. As Palmer remarked, that he was satisfied what should be done must proceed from the concession of the rich, not from the grasping of the poor. Well then, let us begin by habitual imparting. . . . Let my ornamental austerities become natural and dear. The State will frown; the State must learn to humble itself, repent and reform.

A sleeping child gives me the impression of a traveller in a very far country.

1 Here follows the passage beginning thus in "Man the Reformer" (*Nature, Addresses, and Lectures*, p. 234).

"He can toil terribly," said Cecil of Sir Walter Raleigh. Is there any sermon on Industry that will exhort me like these few words? These sting and bite and kick me. I will get out of the way of their blows by making them true of myself.

The conversion of a woman will be the solidest pledge of truth and power.

(From E)

September 17.

I am only an experimenter.[1] Do not, I pray you, set the least value on what I do, or the least discredit on what I do not, as if I had settled anything as true or false. I unsettle all

1 Though printed in "Circles" it seems well to let this whole passage stand here, among the notes of critical years in Mr. Emerson's life. As appears in these pages, all usage in private and public relations was brought to the bar of new theories of independent, self-reliant action. Reforms were rampant, everything questioned by the young radicals who came to Mr. Emerson for backing. To his private journal he confided, not his settled opinion, but the mood or aspect of the moment.

The solid virtue in his character and his good sense carried him safe through the spiritual breakers into serene, happy, and helpful life.

things. No facts are to me sacred, none are profane; I simply experiment, an endless seeker, with no past at my back.

Every hour has its morning, noon, and night.

Alcott said, "Who are these people? there is not one of them whom I cannot offend in any moment."

Ah vast Spirit! I weary of these egotisms. I see well how puny and limitary they are.

September 19.

Life is emblematic to every good mind and is equally profound, let the circumstances or emblems be a kingdom, a camp, a college, or a farm. It is the angle which the object makes to the eye which imports.[1] . . .

September 20.

Can we not trust ourselves? Must we be such coxcombs as to keep watch and ward over our noblest sentiments even, lest they also betray us, and God prove a little too divine? Dare we never say, This time of ours shall be the era

[1] The remainder of the passage is found in "History" (*Essays*, First Series, p. 39); and, as to mere transfer of idolatry, in "Character" (*Essays*, Second Series, p. 98).

of Discovery? These have been the ages of darkness. Wide Europe, wide America lieth in night, turneth in sleep. The morning twilight is grey in the East: the Columbuses, the Vespuccis, the Cabots of moral adventure are loosening their sails and turning their bowsprits to the main. Men have never loved each other. See, already they blush with a kindness which is pure, and Genius, the Inventor, finds in Love the unknown and inexhaustible continent. Love which has been exclusive shall now be inclusive. Love, which once called Genius proud, — behold, they have exchanged names. Love, which was a fat, stupid Shaker, or a maudlin Methodist, or Moravian, now is a brave and modest man of light, sight, and conscience. God hateth the obscure. On the last day, as on the first day, he still says, Let there be Light. Where there is progress in character, there is no confusion of sentiment, no diffidence of self, but the heart sails ever forward in the direction of the open Sea.

Perhaps after many sad, doubting, idle days, days of happy, honest labor will at last come when a man shall have filled up all the hours from sun to sun with great and equal action, shall lose sight of this sharp individuality which

contrasts now so oddly with nature, and, ceasing
to regard, shall cease to feel his boundaries, but
shall be interfused by nature and shall [so] inter-
fuse nature that the sun shall rise by his will as
much as his own hand or foot do now; and his
eyes or ears or fingers shall not seem to him the
property of a more private will than the sea and
the stars, and he shall feel the meaning of the
growing tree and the evaporating waters with
a more entire and satisfactory intelligence than
now attends the activity of his organs of sense.

Every glance we give to the landscape predicts a better understanding, by assuring us we
are not right now. When I am quite alone in
my morning walk, if I lift up my eyes, the
goodly green picture I see seems to call me hypocrite and false teacher — me who stood innocently there with quite other thoughts and had
not spoken a word. For the landscape seems
imperatively to expect a clear mirror, a willing
reception in me, which, not finding, it lies ob-
trusive and discontented on the outward eye,
unable to pass into the inward eye, and breeds
a sense of jar and discord.

The most trivial and gaudy fable, Kehama,
Jack Giant-killer, Red Ridinghood, every grand-
am's nursery rhyme contains, as I have elsewhere

noted, a moral that is true to the core of the world. It is because Nature is an instrument so omnipotently musical that the most careless or stupid hand cannot draw a discord from it. A devil struck the chords in defiance, and his malevolence was punished by a sweeter melody than the angels made.

There is no leap—not a shock of violence throughout nature. Man therefore must be predicted in the first chemical relation exhibited by the first atom. If we had eyes to see it, this bit of quartz would certify us of the necessity that man must exist as inevitably as the cities he has actually built.

September 24.

Cities and coaches shall never impose on me again.[1] . . .

September 26.

You would have me love you. What shall I love? Your body? The supposition disgusts you. What you have thought and said? Well, whilst you were thinking and saying them, but not now. I see no possibility of loving anything but what now is, and is becoming; your cour-

1 See "Man the Reformer" (*Nature, Addresses, and Lectures*, p. 230).

age, your enterprise, your budding affection, your opening thought, your prayer, I can love, — but what else?

"Paradise," said Mahomet, "is under the shadow of swords."[1]

It is easier to distinguish the sweet apples from the sour in a multitude of human faces than it is in an orchard. In the good old women one detects at sight the saccharine principle.

Perhaps it is folly, this scheming to bring the good and like-minded together into families, into a colony. Better that they should disperse and so leaven the whole lump of society.

I will not be chidden out of my most trivial native habit by your distaste, O philosopher, by your preference for somewhat else. If Rhetoric has no charm for you, it has for me and my words are as costly and admirable to me as your deeds to you. It is all pedantry to prefer one thing that is alive to another thing which is also alive. The mystery of God inhabits a nursery tale as deeply as the laws of a state, or the heart of a man.

1 Here other quotations from Simon Ockley's *History of the Saracens* are given.

The Soul. — Do not indulge this rabble of second thoughts. Cast yourself on the hour and the man that now is, nor be so much a *littérateur* as to cast about already for the benefits that shall accrue from this new fact to art. So is your literature thievish.

The Whigs meet in numerous conventions and each palpitating heart swells with the cheap sublime of magnitude and number.[1] . . .

In the history of the world the doctrine of Reform had never such scope as at the present hour.[2] . . . Nations will not shield you, neither will books. . . . Vain is the cumulative fame of Tasso, of Dante, — vain the volumes of Literature which entrench their sacred rhymes, if the passing mystic has no glance for them, not a motion of respect. Alas! too surely their doom is sealed.

Lidian gives the true doctrine of property when she says, "No one should take any more than his own share, let him be ever so rich."

1 For the rest, see "Self-Reliance" (*Essays*, First Series, p. 88).

2 See the second page of "Man the Reformer."

(From F)

September 30.

Yes, I resent this intrusion of a few persons on my airy fields of existence. Shall our conversation when we meet, O wife, or sister Elizabeth, still return, like a chime of seven bells, to six or seven names, nor we freemen of nature be able long to travel out of this narrowed orbit? Rather I would never name these names again. They are beautiful, and therefore we have given them place; but they affront the sun and moon and the seven stars when they are remembered once too often. Beware of Walls; let me keep the open field. Douglas-like, I had rather hear the lark sing than the mouse cheep. Yet though I start like a wild Arab at the first suspicion of confinement, I have drank with great joy the contents of this golden cup hitherto. With great pleasure I heard George Bradford say, that this romance[1] took from the lustre of the Reformers who alone had interested him before. I felt that what was private and genuine in these rare relations was more real, and so more public and

[1] This seems to refer to the engagement and coming marriage of Samuel G. Ward and Anna H. Barker. The friendship with both had made the past year very happy to Mr. Emerson.

universal than conventions for debate, and these weary speculations on reform. The call of a heart to a heart, the glad beholding of a new trait of character, — freedom (derived from the friendly presence of a fellow being) to do somewhat we have never done, — freedom to speak what I could never say, — these are discoveries in the Ocean of life, they are Perus, Brazils, and Plymouth Rocks, which to me were the more inestimable that I had been such a homekeeper, and knew nothing beyond the limits of my own forest and village fair.

(From E)

October 5.

On Saturday evening I attended the wedding of Samuel Gray Ward and Anna Hazard Barker at the house of Mr. Farrar in Cambridge. Peace go with you, beautiful, pure, and happy friends, — peace and beauty and power and the perpetuity and the sure unfolding of all the buds of joy that so thickly stud your branches.

October 7.

Circumstances are dreams, which, springing unawares from ourselves, amuse us whilst we doze and sleep, but when we wake, nothing but causes can content us. The life of man is the true romance which, when it is valiantly conducted and all the stops of the instrument opened, will go nigh to craze the reader with anxiety, wonder and love. I am losing all relish for books and for feats of skill in my delight in this Power.

Do not accuse me of sloth. Do not ask me to your philanthropies, charities, and duties, as you term them;—mere circumstances, flakes of the snow-cloud, leaves of the trees;—I sit at home with the cause, grim or glad. I think I may never do anything that you shall call a deed again. I have been writing with some pains essays on various matters as a sort of apology to my country for my apparent idleness. But the poor work has looked poorer daily, as I strove to end it. My genius seemed to quit me in such a mechanical work, a seeming wise — a cold exhibition of dead thoughts. When I write a letter to anyone whom I love, I have no lack of words or thoughts. I am wiser than myself and read my paper with the pleasure of one who receives a letter, but what I write to fill up the gaps of a chapter is hard and cold, is grammar and logic; there is no magic in it; I do not wish to see it again. Settle with yourself your accusations of me. If I do not please you, ask me not to please you, but please yourself. What you call my indolence, Nature does not accuse; the twinkling leaves, the sailing fleets of water-flies, the deep sky, like me well enough and know me for their own. With them I have no embarrassments, diffidences or compunctions; with them I mean to stay. You think it is because I have an income which exempts me from your day-labor, that I waste (as you call it) my time in sun-gazing and star-gazing. You do not know me. If my debts, as they threaten, should consume what money I have, I should live just as I do now: I should eat worse food, and wear a coarser coat, and should wander in a potato patch instead of in the wood, — but it is I, and not my twelve hundred dollars a year, that love God.

We feel that every one of those remarkable effects in landscape which occasionally catch and delight the eye, as, for example, a long vista in woods, trees on the shore of a lake coming quite down to the water, a long reach in a river, a double or triple row of uplands or mountains seen one over the other, and whatever of the like has much affected our fancy, must be the rhetoric of some thought not yet detached for the conscious intellect.

Virtues are among men rather the exception than the rule. They do what is called a good action, . . . much as they would pay a fine in expiation of daily non-appearance on parade.[1] . . .

I do not give you my time, but I give you that which I have put my time into, namely, my letter, or my poem, the expression of my opinion, or better yet an act which in solitude I have learned to do.

October 17.

A newspaper in a grave and candid tone censures the *Dial* as having disappointed the good expectation of our lovers of literature. I read the paragraph with much pleasure; for the moment we come to sense and candor I know the success of the *Dial* is sure. The *Dial* is poor and low and all unequal to its promise: but that is not for you to say, O Daily Advertiser! but

1 The rest of the paragraph beginning thus is in "Self-Reliance" (*Essays*, First Series, pp. 52, 53). The very next entry in the Journal seems a reflex wave after this misprizing of actions.

for me. It is now better *after your manner* than anything else you have; and you do not yet see that it is, and will soon see and extol it. I see with regret that it is still *after your manner*, and not after mine, and that it is something which you can praise.

"The saugh[1] kens the basket-maker's thumb."
— *Scottish Proverb.*

Go, dear soul,[2] and be scales and sword, an accusation and a terror, a Day of doom and a Future to the world lying in wickedness. The fat and easy and conceited world, the cultivated and intellectual world, takes the prophets by the hand and affects to be of their part and to deplore the general ignorance and sensuality which rejects and derides them. Yet it takes a secret pleasure in the fact that this reprobation reaches not to them, instead of finding therein conviction of sin. This derision is a laurel on the brows of the prophets. This same prelacy, these men of intellect on good terms with the world, are glad to speak the sheriff and the constable fair, for they do not yet see what height and

1 Sallow, willow.
2 Perhaps addressed to the *Dial.*

what debasement are, and that the only asylum and protection and lordship and empire is virtue. . . . Why should I use a means? Why should I not rush grandly to ends?

Yesterday George and Sophia Ripley, Margaret Fuller and Alcott discussed here the Social Plans.[1] I wished to be convinced, to be thawed, to be made nobly mad by the kindlings before my eye of a new dawn of human piety. But this scheme was arithmetic and comfort: this was a hint borrowed from the Tremont House and United States Hotel; a rage in our poverty and politics to live rich and gentlemanlike, an anchor to leeward against a change of weather; a prudent forecast on the probable issue of the great questions of Pauperism and Poverty. And not once could I be inflamed, but sat aloof and thoughtless; my voice faltered and fell. It was not the cave of persecution which is the palace of spiritual power, but only a room in the Astor House hired for the Transcendentalists. I do not wish to remove from my present prison to a prison a little larger. I wish to break all

1 The project of the Community at Brook Farm. Mr. Emerson gives some account of it in " Life and Letters in New England " (*Lectures and Biographical Sketches*).

prisons. I have not yet conquered my own house. It irks and repents me. Shall I raise the siege of this hencoop, and march baffled away to a pretended siege of Babylon? It seems to me that so to do were to dodge the problem I am set to solve, and to hide my impotency in the thick of a crowd. I can see too, afar,—that I should not find myself more than now,—no, not so much, in that select, but not by me selected, fraternity. Moreover, to join this body would be to traverse all my long trumpeted theory, and the instinct which spoke from it, that one man is a counterpoise to a city,—that a man is stronger than a city, that his solitude is more prevalent and beneficent than the concert of crowds.

[Here follow two pages of fine extracts from Beaumont and Fletcher's *Tragedy of Bonduca*, of which three are here given.]

There's not a blow we gave since Julius landed
That was of strength and worth, but, like records,
They file to after ages. Our registers
The Romans are for noble deeds of honour.

Ten times a night
I have swum the rivers when the stars of Rome

Shot at me as I floated, and the billows
Tumbled their watery ruins on my shoulders;
Charging my battered sides with troops of agues.

                              Ye fools,
Ye should have tied up Death first, when ye con-
        quered;
Ye sweat for us in vain else. See him here,
He's ours still, and our friend, laughs at your
        pities,—
And we command him with as easy rein
As do our enemies.

(From F)

The old experiences still return. Society,
when I rarely enter the company of my well-
dressed and well-bred fellow creatures, seems
for the time to bereave me of organs, or perhaps only to acquaint me with my want of them.
The soul swells with new life and seeks expression with painful desire, but finds no outlets.
Its life is all incommunicable. . . . Those who
are to me lovely and dear seem for that reason
to multiply and tighten the folds that envelop
and smother my speech.

A dandy, Mr. Pacelise calls, "*Un mille-fleur
Judas.*"

We need not do what we cannot. Let us go

home again, home to our faculties and work. Is one associate or one circumstance unfit, — in heaven I should hapless be. We use our virtues and their fruits as purchase money for our vices. Not when I walk in the streets of the city, am I earning the prayers of the young and the highly endowed, but when I forget Boston and London in rapid obedience to the Invisible and Only Spirit. Not by wealth and a city consequence, not by skill in arts, nor by the manners and address of the world could I, if these I had, bring any gift worthy of the acceptance of friendship, but only out of a deeper magazine whereto cities and bankers cannot go, out of the realms of an unbroken peace, of loving meditation, of a habitual conversation with nature. Out of these alone can I draw the natural gold which universally commands all other goods and is the royal currency of the world. I love spring water and wild air, and not the manufacture of the chemist's shop. I see in a moment, on looking into our new *Dial*, which is the wild poetry, and which the tame, and see that one wild line out of a private heart saves the whole book.

I wrote C. S. this afternoon that it is not we, but the elements, the destinies and conscience

that make places and hours great, they the omnipresent : — and if we will only be careful not
to intrude or chatter, the least occasion and the
domestic hour will be grand and fated. We shall
one day wonder that we have ever distinguished
days, or circumstances, or persons.

Life only avails, not the having lived.[1] . . .
Neither thought nor virtue will keep, but must
be refreshed by new today. But we get forward
by hops and skips. Shall we not learn one day
to walk a firm continuous step?

As nothing will keep, but the soul demands
that all shall be new today, therefore we reject
a past man, or a past man's teaching. Who is
Swedenborg? A man who saw God and Nature
for a fluid moment. His disciples vainly try to
make a fixture of him, his seeing, and his teaching, and coax me to accept it for God and
Nature.

Dependence is the only poverty.

October 18.
Dr. Ripley is no dandy, but speaks with the
greatest simplicity and gravity. He preaches

1 Continued in "Self-Reliance" (p. 69).

however to a congregation of Dr. Ripleys; and Mr. Frost to a supposed congregation of Barzillai Frosts;[1] and Daniel Webster to an assembly of Websters. Could this belief of theirs be verified in the audience, each would be esteemed the best of all speakers.

The acquirer of riches seems to me a man of energy, good or bad; the inheritor of riches to be a man lamed by his shoes, crippled by his crutches. The respect I pay to a poet I understand; the respect I pay to a ship-master, to a farmer, and to every other conqueror of men, or things; but the deference I pay to wealth is opaque, and not transparent, is a superstition.

"What news?" asks man of man. The only teller of news is the poet.[2]

The history of Jesus is only the history of every man written large. The names he bestows on Jesus belong to himself, — Mediator, Redeemer, Saviour.

1 Dr. Ripley's successor as pastor of the First Church in Concord.

2 See "Poetry and Imagination" (*Letters and Social Aims*, p. 30).

The whole history of the weather is a wonderfully fit symbol of the varying temper of man. The moment we come into such relations to any man or woman that we need consider their moods, we shall find the whole vocabulary of a seaman at our tongue's end.

Captain Pitts did not take out his handkerchief for nothing. The church rung with his echo.[1]

I went to a wedding and the Lord said unto me, Where is thy gift? And I looked and saw that there was nothing in my hand. Then I thought of twenty useful or shining things, and remembered all that I had seen in the goldsmiths' windows, and considered what book or gem or trinket I might buy. But the Lord said, These are no gifts for thee: thy desire for these is not *thy* desire, but the desire of others in thee: thou lookest back on the city and the people thou hast left. The gift which thou canst bring, and which thy friends expect at thy hands, is that which thou alone canst offer them. I

---

1 Mr. Emerson used to say that the old-fashioned nasal trumpeting, "the service of the Lord with trumpets in the sanctuary," seemed to have gone by. It perhaps sometimes uttered comments which church decorum forbade the worshipper to put into words.

have given thee a door of the soul to keep: go in thereat, and hearken to what shall be told thee, for never man stood in that place before; and then go to thy friends, and tell them what thou knowest. They shall hearken to thee and shall forget all that they ever knew. My word is all that thou shalt carry in thy hand.

I ought not to allow any man to feel that he is rich in my presence.[1] . . .

October 23.

And must I go and do somewhat if I would learn new secrets of self-reliance? for my chapter is not finished. But self-reliance is precisely that secret, — to make your supposed deficiency redundancy. If I am true, the theory is, the very want of action, my very impotency, shall become a greater excellency than all skill and toil.

And thus, O Circular philosopher, you have arrived at a fine pyrrhonism.[2] . . .

The good Swedenborg was aware, I believe, of this wonderful predominance and excess of

1 See "Man the Reformer" (*Nature, Addresses, and Lectures*, p. 249).

2 See "Circles" (*Essays*, First Series, p. 317).

the saccharine principle in nature, and noticed that the hells were not without their extreme satisfactions.[1]

October 24.

Osman. — Fine people do not prosper with me: they are so curious and busy with their Claude Lorraine glasses, and their exploration of doves' necks and peacocks' tails, that they do not see the road, and the poor men who go up and down on it. I must go back to my cabin and be, as before, the trusty associate of those whom a household and highway experience has chastened, and be the poor man's poet. I should break with one fine person, if I did not see, or think I see, my own rude self hid under the present mask.

What is the Fall, what Sin, what Death, with this eternal Soul under us originating benefit forever more? We learn that Time is infinite, if we learn nothing else. Is not that lesson enough for a life? The power is dazzling, terrific, inaccessible in its impulses. It now calmly shows us in parts the circle of elements which it also shows us are radically one.

1 In the passage in "Circles" (pp. 317, 318) Swedenborg's name is not used.

It is rhetoric that takes up so much room: The result of the book is very small and could be written down in a very few lines.

To what purpose should you tell me of your faith, of your happiness, if you do not make me feel that you are at rest and blessed? Jones Very's words were loaded with his fact. What he said, held; was not personal to him; was no more disputable than the shining of yonder sun or the blowing of this south wind. But I do not know that you are looking at universal facts.

The fate of the poor shepherd who, blinded and lost in the snow storm, perishes in a drift within a few feet of his own cottage door, is a faithful emblem of the state of man.[1] . . .

Out of doors, in the snow, in the fields, death looks not funereal, but natural, elemental, even fair. In-doors it looks disagreeable.

The Excess of Direction. — Every promise of the soul has twenty or twenty thousand fulfil-

1 The passage thus introduced is in " The Poet " (*Essays,* Second Series, p. 33).

ments. The soul forever tends to the satisfaction of love. It is the promise of all times and of all the faculties. The first friend the youth finds, he cries, "Lo! the hour is come and the man; the promise is fulfilled." But in a few days he finds that it was only a quasi-fulfilment, that the total, inexhaustible longing is there at his heart still; and is aspiring to grander satisfactions. God will not be confuted nor silenced. God kindled this love in me, made me a burning love. I presently dedicate myself to some single object, and find the love insatiate still. How contradictory and unreasonable, you say. Little careth God; he drives me forth out of my cabin, as before, to love and to love. He tells me not what that is I seek, — whether choirs of beatific power and virtue; or the value of nature shut up in a private form; or the total harmony of the universe. From the beginning this is promised us as the crisis and consummation of life, but no final information is ever afforded us.

I value the poet. I think all the argument and all the learning is not in the Encyclopædia, or the Treatise on Metaphysics, or the Body of Divinity, but in the sonnet and the tragedy. In my daily work, I retrace my old steps and do not believe in remedial force, in the power of change and reform; but some Petrarch or Beaumont and Fletcher, filled with the new wine of their imagination, write me a tale or a dialogue in which are the sallies and recoveries of the Soul; they smite and arouse me with the sharp fife, and I open my eye on my own possibilities. They clap wings to the side of all the solid old lumber of the world and I see the old Proteus is not dead.

What a pity that we cannot curse and swear in good society! Cannot the stinging dialect of the sailors be domesticated? It is the best rhetoric, and for a hundred occasions those forbidden words are the only good ones. My page about "Consistency" would be better written thus: Damn Consistency!

The method of advance in nature is perpetual transformation. Be ready to emerge from the chrysalis of today, its thoughts and institutions, as thou hast come out of the chrysalis of yesterday.

Every new thought which makes day in our souls has its long morning twilight to announce its coming.

I dreamed that I floated at will in the great Ether, and I saw this world floating also not far off, but diminished to the size of an apple. Then an angel took it in his hand and brought it to me and said, "This must thou eat." And I ate the world.

October 26.

Theanor said that he saw too much; that he could no longer live at peace with other men for what he saw and they saw not. He said he went to the house of a man who in a dark and stormy night killed his enemy with a sword; "and I," said Theanor, "through the darkness and the storm, sitting myself by the murderer's hearth, saw him go along the road to his victim's house. I saw the sword and the thrust that reached his heart; then new vision came to my eyes and I saw that the sword had a new length, which he saw not, beyond its visible point, and bent about like a cow's horn, and when the short point struck the sleeping enemy, I saw the elongated invisible point reach far back to his own house, in which I sat, and to the body of his own child. The child started in the adjoining room with a loud wailing, and when the haggard man came back his child was dying with black fever. And another man I knew who solaced himself with voluptuous imaginations, and I saw that every pleasure he seemed to himself to steal from his paramours he was tearing away from the scanty stock of his own life."

When I go into my garden with the spade and dig . . . I discover that I have been defrauding myself all this time in letting others do for me what I should have done with my own hands.[1] . . .

I have a pen and learned eyes and acute ears, yet am ashamed before my wood-chopper, my ploughman and my cook, for they have some sort of self-sufficiency. They can contrive without my aid to make a whole day and whole year; but I depend on them.

Our little romances, into which we fling ourselves with so much eagerness, end suddenly, and we are almost sad to find how easily we can brook the loss. Let us learn at last that the tragedy of other men, of the sufferers in the old world, was as slight and medicable. We are made

[1] Here follows the long passage on the education and manliness given by personal work, found in " Man the Reformer " (p. 337).

for joy and not for pain. We are full of outlets; full of resources; made of means, as the infusories are said to be the genetical atoms of which we are made.

Literature. — O pardon it, for it is the effort of man to indemnify himself.

Air is matter subdued by heat. Order is matter subdued by mind.

It does not help the matter much that you live and write according to Milton, and not according to what cheap contemporary models, what Wordsworth, Carlyle, or Webster, may happen to stand in your sunlight.

November 5.

In nature there is a mystical equality; nothing is low. It costs the exertion of the very highest principle to effect the feeblest function of vegetable life. The total God meets you everywhere in the bract or stipule of the most unobserved weed. The least seed is of new significance to the oldest cherub as well as to the child; but every new thought whose light we drink adds new scores of works of art to the obsolete and unmeaning.

Art is cant and pedantry; it is not practical and moral, that is, if it do not make the poor and uncultivated feel that it addresses them also and brings with it the oracle of Conscience. And I find this power of art in the fact that human power grows with virtue; that virtue transfigures the face into its own glorious likeness, and of course redeems and purifies and beautifies posterity. A grand soul flings your gallery into cold nonsense, and no limits can be assigned to its prevalency and to its power to adorn.

The past combines with the present in every object. You admire the graceful convolutions of the seashell.[1] . . .

The moon keeps its appointment. Will not the good Spirit? Wherefore have we labored and fasted, say we, and thou takest no note? Let him not take note, if he please to hide, — then it were sublime beyond a poet's dreams still to labor and abstain and obey, and if thou canst, *to put the good Spirit in the wrong*.[2] That

[1] The rest of the paragraph is in "The Conservative" (*Nature, Addresses, and Lectures*, p. 300).

[2] This passage may be found in pleasing form in "The Poet" (*Poems*, pp. 319, 320).

were a feat to sing in Elysium, on Olympus, by the waters of life in the New Jerusalem. Yet no thought dawns on me. This morning I woke with a gleam of the true light, but it faded away as the old trifles reappeared. Will it reappear? Yea. I know something of these mysterious approaches of a thought.

Every moment compromises the last; every moment, but not the man. The fountain is always superior to the stream, the life to the phenomena.

Nature delegates her smile to the morning. . . . I was ashamed before the laborer cutting peat in the meadow, though I could well see that his life at last was as superficial as mine, save — if save — that more necessity entered into it and made it sublime. How, then, should I not be ashamed before that pending bulrush into which Nature had flung her soul? Every moment instructs, though we know it not, and call today trivial, for wisdom is so melted and disguised into every form that we know not it is wisdom.[1] . . .

[1] What follows, and the omitted sentence above, are found in the concluding paragraph of "Nature" (*Essays*, Second Series).

It is not irregular hours or irregular diet that make the romantic life. A sylvan strength, a united man, whose character leads the circumstances, and is not led by them, — this makes romance, and no condition.

Calmness is fabulous. The most iron men give to the spiritual eye the impression of leaning, mendicant manners. Calmness is always Godlike.

Funestes are these French novels with their pistols.

A career, say the French, — "*il aurait en des talents, de l'ambition, et une carrière.*" (*Valentine.*)

Circles. — What avail marble brows and inscrutable purposes? Bring in a new man with a truth that commands the last, and the marble brow becomes a rippled wave, the inscrutable purposes are exposed and scattered.

In Boston, at Dr. Jackson's, I saw five or six persons take the nitrous-oxide gas. It looked very much as if the bladder was full of opinions.

When Jesus bade the disciples not tell of this or that, he would say, "The last thing you shall do is to gossip of this; lie low in the Lord's power. Receive this fact into your mind in silence." He had no ways of Prudence, as we call it. The main end to be answered by each man's working is, his own character; and if what you call his imprudence, that is, his directness, thwarts his private ends, it may yet answer this end; then I call it success.

November 21.

Swedenborg exaggerates the circumstance of marriage.[1] . . .

I make my own temptations. If I am clean and sound, the heavens and earth are new and glorious; they are my hands and feet, my willing instruments, my means, my organ, my element, and language. If I am imperfect, everything I touch I turn into an enemy and hurt; I make the bread I eat and the air I inhale a temptation.

It is more elegant to answer one's own needs than to be richly served; inelegant, perhaps, it

1 Here follows the substance of two pages in "Swedenborg" (*Representative Men*, pp. 128, 129).

may look today, and to a few, but elegant forever and to all.

I hear much that is ridiculous in music. You would laugh to know all that passes through my head in hearing a concert. Not having an ear for music, I speculate on the song and guess what it is saying to other people; what it should say to me. It is Universal and seems to hint at communication more general than speech, more general than music also. What mystic obscurities in every breast do these lovesongs accost?

How fast these wrinkles come! Adust complexions with burning eyes.

" Pales filles du Nord! vous n'êtes pas mes sœurs." [1]

The circulation of the waters, the circulation of sap, the circulation of the blood, the immor-

---

1 With regard to complexions Mr. Emerson was rather a fatalist. He would remark on the thick, saddle-leather complexion which, with dark coarse hair and a strong jaw, often marked a Calvinist. He would say of a spirited youth, "Ah, but he has the hopeless adust complexion which augurs no good." The French quotation — its source not given — evidently suggested his Romany Girl's

> Pale Northern girls! you scorn our race,
> You captives of your air-tight halls.

tality of an animal species through the death of
all the individuals, the balance and periods of
planetary motion;—these are works of art,
quick, and eternal. In the presence of these his
[man's] proudest works seem to be the puppets
and scratch-cradles and toy-mills which betray
the incessant instinct of his infant hands.

Whatever is divine will share the self-exist-
ence of God. Every true institution will be self-
existent.

Present a poetic design to people and they will
tear it to mammocks. Yet how subtle an auxiliary
is Nature; I knew a man who learned that his
modes of living were false and mean by looking
at the hill covered with wood which formed the
shore of a small but beautiful lake which he
visited in his almost daily walk. He returned to
his gossips and told them his schemes of reform
and they contradicted and chided and laughed
and cried with vexation and contempt and shook
his confidence in his plans. But when he went
to the woods and saw the mist floating over the
trees on the headland which rose out of the
water, instantly his faith revived. But when he
came to his house, he could not find any words

to show his friends in what manner the beautiful shores of the lake proved the wisdom of his economy. He could not show them the least connexion between the two things. When he once tried to speak of the bold shore, they stared as if he were insane. Yet whenever he went to the place and beheld the landscape his faith was confirmed.

Beauty can never be clutched; in persons and in nature is equally inaccessible.[1] . . . Glory is not for hands to handle.

I shed all influences. A. is a tedious archangel. How few have faith enough to treat a man of genius as an exiled prince of the blood, who must presently come to his own, and it will then appear that it had been best to have been of the same household all the time. *Yet if you have not faith in you, how can I have faith in you?*

Nature ever flows; stands never still. Motion or change is her mode of existence. The poetic eye sees in Man the Brother of the River, and in Woman the Sister of the River. Their life is always transition. Hard blockheads only drive

1 The substance of what follows is in " Nature " (*Essays*, Second Series).

nails all the time; forever remember; which is fixing. Heroes do not fix, but flow, bend forward ever and invent a resource for every moment. A man is a compendium of nature, an indomitable savage; . . . as long as he has a temperament of his own, and a hair growing on his skin, a pulse beating in his veins, he has a physique which disdains all intrusion, all despotism; it lives, wakes, alters, by omnipotent modes, and is directly related there, amid essences and *billets doux*, to Himmaleh mountain chains, wild cedar swamps, and the interior fires, the molten core of the globe.

Over every chimney is a star; in every field is an oaken garland, or a wreath of parsley, laurel, or wheat-ears. Nature waits to decorate every child.

> Diamond sparks and beryl beads,
> Carbuncles and pearls in seeds,
> Drops of amber, golden thread
> From the rock unravellèd, —
> Prize not these, thou blessed child,
> Be they trampled and defiled;
> But the life that in thee flows
> Each drop of blood a blessing owes.
> Each drop did infinite time distil

From all the flowers that Nature fill,
From all the hidden crafts that lie
In stone, plant, worm, wave, star, or sky, —
From all the magic light intrudes,
Gilding the starry multitudes. . . .

Waldo declines going to church with Mrs. Mumford, "because Mrs. Mumford is not beautiful; she has red hands and red face." The next week, when reminded that he does not like Mrs. Mumford, he tells Louisa, " I have made a little prayer that Mrs. Mumford might be beautiful, and now I think her beautiful."

Louisa proposed to carry Waldo to church with her, and he replies, " I do not wish to go to Church with you, because you live in the kitchen."

December 20.

I think nothing is of any value in books excepting the transcendental and extraordinary.[1] . . .

People are uneasy because the philosopher seems to compromise their personal immortality.

1 The rest of the passage is in " The Poet " (*Essays*, Second Series, p. 32).

Mr. Quin thinks that to affirm the eternity of God and not to affirm the reappearance of Mr. Quin bodily and mentally with all the appearances and recollections of Mr. Quin, excepting of course his green surtout and bank-stock scrip, is to give up the whole ship. But Mr. Quin is a sick God. All that sin and nonsense of his, which he parades these many summers and winters so complacently, which seem to him his life, his stake of being, in losing which he would lose all, are the scurf and leprosy which do not perish and smell in the nostril only because the divine Life has not yet ebbed quite away from them. But it is the Life, it is the incoming of God by which that Individual exists. It is the God only which he values and pleads for, though to his diseased eye that poor skin and raiment seem to have an intrinsic price. When that Divine Life shall have more richly entered and shed itself abroad in him, he will no longer plead for Life, he will live. Do not imagine that the Universe is somewhat so vague and aloof that a man cannot be willing to die for it. If that lives, I live. I am the Universe. The Universe is the externisation of God.[1] . . .

[1] The rest of the paragraph is found in "The Poet" (pp. 14, 15).

But there is no interval between this perception of Identity of the growing God and littleness. If you do not see your right to all, and your being reflected to you from all things, then the world may easily seem to you a hoax, and man the dupe. Yet the little fellow takes it so innocently, works in it so earnest and believing, blushes and turns pale, talks and sweats, is born red and dies grey, thinking himself an adjunct to the world which exists from him, that, until he is explained to himself, he may well look on himself as the most wronged of victims.

Everything is worshipped in the world but God. The new inspiration is always rejected. The world is bowing to a past revelation of God, to God seen through the lens of time, and so shorn of his dazzling rays, which offend weak eyes — diluted by much time; Homer, Jesus, Shakspear may pass and be suffocated with incense — Yet by how much these revelations are old, by so much do they cease to be divine. The Omnipresent exacts a total devotion to the present and Impending, — hands and hearts, and not a lazy gazing at old pictures. Yet genius always finds itself a century too early. But let not genius complain of its cold welcome and hard fare. Hath it not God? Let it cease from man.

A droll dream last night, whereat I ghastly laughed. A congregation assembled, like some of our late conventions, to debate the institution of Marriage; and grave and alarming objections stated on all hands to the usage; when one speaker at last rose and began to reply to the arguments, but suddenly extended his hand and turned on the audience the spout of an engine which was copiously supplied from within the wall with water, and whisking it vigorously about, up, down, right, and left, he drove all the company in crowds hither and thither and out of the house. Whilst I stood watching, astonished and amused at the malice and vigor of the orator, I saw the spout lengthened by a supply of hose behind, and the man suddenly brought it round a corner and drenched me as I gazed. I woke up relieved to find myself quite dry, and well convinced that the institution of marriage was safe for tonight.

And why, as I have written elsewhere, not be Universalists, or lovers of the whole world? Why limit our zeal and charity to such narrow parochial bounds? Are there black, bilious, sad tem-

peraments? They accuse me and thee. Let us
arise and redeem them and purge this choler and
sediment out of nature by our calmness and
immoveable love.[1]

(From E)

December 26.

We all know why Jesus serves men so well
for a deity: why pure and sublime souls like À
Kempis and Herbert can expend their genius
and heart so lavishly on his name and history,
and feel no check; why he stands ambassador
or proxy for the sovereign, and receives homage
of the lieges without any cloud of shame dark-
ening the brow of the noblest among them. We
all know, yet we cannot easily tell. It is for the
same reason that the Koran and the Vedas and
Buddhism have their martyrs and their sages.
It is for the same reason that Swedenborg's
Mythus is so coherent and vital and true to
those who dwell within; so arrogant or limitary
to those without.

There is nothing that comes out of the human
heart — the deep aboriginal region — which is
not spheral, mundane, thousand-faced — so re-

1 This passage is followed by the last two pages of " History " (*Essays*, First Series).

lated to all things that if perchance intense light falls on it and immense study be given to it, it will admit of being shown to be related to all things. The rose is a type of youth and mirth to one eye, of profound melancholy to another. There is nothing in nature which is not an exponent of nature. I feel this in nature constantly.

If you criticise a fine genius, as Burns or Goethe, the odds are that you are quite out of your reckoning.[1] . . .

AUTHORS OR BOOKS QUOTED OR REFERRED TO IN JOURNAL FOR 1840[2]

Buddha; Vedas; Zoroaster;

Æschylus, *Prometheus Bound*, *Seven against Thebes*; Sophocles, *Electra*; Plato, *Politicus*, *apud* Cousin; Vitruvius;

St. Augustine, *Confessions*; Koran;

Petrarch; Dante; Thomas à Kempis; Chaucer; Luther; Rabelais; Hans Sachs; Chapman;

1 For the rest of this paragraph, see "Nominalist and Realist" (*Essays*, Second Series, p. 241).

2 Including books from the Boston Athenæum charged to Mr. Emerson.

Spenser; Donne; Hampden, *Memoir* by Nugent;

Fuller; Gilbert Burnet, *History of his own Times;*

Count Anthony Hamilton, *Mémoires du Comte de Gramont;* Simon Ockley, *History of the Saracens;* André Michaux, *Les Chênes d'Amérique Septentrionale;* D'Abrantès, *Mémoires;*

Sir William Jones; Goethe, *Wilhelm Meister;* Lives of Haydn and Mozart; Karoline von Günderöde; Bettina von Arnim;

Burns; Dr. Abernethy;

Cousin; Fourier, *Social Destiny of Man;* Mignan, *Travels in Chaldea;*

Webster, *Speeches;* Bryant, *Ancient Mythology;* Carlyle;

Harriet Martineau, *Deerbook;* R. H. Dana, Jr., *Two Years Before the Mast;*

Tennyson; Balzac, *Le Livre Mystique;* French Novels; *Valentine;* W. Ellery Channing, *Poems;* Mrs. Wells, *Poem,* "My own delighted, laughing boy."

JOURNAL

FIRST ESSAYS PRINTED
REFORMS

JOURNAL XXXII

1841

(From Journals E, F, G, H, and J)

[IN January, Mr. Emerson — his book of Essays sent to the printer — had to prepare the lecture "Man the Reformer," which he delivered before the Mechanics' Apprentices' Library Association in Boston on the 25th of the month. His sedentary work and the severe winter seem to have left him in bad condition in the spring, and in April a pleasant and successful alliance was made with Henry Thoreau, then twenty-four years old, which lasted for two years. Thoreau became, as it were, an elder son in the family, attended to the gardening, established a poultry-yard, grafted the trees, and skilfully did odd jobs and repairs in the house. He was man of the house during Mr. Emerson's absences, and was most respectfully attentive to Mrs. Emerson, to whom he always looked up as a sort of lady-abbess. He was a delightful friend to the children, and had great gifts of amusing and helping them. He reserved what time he wished for studies, afield and at home. Sometimes he walked with Mr. Emerson and showed him Nature's secrets in the woods or swamps or on the river. Mr. Emerson's lack of skill in gardening or household emergencies was admirably supplemented by his young friend.]

(From E)
January 1, 1841.

I begin the year by sending my little book of Essays to the press. What remains to be done to its imperfect chapters I will seek to do justly. I see no reason why we may not write with as much grandeur of spirit as we can serve or suffer. Let the page be filled with the character, not with the skill of the writer.

Goethe is right in his mode of treating colors, i. e., poetically, humanly. Beethoven is too proud, yet is grand.

(From F)

I wondered at the continence of Nature under the glittering night sky, and truly Pan ought to be represented in the Mythology as the most continent of Gods. But not less admirable is the phlegm of the good ghost that inhabits it. For can I, can any, spare the next day, the next year of our lives? Can any consent to die now? Are we not always expecting that this marvellous moderation which refuses to blab the secret, and yields us no rapturous intelligence such as all feel must lie behind there, will give way at last to the necessity of imparting the Divine Miracle?

This reserve and taciturnity of time.[1]

January 11.

The Confessional. — Does Nature, my friend, never show you the wrong side of the tapestry? Never come to look dingy and shabby? Do you never say, "Old stones! old rain! old landscape! you have done your best; there is no more to be said; praise wearies; you have pushed your joke a little too far"? — Or, on the other hand, do you find Nature always transcending and as good as new every day? I know, I know, how nimble it is, — the good monster. You have quite exhausted its power to please, and to-day you come into a new thought, and lo! in an instant there stands the entire world converted suddenly into the cipher or exponent of that

1 And matched his sufferance sublime
  The taciturnity of time.
            "The Poet," *Poems,* Appendix.

very thought, and chanting it in full chorus from every leaf and drop of water. It has been singing that song every day since the Creation in your deaf ears.

Away with your prismatics, I want a spermatic book. Plato, Plotinus, and Plutarch are such.

It is necessary in considering the nature of everything to direct our attention to the purity of it. (Plotinus.)

Every soul pays a guardian attention to that which is inanimate. (Plato in *Phædrus*.)

Necessity indeed is in intellect, but persuasion in soul. (Plotinus.)

(From E)

January 17.

It appears sometimes what Prudence stands for. The true prudence is no derogation from the lofty character. The man who moved by interrupted impulses of virtue would lead a violent and unfortunate life. These continent, persisting, immoveable persons who are scattered up and down for the blessing of the world, howsoever named, Osiris or Washington or Samuel Hoar, have in this phlegm or gravity of their nature a quality which answers to the fly-wheel in a mill which distributes the motion equably over all the wheels and hinders it from falling unequally and suddenly in destructive shocks.[1] . . .

He did not get it from the books, but where the bookmaker got it.

Books lead us from ecstasy.

We look at the mercury to know the heat, but Nature is the mercury of our progress. Do we dissolve the sun or the sun us? do we freeze the January, or January us?

We have exhausted Nature, but we read one of the masters and instantly are made aware of new classes of laws, and the world casts itself into types so smiling grand and so equal to the sense that we get a new idea of wealth, and grow impatient of our words and think we will never use them again; like boys who have had a rocking-horse or boat and then are mounted on a live horse or a sailboat — they despise their toys.

[1] Much of this in substance, but without naming men, occurs at the end of "Man the Reformer" (*Nature, Addresses, and Lectures*).

Powerful influence should never let us go; never be out of the mind, sleeping or waking: his name is on our lips, though we do not frequent his society.

Thou, O Truth, never lettest us go.

The love of Nature,—what is that but the presentiment of intelligence of it? Nature preparing to become a language to us.

Mechanics easily change their trades, for that which they learn in their apprenticeship is the use of tools, and, having learned that, they can readily turn themselves to any new work. All knowledge is thus eccentric, and of course the progress of knowledge geometric. Are there three rates of increase, arithmetical, geometrical, and circumferential, or from the centre on all sides out?

January 20.

Of these unquiet dæmons that fly or gleam across the brain what trait can I hope to draw in my sketch-book? Wonderful seemed to me as I read in Plotinus the calm and grand air of these few cherubim — great spiritual lords who have walked in the world — they of the old religion — dwelling in a worship that makes the sanctities of Christianity *parvenues* and merely popular.[1] . . .

"Blessed," said the Review which pleased me so well, "is the man who has no powers," and, as I had written long ago, Happy is the man who hears: unhappy the man who speaks. The reason is obvious: it is better to be poor and helpless in doing, because our heart is preoccupied and astonished with the immensities of God, than to be at leisure to adorn and finish our trivial works because communication with the Deity is no longer open to us. Therefore very wisely did the ancients represent the Muses as daughters of Memory. But when vision and union come, there is no leisure for memory or muses.

The ploughman and the ox, or a rider and his horse, indicate the natural society of wisdom and strength: each is necessary to the other.

[1] The rest of this passage on the philosophers of Ancient Hellas and the Neoplatonists forms the conclusion of "Intellect" (*Essays*, First Series), and it is, in the Journal, immediately followed by the opening passage of the same essay.

January 21.

A man should think much of himself because he is a necessary being: a link was wanting between two craving parts of Nature and he was hurled into being as the bridge, over that yawning need.[1] . . .

When I look at the sweeping sleet amid the pine woods, my sentences look very contemptible, and I think I will never write more: but the words prompted by an irresistible charity, the words whose path from the heart to the lips I cannot follow, — are fairer than the snow. It is pitiful to be an artist.[2] . . .

We are to come into Nature from a higher law, and classify it anew. There is no mire, no dirt to chemistry: the ignorant, the foul, know of dirt: the chemist sees all dissolved into a chain of immaterial, immortal, irresistible laws. Even so must we come into Nature, that is, so walk and work and build and associate. We

1 The rest of this paragraph is found in "The Method of Nature" (*Nature, Addresses, etc.*, p. 207.)

2 The rest is in the above address (p. 110) and is immediately followed here by the concluding passage in "Man the Reformer" in the same volume.

must not scold, we must not lay hands on men, but, being inspired, must awe their violence and lead them by our eye into harmonic choirs.

A man is a poor, limitary benefactor,[1] . . .

January 31.

God gives us facts and does not tell us why; but the reason lives in the fact; we are sure their order is right : there is no interpolation : and they only await our riper insight to become harmonious in their order and proportion. God knows all the while their divine reason. Swedenborg writes history after ideas. If he names Jew or Persian, Moravian or Lutheran, Papist or African, he gives us the reason in their character for the fact he names. I hope that day will come when no man will pretend to write history but he who does so by divine right. A man being born to see the order of certain facts, is born to write that history. Every other person, not so qualified, who affects to do this work is a pretender, and the work is not done. . . .

All my thoughts are foresters. I have scarce a day-dream on which the breath of the pines

[1] The passage thus beginning is in " The Transcendentalist " (*Nature, Addresses, etc.,* p. 346).

has not blown, and their shadows waved. Shall I not then call my little book Forest Essays?

Ecstasy, religion, are essentially self-relying, the entranced instantly speak down as from an immeasureable height to him who but yesterday was walking at their side. They ask no sympathy. But the soul which enters its noviciate in the temple, when it has prayed or chaunted inquires of its old friends, whether this was verily prayer and music?

The Present. — Cannot all literature, and all our own remote experience avail to teach us that the To-day which seems so trivial, the task which seems so unheroic, the inexpressive blank look of the Present moment, . . . cannot all avail to teach us that these are wholly deceptive appearances, and that as soon as the irrecoverable Years have placed their Blue between these and us, these things shall glitter and attract us, seeming to be the wildest romance, and — as far as we allowed them in passing to take their own way and natural shape — the homes of beauty and poetry?

Novels. — To find a story which I thought I remembered in *Quentin Durward*, I turned over the volume until I was fairly caught in the old foolish trap and read and read to the end of the novel. Then, as often before, I feel indignant to have been duped and dragged after a foolish boy and girl, to see them at last married and portioned, and I instantly turned out of doors like a beggar that has followed a gay procession into the castle. Had one noble thought opening the abysses of the intellect, one sentiment from the heart of God been spoken by them, I had been made a participator of their triumph, I had been an invited and an eternal guest, but this reward granted them is property, all-excluding property, a little cake baked for them to eat and for none other, nay, which is rude and insulting to all but the owner.[1] In *Wilhelm Meister*, I am a partaker of the prosperity.

Yet a novel may teach one thing as well as my choosings at the corner of the street which way to go, — whether to my errand or whether to the woods, — this, namely, that action inspires respect; action makes character, power, man, God.

[1] Compare the passage in "Behaviour," where the same complaint is made in a more general way (*Conduct of Life*, pp. 191, 192).

These novels will give way, by and by, to diaries or autobiographies;—captivating books, if only a man knew how to choose among what he calls his experiences that which is really his experience, and how to record truth truly!

February 4.

I am dispirited by the lameness of an organ: if I have a cold, and the thought I would utter to my friend comes forth in stony, sepulchral tones, I am disgusted, and I will not speak more. But, as the drunkard who cannot walk can run, so I can speak my oration to an assembly, when I cannot without pain answer a question in the parlor. But lately it is a sort of general winter with me. I am not sick that I know, yet the names and projects of my friends sound far off and faint and unaffecting to my ear, as do, when I am sick, the voices of persons and the sounds of labor which I overhear in my solitary bed. A puny, limitary creature am I, with only a small annuity of vital force to expend, which if I squander in a few feast-days, I must feed on water and moss the rest of the time.

I went to the Rainers' concert last night in our Court-House. When I heard them in Boston, I had some dreams about music: last night, nothing. Last night I enjoyed the audience. I looked with a great degree of pride and affection at the company of my townsmen and townswomen, and dreamed of that kingdom and society of Love which we preach.

His virtues were virtues of the senses. You can't tell how much good nature and generosity is to be ascribed to a good dinner, and how much to the character. There is a great deal of poetry and fine sentiment in a chest of tea. . . .

If I judge from my own experience I should unsay all my fine things, I fear, concerning the manual labor of literary men. They ought to be released from every species of public or private responsibility. To them the grasshopper is a burden. I guard my moods as anxiously as a miser his money; for company, business, my own household chares, untune and disqualify me for writing. I think then the writer ought not to be married; ought not to have a family. I think the Roman Church with its celibate clergy and its monastic cells was right. If he must marry, perhaps he should be regarded happiest who has a shrew for a wife, a sharp-tongued notable dame who can and will assume the total economy of the house, and, having some sense that her philosopher is best in his study, suffers him not to intermeddle with her thrift. He shall be master but not mistress, as Elizabeth Hoar said.

February 10.

Prudence. — What right have I to write on Prudence whereof I have but little and that of the negative sort?[1] . . .

February 12.

There is no Time. — If the world would only wait one moment, if a day could now and then be intercalated, which should be no time, but pause and landing-place, a vacation during which sun and star, old age and decay, debts and interest of money, claims and duties, should all intermit and be suspended for the halcyon trance, so that poor man and woman could throw off the harness and take a long breath and consider what was to be done, without being fretted by the knowledge that new duties are gathering for them in the moment when they are considering the too much accumulated old duties! But this

1 The rest of the passage is the opening paragraph of "Prudence" (*Essays*, First Series).

on, on, forever onward, wears out adamant. All families live in a perpetual hurry. Every rational thing gets still postponed and is at last slurred and ill-done or huddled out of sight and memory.

March 1.

In March many weathers. March always comes if it do not come till May. May generally does not come at all.

The poorness or recentness of my experience must not deter me from affirming the law of the soul : nay, although there was never any life which in any just manner represented the facts. We are bound to say what already is, and is explained and demonstrated by every right and every wrong of ours, though we are far enough from that inward health which would make this true order appear to be the order of our lives.

What a coxcomb is our experience which decides that such a fact or character cannot be because it has never been, as if that was not the reason why it should now be.

March 19.

Sent copies of my essays to Nathaniel L. Frothingham, Sam G. Ward, J. G. Palfrey, N. I. Bowditch, Margaret Fuller, Caroline Sturgis, W. H.

Furness, [Rev.] Dr. Francis, Samuel Ripley, F. H. Hedge, George Ripley, Abel Adams, J. R. Lowell, Dr. James Jackson, Dr. Charles T. Jackson, [Aunt] Mary Moody Emerson, William Emerson, Henry Ware, Jr., George P. Bradford, D[avid] H[enry] Thoreau, A. B. Alcott, W. Ware, Mrs. Lucy C. Brown, F. A. Farley, Elizabeth Hoar, William Henry Channing, W. E. Channing, Jr., [Rev.] Barzillai Frost, J. M. Cheney, Rockwood Hoar, Mother, Lidian, H. Colman, Thomas W. Haskins, Sarah Searle, Edward Palmer, William Wordsworth, Thomas Carlyle, John Sterling, Harriet Martineau, J. W. Marston, Sophia Peabody [Mrs. Hawthorne], Wm. M. Jackson, H. Bulfinch, Mary Russell, M. W. Willis, *N. Y. Review*, *Knickerbocker*.

April 10.

Do not judge the poet's life to be sad because of his plaintive verses and confessions of despair. Because he was able to cast off his sorrows into these writings, therefore went he onward free and serene to new experiences. You must be a poet also to draw any just inference as to what he was from all the records, be they never so rich, which he has left. Did you hear him speak? His speech did great injustice to his thought. It was either

better or worse. He gave you the treasures of
his memory, or he availed himself of a topic rich
in allusions to express hopes gayer than his life
entertains, or sorrows poured out with an energy
and religion which was an intellectual play and not
the habit of his character. You shall not know
his love or his hatred from his speech and behaviour. Cold and silent he shall be in the circle
of those friends who, when absent, his heart
walks with and talks with evermore. Face to
face with that friend who for the time is unto him
the essence of night and morning, of the sea and
the land, the only equal and worthy incarnation
of Thought and Faith, — silence and gloom shall
overtake him; his talk shall be arid and trivial.
There is no deeper dissembler than the sincerest
man. Do not trust his blushes, for he blushes
not at his affection, but at your suspicion. Do
not trust his actions, for they are expiations and
fines often, with which he has amerced himself,
and not the indications of his desire. Do not
conclude his ignorance or his indifference from
his silence. Do not think you have his thought,
when you have heard his speech to the end. Do
not judge him worldly and vulgar, because he
respects the rich and the well-bred, for to him the
glittering symbol has a surpassing beauty which

it has not to other eyes, and fills his eye, and his heart dances with delight in which no envy and no meanness are mixed. Him the circumstance of life dazzles and overpowers whilst it passes because he is so delicate a meter of every influence. You shall find him noble at last, noble in his chamber.

France. — "But Gymnast said, 'My sovereign lord, such is the nature and complexion of the French that they are worth nothing but at the first push.'" — (Rabelais.)

I read with joy the life of Pythagoras by Iamblichus; and the use of certain melodies to awaken in the disciple now purity, now valor, now gentleness. That *Life* is itself such a melody, and proper to these holy offices. Especially I admire the patience and longanimity of the probation of the novice. His countenance, his gait, his manners, diet, conversation, associates, employments, were all explored and watched; then the long discipline, the long silence was imposed, the new and vast doctrines taught, and then his vivacity and capability of virtue explored again. — If all failed, then his property (otherwise made common) was restored to him, a tomb built to his memory, and he was thenceforward spoken of and regarded by the School as *dead.* The long patience in this fugitive world is itself an affecting argument of the eternity of soul, affirms the faith of those who thus greatly slight our swift almanacs. He who treats human beings as centennial, millennial natures, convinces me of his faith. . . . Yet how much I admire their use of music as a medicine. But for me, with deaf ears, Order and Self-control are the "melodies" which I should use to mitigate and tranquillize the ferocity of my animal and foreign elements.

I saw with great pleasure the plates of the French artist of the ruins of Palenqua in Mexico: Cyclopean remains of a simple and original architecture that compares at once with what is best of Egyptian, Doric, or Gothic. Its great value to the eye is the emancipation of the spirit which it works. Everything is again possible. We are no longer forced to reproduce buildings in one of five or six foolish styles, but are as free as dreams, free as wishes, free as new necessities can make us.

Seest thou not how social and intrusive is the nature of all things? Ever they seek to penetrate and overpower each the nature of every other creature, and itself alone in all modes and throughout space and spirit to prevail and possess.[1] . . .

Man is the tender, irritable, susceptible matrix or receiver. The pollen of all these grand flowers, these savage forests, blows up and down and is lodged in him, and he bears a universal variegated blossom, rich with the qualities of every nature.

There is nothing man meditates but he tends presently to re - create, — whether a gallery of sculpture, or economical machines, or a government, or a bank, or the starry heaven, or a field of flowers, — a ship or a picture, music or a farm, a whaling voyage, or a war. Soft and facile all images float freely over his retina: the poet is he who can fix the grandest image and keep the vividness of a brisk conversation to a millennium. What are all these artists and masters of commerce, war, science, art, who go up and down so energetically, but the celebrators and worshippers and minions, one may say, each of some substance or relation in Nature? That shining, alluring property did first sing in his ear a syren

1 The rest of this long and striking passage is in "The Method of Nature" (*Nature, Addresses, etc.,* p. 212).

all the running sea of forms, I am truth, I am love, and immutable I transcend form as I do time and space.

Is a service of plate a fit reward of a virtuous action? or, is the friend whom it has won, and the insight it has given, and the reaction it has caused, the fit reward? And is Science to be learned always in laboratories, or will it one day be eaten and drunken, be smelled and tested, be digged and swum and walked and dreamed?

Every man tries his hand at poetry some-where, but most men do not know which their poems are.

Φυγὴ μόνου πρὸς μόνον.[1]

April 19.

Saint-Simon paints Fénelon as he sees him from the army and the saloons of Versailles, so that his Fénelon is a Saint-Simon in surplice, and no Fénelon at all.

I am tempted lately to wish, for the benefit of our literary society, that we had the friendly institution of the *Café.* How much better than Munroe's bookshop would be a coffee-room

1 The flight of the Only to the Only.

wherein one was sure at one o'clock to find what scholars were abroad taking their walk after the morning studies were ended.

Education. — We assume a certain air of holiness when we go to deal with our children, and appeal at that moment to a principle to which we do not appeal at other times. Of course, we do not succeed: the child feels the fraud. Simply the Holy Spirit is not there, and the effects cannot appear.

April 20.

Would it not be well to write for the young men at Waterville a history of our present literary and philosophical crisis, a portrait of the parties, and read the augury of the coming hours? In England, ethics and philosophy have died out. How solitary is Coleridge and how conspicuous, not so much from his force as from his solitude. In this country, a throng of eager persons read and hear every divine word. Yet for the most part there is great monotony in the history of our young men of the liberal or reforming class. They have only got as far as rejection, not as far as affirmation. They seem therefore angry and railers: they have nothing new or memorable to offer; and that is the vice of their writings, —

SAMUEL T. COLERIDGE

profuse declamation, but no new matter: after a very short time, this becomes to the reader insufferably wearisome, and the fine young men and women who looked but the other day in that direction, with eyes of hope like the first rays of morning, are turning away with a kind of bitterness from the saturation of talk, of promise, and of preaching. Silence, personal prowess, cheerfulness, solid doing, seem to be the natural cures.

We are a puny and fickle folk. Hesitation and following are our diseases. The rapid wealth which hundreds in the community acquire in trade or by the incessant expansions of our population and arts, enchants the eyes of all the rest, the luck of one is the hope of thousands, and the whole generation is discontented with the tardy rate of growth which contents every European community. America is . . . the country of small adventures, of short plans, of daring risks, not of patience, not of great combinations, not of long, persistent, close-woven schemes, demanding the utmost fortitude, temper, faith, and poverty. Our books are tents, not pyramids: our reformers are slight and wearisome talkers, not man-subduing, immutable, all-attracting; discharging their own task and so " charming the eye with dread," and persuading without knowing that they do so. There are no Duke Wellingtons, no George Washingtons, no Miltons, Bentleys, or Hearns among our rapid and dashing race; but abundance of Murats, of Rienzis, of Wallers, and that slight race who put their whole stake on the first die they cast.

The great men bequeath never their projects to their sons to finish: these eat too much pound cake.

The most interesting class of people are those who have genius by accident and are powerful obliquely.[1] . . .

Beautiful to me, among so many ordinary and mediocre youths as I see, was Sam Ward when I first fairly encountered him, and in this way just named.

There are two theories of life, — one, for the demonstration of our talent, and the other for the education of the man. The life of politics, of the college, of the city, is very seductive, as it invites to the former, but sincerity counts all the time spent in the former lost, or all but a little. But obey the Genius when he seems to

[1] The rest of the passage is printed in "Experience" (*Essays*, Second Series, p. 68).

lead to uninhabitable deserts, penetrate to the bottom of the fact which draws you, although no newspaper, no poet, no man, has ever yet found life and beauty in that region, and presently when men are whispered by the gods to go and hunt in that direction, they shall find that they cannot get to the point which they would reach without passing over that highway which you have built. Your hermit's lodge shall [be] the Holy City and the Fair of the whole world.

War was courteously carried on, as a tournament of the aristocracy, in Louis Quatorze's time. Duc de Saint-Simon relates that when the Maréchal de Lorges, general of the army on the Rhine, fell sick, Louis of Baden, the general of the enemy, sent by trumpet offers of his physicians, of supplies, and every courtesy and attention in his power.

April 21.

America, and not Europe, is the rich man. According to De Tocqueville, the column of our population on the western frontier from Lake Superior to the Gulf of Mexico (twelve hundred miles as the bird flies) advances every year a mean distance of seventeen miles. He adds, " This gradual and continuous progress of the European race towards the Rocky Mountains has the solemnity of a providential event ; it is like a deluge of men rising unabatedly, and daily driven onward by the hand of God."

Animals. — Pirates do not live on nuts and herbs. The use of animal food marks the extremely narrow limits of our ideas of justice. We confine our justice to men alone, according to Porphyry's remark. Certainly our whole life ought to be a benefit, and the heliotrope and sweetbriar and thyme should not smell sweeter.

April 22.

Whenever the Church is restored, the culture of the Intellect will be enjoined in it, not, as now, with an apology and reservations, but conscientiously and to the shame and repentance of our fat, sluggish, and trivial modes of living. And I think that the labor in a college should be as strenuous and rugged, I may say as audacious as any labor that is undertaken in agriculture or in war. And the student ought to feel a poignant shame if when he reads the marches of Hannibal or Napoleon across the Alps, or the hardships of Hudson and Parry in their

polar voyages, or the patience of Columbus,
these eminent pieces of endurance appear to him
to indicate a greater manhood and resolution,
a more incessant industry, or a ruder courage
than that which he exercises in his silent library.
Does he wish to be a placid smiler, a demure,
inoffensive reader of such books as the newspapers applaud, to be helped over a fence when
he walks with a man, as if he were a girl (like
my dear Rev. Mr. A.), — I see not how he is
better than a lacquey hired to read, instead of
one hired to wait on table or to polish boots.
His courage is[1] not that of a soldier or a sailor,
but that of a scholar, and as worthy of their
admiration as theirs is worthy of his.

Should not man be sacred to man? What
are these thoughts we utter but the reason of our
incarnation? To utter these thoughts we took
flesh, missionaries of the everlasting Word which
will be spoken.

April 23.

Do not cast about for reasons among their
shop of reasons, but adduce yourself as the only
reason. We forget daily our high call to be
discoverers — we forget that we are embarked

1 i. e., the scholar's should be.

on a holy, unknown sea in whose blue recesses
we have a secret warrant that we shall yet arrive
at the Fortunate Isles hid from men; and at each
saucy wood-craft or revenue cutter or rum-boat
that hails us, we are astonished, and put off from
our purpose, and ready to return to the rotten
towns we have left, and quit our seeking of the
Virgin Shore.

No great man ever complains of want of opportunity,— no, nor of any want except of
being wanting to himself. All that he lays to
the charge of his fortune accuses himself only.
Want of opportunity! Why, did not divine
necessity create him? Did he not come into
being because something must there be, and be
done, which thing he and none other is and
does? If *I see*, the world is visible enough,
clothed in brightness and prismatic hues. If
again I see from a deeper energy, — I pierce
the gay surface on all sides, and every mountain
and rock and man and operation grows transparent before me.[1] . . .

When I wish, it is permitted me to say, These
hands, this body, this history of Waldo Emerson
are profane and wearisome, but I, I descend not

[1] The rest of the paragraph is found in "The Method
of Nature" (*Nature, Addresses, etc.*, pp. 207, 208).

to mix myself with that, or with any man. Above his life, above all creatures, I flow down forever, a sea of benefit into races of individuals. Nor can the stream ever roll backward, or the sin or death of a man taint the immutable energy which distributes itself into men, as the sun into rays, or the sea into drops.[1]

When Coleridge converses, or Scott romances, or Wordsworth writes poems, there is an admirable fact; and now the activity of the engineer, of the railroad builder, and the manufacturer is real and inventive, and deserves regard. Commerce, speculation overflow their old boundaries and run into new paths. Reform is to-day creative and not slavish. But the only rule and condition of merit and noteworthiness is not renown, nor number, nor property, nor geography, but only vitality. Its title to be studied is not to be measured by anything but persons. . . . If you would know what was done long ago, examine the institutions, the millions, the wealth, the laws. If you would know what God now hath at heart, behold the bright eye, hear the melodious speech, mark the irresistible hand

[1] The doctrine of the Universal Mind or the Over-Soul. See also " Pan " in the Appendix to the *Poems*.

which that energy now flows into. It matters not what topic men prefer, but what subject or instance they select to study the same upon. Not divination or ethics or astronomy is better than farriery or the rules of chess, but the one object of study is a great man. A great personal ascendancy is an inundation of reason, and therein they shall read the laws of gods and men and atoms. But scholars who should be diviners, Ephori, Judges, Eyes and Souls, bow to badges and officers, and do not require of every man whom they meet, that he should be the Founder of a Family, or a Profession, the Inventor of a way of life. Geology, Chemistry, Animal Dynamics, Electricity, the law of day and night, and of all material relation is being read aloud.

We must distinguish between the hero's greatness and his foible, and not consecrate so much nonsense as we do because it was allowed by great men. There is none without his foible.[1] . . .

1 Here follow the passages in "Nominalist and Realist" (p. 227) about the fear of angels' foibles ; and that in "New England Reformers" (pp. 265, 266), about true and false concert of men (*Essays*, Second Series).

April 24.

I beheld him and he turned his eyes on me, his great serious eyes.[1] Then a current of spiritual power ran through me, and I looked farther and wider than I was wont, and the visages of all men were altered and the semblances of things. The men seemed to me as mountains, and their faces seamed with thought, and great gulfs between them, and their tops reached high into the air. And when I came out of his sight, it seemed to me as if his eyes were a great river, like the Ohio or the Danube, which was always pouring a torrent of strong, sad light on some men, wherever he went, and tingeing them with the quality of his soul.

The balance must be kept, — the power to generalize and the power to individualize must coexist to make a poet; Will and Abandonment, the social and the solitary humour, man and opportunity.

Beauty is the only sure sign, so that if your word threatens me, I know it is a bully, I know it is weak, I know there is a better word discoverable and returnable. That word only which is

1 Perhaps some vision.

fair and fragrant, which blooms and rejoices, which runs before me like verdure and a flowering vine, sowing an Eden in the path, is truth. I hate, therefore, to hear that a cloud always hangs on an American's brow.

I frequently find the best part of my ride in the Concord Coach from my house to Winthrop Place to be in Prince Street, Charter Street, Ann Street, and the like places at the North End of Boston. The dishabille of both men and women, their unrestrained attitudes and manners, make pictures greatly more interesting than the clean-shaved and silk-robed procession in Washington and Tremont streets. I often see that the attitudes of both men and women engaged in hard work are more picturesque than any which art and study could contrive, for the Heart is in these first. I say *picturesque;* because when I pass these groups, I instantly know whence all the fine pictures I have seen had their origin : I feel the painter in me : these are the traits which make us feel the force and eloquence of *form* and the sting of color. But the painter is only *in* me; it does not come to the fingers' ends. But whilst I see a true painting, I feel how it was made; I feel that genius organizes, or it is lost. It is the gift of God ; as Fanny Elssler can dance and Braham can sing, when many a worthy citizen and his wife, however disposed, can by no culture either paint, dance, or sing. Do not let them be so ridiculous as to try, but know thou, know all, that no citizen, or citizen's wife, no soul, is without organ. Each soul is a soul or an individual in virtue of its having, or I may say being, a power to translate the universe into some particular language of its own : . . . into something great, human, and adequate which, if it do not contain in itself all the dancing, painting, and poetry that ever was, it is because the man is faint-hearted and untrue.

Wouldest thou see the wonders of art and the graces of society without a sense of inferiority, make thy life secretly beautiful.

[Here follow passages on genius and on talent, which are printed in "The Method of Nature" (pp. 204 and 218). The following reference to Miss Mary Moody Emerson occurs, in the Journal, in the middle of the latter passage.]

May 4.

Aunt Mary, whose letters I read all yesterday

afternoon, is Genius always new, subtle, frolic-
some, musical, unpredictable. All your learning
of all literatures and states of society, Platon-
istic, Calvinistic, English or Chinese, would
never enable you to anticipate one thought or
expression. She is embarrassed by no Moses
or Paul, no Angelo or Shakspeare, after whose
type she is to fashion her speech: her wit is
the wild horse of the desert, who snuffs the si-
rocco and scours the palm-grove without having
learned his paces in the Stadium or at Tatter-
sall's. What liberal, joyful architecture, liberal
and manifold as the vegetation from the earth's
bosom, or the creations of frostwork on the
window! Nothing can excel the freedom and
felicity of her letters, — such nobility is in this
self-rule, this absence of all reference to style
or standard: it is the march of the mountain
winds, the waving of flowers, or the flight of
birds. But a man can hardly be a reader of
books without acquiring their average tone, as
one who walks with a military procession involuntarily falls into step.

In every family is its own little body of literature, divinity, and personal biography, — a
common stock which their education and cir-

cumstance have furnished, and from which they all draw allusion and illustration to their conversation whilst it would be unintelligible (at least in the emphasis given to it) to a stranger. Thus, in my youth, after we had brought home *Don Juan* and learned to pester Aunt Mary with grave repetition of the lines from the shipwreck:

" They grieved for those who perished in the cutter,
  And likewise for the biscuit-casks and butter,"

— these became the byword for the mean spirit of derision that characterised the present age, in contrast with the alleged earnest and religious spirit of the Puritans, and especially the austere saints of Concord and Malden, she was so swift to remember.

I find a letter of hers to Charles, dated Waterford, October, 1831 : —

"O could you be here this afternoon — not a creature but the dog and me — we don't go to four-days-meeting.¹ There's been one at the Methodists', closing to-day, and such a rush from the other society. But such a day ! Here's one balm-of-gilead tree — but a few leaves left, as though on purpose to catch the eye to see them play in the wind day after day, — and the

1 A " Revival " then going on in Waterford, Maine.

deserted nest. Ah! where are its anxious parents
and their loved brood? Dead? Where the mysterious principle of life? . . . Past nine o'clock.
The vision of beauty has changed — a white
mist has risen which hides the venerable mount,[1]
but shows the trees in fine picturesque, and the
deserted nest is sheltered with a soft pall, like
the oblivion which rests on the miseries of the
wretched. Just after the house was left for the
evening vigils at the chapel, a man came for me
to write a note he was going to carry. The peculiarity of notes here, is, a friend asks for another's conversion — thus the best of human
feelings are brought into action. But note the
Cracker's;[2] I brought down by mistake the only
pen which is good of the four (one which I don't
use to you or Brother S.[3]) and I persuaded him to
shorten his petitions; and, as he was satisfied,
surely there was no harm. And here comes a
living voice — the charm too is gone from the

1 Bear Mountain, with a beautiful lake at its foot.

2 Perhaps the humble revivalists were so called. The
"notes" referred to were written requests sent up to the
minister in the pulpit for special remembrance in his prayer in
cases of suffering or death of relatives, or for thanksgiving for
happy events.

3 Rev. Samuel Ripley of Waltham, her half-brother.

moon — she rides full brightly — the tarn has gathered her misty wanderers in her bosom, and the trees stretch their naked arms to the skies like the scathed martyrs of Persecution."

New England Theology. — The new relations we form we are apt to prefer, as *our own ties*, to those natural ones which they have supplanted. Yet how strict these are, we must learn later, when we recall our childhood and youth with vivid affection, and feel a poignant solitude, even in the multitude of modern friends. In reading these letters of M. M. E. I acknowledge (with surprise that I could ever forget it) the debt of myself and my brothers to that old religion which, in those years, still dwelt like a Sabbath peace in the country population of New England, which taught privation, self-denial, and sorrow.[1] A man was born, not for prosperity, but to suffer for the benefit of others, like the noble rock-maple tree which all around the villages bleeds for the service of man. Not praise, not men's acceptance of our doing, but the Spirit's holy errand through us, absorbed the thought.

[1] This passage, although much of it is printed in "The Method of Nature," is so intimate and personal that it is kept here.

How dignified is this! how all that is called talents and worth in Paris and in Washington dwindles before it! How our friendships and the complaisances we use, shame us now, — they withdraw, they disappear, and the gay and accomplished associates, — and our elder company, the dear children and grave relatives with whom we played and studied and repented, they return and join hands again. I feel suddenly that my life is frivolous and public; I am as one turned out of doors, I live in a balcony, or on the street; I would fain quit my present companions as if they were thieves or pot-companions, and betake myself to some Thebais, some Mount Athos, in the depths of New Hampshire or Maine, to bewail my innocency and to recover it, and with it the power to commune again with these sharers of a more sacred idea. I value Andover, Yale, and Princeton as altars of this same old fire, though I fear they have done burning cedar and sandalwood there also, and have learned to use chips and pine.

But I meant to say above, that we are surprised to find that we are solitary, that what is holiest in our character and faculty is unappreciated by those who stand around us, and so lies uncalled for and dormant, and that it needs

that our dear ghosts should return, or such as
they, to challenge us to right combats.

Charles and Edward. — I ought to record the
pleasure I found, amid all this letter-reading, in
some letters to C. C. E. from his college mates,
in the uniform tone of affection and respect with
which these boys — for such they still were —
accost him. Edward also was respected, admired
by his mates, but, I suspect, never loved, — not
comprehended, not felt, — he puzzled them.
Yet I still remember with joy Charles's remark
when he returned from visiting Edward at Porto
Rico, that the tone of conversation there was
the most frivolous and low that could be, yet
that Edward never suffered anything unworthy
to be said in his presence, without speaking for
the right, and so good-humoredly and so well,
as invariably to command respect, and be a check
on the company.[1] But Charles always, from his

1 Of Edward Emerson, Dr. Oliver Wendell Holmes thus
spoke at a Meeting of the Massachusetts Historical Society in
his tribute to the elder brother, in 1882: —

"Children of the same family, as we well know, do not alike
manifest the best qualities belonging to the race. But the two
brothers of Ralph Waldo Emerson whom I can remember were
of exceptional and superior natural endowments. Edward Bliss
Emerson, next to him in order of birth, was of the highest

school days, had this *following*, and that of the best who were about him ; it was true, leal service, homage to something noble and superior, which the giver felt it was a compliment to himself to pay. Thus he brought boarders to the houses where he went, to Danforth's in Cambridge, and Pelletier's in Boston.

May 6.

These letters revive my faded purpose of writing the oft-requested memoir of Charles. That certainly would have been unfit : it was right for the young and the dear friend to ask : it had been wrong in me to undertake ; the very nobleness of the promise should make us more reluctant to recite the disappointment of the promise. Let us not stoop to write the annals of sickness and disproportion. Charles delighted in strength, in grace, in poetry, in success ; — shall we wrong

promise, only one evidence of which was his standing at the head of his college class at graduation. I recall a tender and most impressive tribute of Mr. Everett's to his memory at one of our annual Φ B K meetings. He spoke of the blow which had jarred the strings of his fine intellect and made them return a sound,

‘ Like sweet bells jangled, out of tune and harsh,’

in the saddened tones of that rich, sonorous voice still thrilling in the ears of many whose hearing is dulled for all the eloquence of to-day.’’

him so far as to make him the unwilling object of pity, the centre of a group of pain, a caryatid statue in our temple of Destiny? Yet now, as I read these yellowing letters of Aunt Mary, I begin to entertain the project in a new form. I doubt if the interior and spiritual history of New England could be trulier told than through the exhibition of family history such as this, the picture of this group of Aunt Mary and the boys, mainly Charles. The genius of that woman, the key to her life is in the conflict of the new and the old ideas in New England. The heir of whatever was rich and profound and efficient in thought and emotion in the old religion which planted and peopled this land. She strangely united to this passionate piety the fatal gifts of penetration, a love of philosophy, an impatience of words, and was thus a religious skeptic. She held on with both hands to the faith of the past generation as to the Palladium of all that was good and hopeful in the physical and metaphysical worlds; and in all companies, and on all occasions, and especially with these darling nephews of her hope and pride, extolled and poetised this beloved Calvinism. Yet all the time she doubted and denied it, and could not tell whether to be more glad or sorry to find that these boys

were irremediably born to the adoption and fur-
therance of the new ideas. She reminds me of
Margaret Graeme, the enthusiast in Scott's
Abbot, who lives to infuse into the young Roland
her enthusiasm for the Roman Church; only that
our Margaret doubted whilst she loved. Milton
and Young were the poets endeared to the generation she represented. Of Milton they were
proud, but I fancy their religion has never found
so faithful a picture as in the *Night Thoughts*.
These combined traits in Aunt Mary's character gave the new direction to her hope, that these
boys should be richly and holily qualified and
bred to purify the old faith of what narrowness
and error adhered to it, and import all its fire
into the new age, — such a gift should her Prometheus bring to men. She hated the poor, low,
thin, unprofitable, unpoetical Humanitarians as
the devastators of the Church and robbers of
the soul, and never wearies with piling on them
new terms of slight and weariness. "Ah!" she
said, "what a poet would Byron have been, if
he had been born and bred a Calvinist."

Sunday.

Beautiful, eloquent day, rich with more than
I have skill to tell, though I have attempted it

in verses. We rightly call the woods enchanting, they so confound all our measures, and upset our whole system of tradition.[1] . . . Here reigns eternal Sabbath, and the hours so ample and profound, they seem to stretch to centuries. . . . How far off is man and his works; Babylon and Britain draw very near together, and are not to be discriminated. The Circumstance is here emphatically felt to be nothing.

The Present Age will perhaps be characterised long hence by the importance now for several centuries attached to two words, namely, *Gentleman* and *Christian*. Yet see how this is the prevalence or inundation of an idea, and not of any person or purpose. Who did this? Who elevated these two words to their dignity in the metaphysical and practical world? Was any man a party to this exaggeration? Plainly no man, but all men. Well, there is no fact and no thought which shall not equally come in turn to the top and be celebrated.

General Harrison was neither Whig nor Tory, but the Indignation President; and, what was

1 The omitted sentences are in the first pages of " Nature " (*Essays*, Second Series).

not at all surprising in this puny generation, he could not stand the excitement of seventeen millions of people, but died of the Presidency in one month. A man should have a heart and a trunk vascular and on the scale of the Aqueducts or the Cloaca Maxima of Rome to bear the friction of such a Mississippi stream.

The dew-drops which are only superficial, what a depth do they give to the aspect of the morning meadows as you walk! So do manners, so do social talents to frivolous society.

We know as little of men as we do of plants. We doubt not that every weed in our soil hath its uses, and each no doubt excellent and admirable uses; yet now how poorly they figure in our Materia Medica! And is not a man better than a mullein or a buckthorn?

I walked in my dream with a pundit who said, . . . he could not speak with me many words, for the life of incarnate natures was short, but that the vice of men was old age, which they ought never to know; for, though they should see ten centuries, yet would they be younger than the waters, which — hearken unto their sound!

how young is it, and yet how old! Neither, said
he, ought men ever to accept grief from any external event; for, poverty, death, deluges, fires,
are flaws of cold wind or a passing vapor which
do not affect a constant soul. He added, that,
as the river flows, and the plant flows (or emits
odours), and the sun flows (or radiates), and the
mind is a stream of thoughts, so was the universe the emanation of God.[1] . . . Therefore,
he added, they mistake who seek to find only
one meaning in sacred words and images, in the
name of gods, as Jove, Apollo, Osiris, Vishnu,
Odin: or in the sacred names of Western Europe and its colonies, as Jesus and the Holy
Ghost: for these symbols are like coins of different countries, adopted from local proximity
or convenience, and getting their cipher from
some forgotten accident, the name of a consul,
or the whim of a goldsmith; but they all represent the value of corn, wool, and labor, and are
readily convertible into each other, or into the
coin of any new country. That sense which is
conveyed to one man by the name and rites
of Pan or Jehovah, is found by another in the
study of earthquakes and floods, by another in

[1] The omitted passage about emanations is found in "The
Method of Nature" (p. 199).

the forms and habits of animals; by a third in trade, or in politics; by a fourth in electro-magnetism. Let a man not resist the law of his mind and he will be filled with the divinity which flows through all things. He must emanate; he must give all he takes, nor desire to appropriate and to stand still.

He also said, that the doctrine of Pantheism or the Omnipresence of God would avail to abolish the respect of circumstance, or the treating all things after the laws of time and place, and would accustom men to a profounder insight. Thus Hospitality, he said, was an external fact. The troops of guests who succeed each other as inmates of our houses and messmates at our tables, week after week, are recording angels who inspect and report our domestic behaviour, our temperance, our conversation, and manners. Therefore, the pure in heart, having nothing to hide, are the most hospitable, or keep always open house. But to those who have somewhat to conceal, every guest is unwelcome.

A man is a gate betwixt Hell and Heaven. Through his heart streams a procession, when he wills good, of all angels and mights; when he wills evil, of all cattle and devils. Thou saidst of thy heart just now that it was cold, that it was broken, and thou wonderest why God should create it to be pained; and other the like things. What is the Heart, but the power to give and receive which varies every moment with the action? Whoso blesseth all beings or any being, — to him, to her, bend all the world of Spirits, as the brothers' sheaves to Joseph's sheaf. Whoso curseth any, by word or deed, from him, from her, all spirits in all worlds turn their backs. You cannot will without turning the key of Nature and opening or shutting the door of Light and of Darkness. There where you are, create value, and you publish yourself on the wings of every wind, every ray of light becomes your advertisement, and all souls shall bid on you until your just wages are paid.

I owe to genius always the same debt of lifting the curtain from the common, and showing me that gods are sitting disguised in this seeming gang of gypsies and pedlars.[1] And why should I owe it to a book or a friend, and not myself pierce the thin *incognito*? A question I may well ask, but I must ask it of my hands and of my

1 This sentence occurs in "Works and Days" (*Society and Solitude*, p. 176).

will. Holiness is the only stair to the mount of God. Yet am I continually tempted to sacrifice genius to talent, the hope and promise of insight (through the sole door of better being) to the lust of a freer play and demonstration of those gifts I have. We seek that pleasurable excitement which unbinds our faculties and gives us every advantage for the display of that skill we possess, and we buy this freedom to glitter by the loss of general health. Humility, patience, abstinence, mortification, nakedness (stripping off these clothes of law, custom, fortune, and friends), they can teach a philosophy, a rhetoric, and a poetry which the world has not heard these thousand years. Coffee is good for talent, but genius wants prayer. — Dost thou not fear that this perception, so keen, of right and wrong thou hast, of the true and the ridiculous in reform, will some time vanish and not be, and dost thou not wish to hold it to thee? I know thou dost. Do then what thou knowest.[1] . . .

What is strong but goodness, and what is energetic but the presence of a good man? It is time that this doctrine of the Presence[2] . . .

1 " Method of Nature " (p. 222).
2 Ibid. (p. 216).

The crystal sphere of thought is as concentrical as the geological globe we inhabit.[1] . . .

The various matters which men magnify, as trade, law, creeds, sciences, paintings, coins, manuscripts, histories, poems, are all pieces of *virtu* which serve well enough to unfold the talents of the man, but are all diversions from the insight of the soul. Saints' worship is one of these,—the worship of Mahomet or Jesus,— like all the rest, a fine field of ingenuity wherein to construct theories : a fine, capacious platform whereon to build institutions and societies, poetry, eloquence, and reputation — nay, a drug, a specific for the present distress, a crutch for fainting virtue, a lozenge for the sick ;— but, seriously and sadly considered, a remedy more dangerous than the disease. The soul will none of this roving. Why goest thou boswellizing this saint or that? It is *lèse-majesté*, it is the razor to the throat : here art thou, with whom so long the universe travailed in labor. Darest thou to think meanly of thyself — thee whom the stalwart Fate brought forth to unite his ragged sides ; to shoot the gulf ; to reconcile the erst irreconcileable ? As long as thou magnifiest anything, thou accusest thyself

1   "Method of Nature " (pp. 195, 196).

of trifling, of dallying and postponing thy own
deed, for, when once thou graspest the handles
of thy plough, thou wilt put all names behind
thee as living nature forces us to put all dead
bodies under ground. In the infinite disparity
between the soul and any one incarnation of it,
though holiest and grandest, all differences between one and another disappear, — they have
no parallax at a distance so vast.

In every pulse of virtue, in every revelation,
tho' slightest, of the soul, the soul affirmeth the
kingdom of the universe, the descent of itself
into man.

May 28.

Can I not learn that there is nothing settled
in manners?[1] . . .

Good sense is the leader of fashion as of
everything else. A man has strong sense to
write or to command armies, but he makes no
figure in society, simply because there his sense
does not work, — is dismounted by his self-
consciousness, or excessive desire to please, or
some other superstition; but the reason why he
yields so readily to the victors of the carpet is,

---

[1] The rest is in "Manners" (*Essays*, Second Series,
pp. 131, 132).

that he feels and sees that they carry the matter more sensibly than he.

[In his letter to Carlyle, May 30, Mr. Emerson said: —

"One reader and friend of yours dwells now in my house, and, as I hope, for a twelvemonth to come, — Henry Thoreau, — a poet whom you may one day be proud of; — a noble, manly youth, full of melodies and inventions. We work together day by day in my garden, and I grow well and strong." — (*Carlyle - Emerson Correspondence*, vol. i, Letter LX.)]

June 6.

I am sometimes discontented with my house because it lies on a dusty road, and with its sills and cellar almost in the water of the meadow. But when I creep out of it into the Night or the Morning and see what majestic and what tender beauties daily wrap me in their bosom, how near to me is every transcendent secret of Nature's love and religion, I see how indifferent it is where I eat and sleep. This very street of hucksters and taverns the moon will transform to a Palmyra, for she is the apologist of all apologists, and will kiss the elm trees alone and hides every meanness in a silver-edged darkness. Then the good river-god has taken the form of my valiant Henry Thoreau here and introduced me to the riches of his shadowy, starlit, moonlit stream, a lovely new world lying as close and yet as unknown to this vulgar trite one of streets and shops as death to life, or poetry to prose. Through one field only we went to the boat and then left all time, all science, all history, behind us, and entered into Nature with one stroke of a paddle. Take care, good friend! I said, as I looked west into the sunset overhead and underneath, and he with his face toward me rowed towards it, — take care; you know not what you do, dipping your wooden oar into this enchanted liquid, painted with all reds and purples and yellows, which glows under and behind you. Presently this glory faded, and the stars came and said, "Here we are"; began to cast such private and ineffable beams as to stop all conversation. A holiday *villeggiatura*, a royal revel, the proudest, most magnificent, most heart-rejoicing festival that valor and beauty, power and poetry ever decked and enjoyed — it is here, it is this. These stars signify it and proffer it: they gave the idea and the invitation,[1] . . .

1 Portions of this passage are printed in "Nature" (*Essays,* Second Series, pp. 172-174).

these beguiling stars, soothsaying, flattering, persuading, who, though their promise was never yet made good in human experience, are not to be contradicted, not to be insulted, nay, not even to be disbelieved by us. All experience is against them, yet their word is Hope and shall still forever leave experience a liar. . . .

Yes, bright Inviters! I accept your eternal courtesy.[1] . . .

But on us, sitting darkling or sparkling there in the boat, presently rose the moon, she cleared the clouds and sat in her triumph so maidenly and yet so queenly, so modest yet so strong, that I wonder not that she ever represents the Feminine to men. There is no envy, no interference in Nature. The beauty and sovereignty of the moon, the stars, or the trees, do not envy; they know how to make it all their own. As we sail swiftly along, and so cause the moon to go, now pure through her amber vault, and now through masses of shade, and now half-hid through the plumes of an oak or a pine, each moment, each aspect is sufficient and perfect; there is no better or worse, no interference, no preference; but every virtuous act of man or woman accuses other

1 Compare lines in "The Poet" (*Poems*, Appendix, p. 314).

men and women; shames me; and the person of every man or woman as in my varying love slighted or preferred. Blessed is Law. This moon, the hill, the plant, the air, obey a law, they are but animated geometry and numbers; to them is no intemperance; these are through law born and ripened and ended in beauty: but we through the transgression of Law sicken and inveterate.

June 7.

[Here follow several sentences from the " Chaldæan Oracles" attributed to Zoroaster.]

Things divine are not attainable by mortals who un-
derstand body;
But only as many as are lightly armed arrive at the
summit.
It is not proper to understand the Intelligible with
vehemence
But with the extended flame of an extended mind
measuring all things
Except that Intelligible. But it profits to understand
this
For if you incline your mind you will understand it
Not earnestly, but it becomes you to bring with you
a pure and inquiring eye;
To extend the void mind of your soul to the Intelligible
Because it subsists beyond mind.

You will not understand it as when understanding
    some particular thing.
There is a certain Intelligible which it becomes you
    to understand with the flower of the mind.
Let the immortal depth of your soul lead you.
Enlarge not thy destiny.

To every tree its own leaf and fruit, and every
man; are you a juniper or are you an orange:
but if the tree is pruned and exposed to the
South wind and manured, then it will bear a cart-
load of oranges; if neglected, few and bad. So
it seems more the pity if you are a man of genius, the sweetest of all poets, that you should pine
in bad condition and yield one song in a year.

We are too civil to books. For a few golden
sentences we will turn over and actually read a
volume of four or five hundred pages. Even the
great books, — "Come," say they, "we will
give you the key to the world." — Each poet,
each philosopher says this, and we expect to go
like a thunder-bolt to the centre.[1] . . . Ever
and forever Heraclitus is justified, who called
the world an eternal inchoation.

Critics. — The borer on our peach trees bores

1 See "The Method of Nature" (p. 196).

that she may deposit an egg: but the borer into theories and institutions and books bores that he may bore.

The man of practical or worldly force requires of the preacher a talent, a force like his own.[1] . . .

You defy anybody to have things as good as yours. Hafiz[2] defies you to show him or put him in a condition inopportune and ignoble. Take all you will, and leave him but a corner of Nature, a lane, a den, a cowshed, out of cities, far from letters and taste and culture; he promises to win to that scorned spot, the light of moon and stars, the love of men, the smile of beauty, the homage of art. It shall be painted, and carved, and sung and celebrated and visited by pilgrimage in all time to come.

(From G)

July.

The Actual. — O Protean Nature, whose energy is change evermore, thou hurlest thyself

1 The rest of the passage is printed in "The Preacher" (*Lectures and Biographical Sketches*, p. 230).

2 Mr. Emerson uses the name of Hafiz, as he more frequently did that of Saadi (Seyd or Said), in describing a poet's life or ideal. (See "Saadi," "Beauty," and "Fragments on the Poet and the Poetic Gift" in the *Poems*.)

into a berry or a drop, thou lodgest all thought in a word, all moral quality in the glance of an eye, but tell me, art thou only such a creator as bards and orators? Is thy power only for display? Or canst thou change the form of this waste and unnecessary day into an hour of love and fitness? When I see what waste strength is in friendship and in the writing and reading of modern society, the world seems to exist to dilettantism.

OSMAN AND SCHILL [1]

Schill. No tea! no wine! How are you the better or how am I the worse?

Osman. You are wise for me now. I am dull and you are inspired. But I know what you say, and shall remember it when you cannot.

Schill. How mean you that?

Osman. Time is my friend and not yours. The vital force is more ductile than gold, and the coin which you throw into a gambler's hand may be beaten into a leaf which shall gild the globe.

Schill. Whilst I confess I come eating and drinking, I praise your self-denial which I also

---

1 There seems to be no reason to be given for the choice of the name Schill for one of the interlocutors. It has nothing to do with the hero of Wordsworth's sonnet.

think is *ton* and *tournure* which makes kings vulgar.

Osman. It is no virtue in me, Sir. My father gave me a good constitution, which makes the taste of berries as grateful to me as pears or pineapples to you; and my temperance is no more to be imputed to me for righteousness than is the fact that a straw hat protects my head for all these years as well as an iron helmet. I think myself master of Assyrian luxury when I walk in the woods through sweet-fern and sassafras, or pass to the leeward of an elder bush in flower, or blacken my teeth with the betel nuts we have now plucked. One thing fell from you just now concerning fashion, which, though I did not quite understand it, may be the same thing which I have often thought, — that the best teachers of elegance are the stars which shine so delicately in yonder amber sky; and in the presence of the woodland flowers and the birds, I am ashamed to be coarse in my costume or behavior.

Character. — A word warm from the heart written or spoken, *that* enriches me. I surrender at discretion;[1] . . .

1 For the rest of the passage, see " Character " (*Essays,* Second Series, pp. 104, 105).

I value my welfare too much to pay you any longer the compliment of attentions. I shall not draw the thinnest veil over my defects, but if you are here, you shall see me as I am. You will then see that, though I am full of tenderness, and born with as large hunger to love and to be loved as any man can be, yet its demonstrations are not active and bold, but are passive and tenacious. My love has no flood and no ebb, but is always there under my silence, under displeasure, under cold, arid, and even weak behavior.

I think not of mean ages, but of Chaldæan, Egyptian, or Teutonic ages, when man was not featherbrained, or French, or servile, but, if he stooped, he stooped under Ideas : times when the earth spoke and the heavens glowed, when the actions of men indicated vast conceptions, and men wrote histories of the world in prison, and builded like Himmaleh and the Alleghany chains. I think that only is real which men love and rejoice in.[1] . . .

Men do not to-day believe in one who ascribes to man the attributes of the soul : even they who

[1] Most of what follows is in the " Lecture on the Times " (*Nature, Addresses, etc.*, p. 264).

speak that speech will scarcely stick to it, and if a man assert that great mystery, every little scribbler in the newspaper shall make great eyes, and point at his own little brain, and say, He is mad; and it may and does happen that the man who spoke it shall flee before the word of this newspaper written by some shallow boy in the dark, who wrote he knew not what, dipping his pen in mire and darkness. And yet night and morning, earth and heaven, and the soul of man are not to be so easily disposed of. It is true that there is another side to man. The other side, of fugitiveness, of frailty, that man is moth, or bubble, or gossamer, they readily hear and say: but that man is necessary and eternal they unwillingly hear. A man must reach the whole extent from Heaven to Earth. But it is possible that a man may come to subsist in some other way than that which the prudent think of. Hateful it is that transcendent men should only come to us in obscure and lurid forms, and not like sunshine and blue sky. Yet when they come, they will not be reported: they will affect men in a rapturous and extraordinary way, and the last thing they will think of will be to take notes.

The Age once more should appear capacious, undefinable, far retreating, still renewing, as the depths of the horizon do when seen from the hills.

You have many coats in your wardrobe, for you are rich. You need many for your conversation; and your action I am heartily tired of, —— old, musty, and stale. But Godfrey, who has but one coat to his back, has as many to his thought as Nature has days or plants or transformations.

July 6.

Ah, ye old ghosts! Ye builders of dungeons in the air! Why do I ever allow you to encroach on me a moment; a moment, to win me to your hapless company? In every week there is some hour when I read my commission in every cipher of Nature, and know that I was made for another office, a professor of the Joyous Science, a detector and delineator of occult harmonies and unpublished beauties, a herald of civility, nobility, learning, and wisdom; an affirmer of the One Law, yet as one who should affirm it in music or dancing. A priest of the Soul, yet one who would better love to celebrate it through the beauty of health and harmonious power.

My trees teach me the value of our circumstance or limitation. I have a load of manure, and it is mine to say whether I shall turn it into strawberries, or peaches, or carrots. I have a tree which produces these golden delicious cones called Bartlett pears, and I have a plant of strong common-sense called a Potato. The pear tree is certainly a fine genius, but with all that wonderful constructive power it has, of turning air and dust, yea, the very dung to Hesperian fruit, it will very easily languish and bear nothing, if I starve it, give it no southern exposure, and no protecting neighborhood of other trees. How differs it with the tree-planter? He too may have a rare constructive power to make poems, or characters, or nations, perchance, but though his power be new and unique, if he be starved of his needful influences, if he have no love, no book, no critic, no external call, no need or market for that faculty of his, then he may sleep through dwarfish years and die at last without fruit.

Colombe prefers to take work of Edmund Hosmer by the job, "for the days are damn long." [1]

1 A French-Canadian laborer. Edmund Hosmer was a neighbor and friend of Mr. Emerson's, a farmer of the old-fashioned thrifty type. His virtues are told by Mr. Emerson in "Agriculture in Massachusetts," first printed in the *Dial*, now included in the Works (*Natural History of Intellect*, p. 358).

Sunday.

If I were a preacher, I should carry straight to church the remark Lidian made to-day, that "she had been more troubled by piety in her help than with any other fault. The girls that are not pious, she finds kind and sensible, but the church members are scorpions, too religious to do their duties, and full of wrath and horror at her if she does them."

Every man has had one or two moments of extraordinary experience, has met his soul, has thought of something which he never afterwards forgot, and which revised all his speech, and moulded all his forms of thought.

I resent this intrusion of alterity. That which is done, and that which does, is somehow, I know, part of me. The Unconscious works with the Conscious, — tells somewhat which I consciously learn to have been told. What I am has been conveyed secretly from me to another whilst I was vainly endeavoring to tell him it. He has heard from me what I never spoke.

If I should or could record the true experience of my late years, I should have to say that I skulk and play a mean, shiftless, subaltern part

much the largest part of the time. Things are
to be done which I have no skill to do, or are
to be said which others can say better, and I lie
by, or occupy my hands with something which
is only an apology for idleness, until my hour
comes again.[1]

But woe to him who is always successful, who
still speaks the best word, and does the hand-
iest thing, for that man has no heavenly moment.

I find an analogy also in the Asiatic sentences
to this fact of life. The Oriental genius has no
dramatic or epic turn, but ethical, contempla-
tive, delights in Zoroastrian oracles, in Vedas,
and Menu and Confucius. These all embracing
apophthegms are like these profound moments
of the heavenly life.[2]

Lidian says that the only sin which people
never forgive in each other is a difference of
opinion.

[1] The rest of the passage, in an impersonal form, is found in
"The Transcendentalist" (*Nature, Addresses, etc.*, pp. 353,
354).

[2] The *Dial* was printing, under the title "Ethnical Scriptures," sentences from the above sources.

Carlyle with his inimitable ways of saying the thing is next best to the inventor of the thing. " I King Saib built this pyramid. I, when I had built it, covered it with satin. Let him that cometh after me and says he is equal to me cover it with mats."

END OF VOLUME V

The Riverside Press

CAMBRIDGE . MASSACHUSETTS

U . S . A